Abnormal Psychology 2AP3 Handbook

Dick Day

With thanks to Dr. Deborah Truscott
for her invaluable editorial and proofreading assistance

Winter, 2014 - 2015

Copyright 2014
Richard B. Day

Table of Contents

Course Outline . . . . Page   ii

Using This Handbook and Other Course Materials . . . . Page   v

Getting Listed References . . . . Page   ix

Introduction to Abnormal Psychology . . . . Page   1

Neurodevelopmental Disorders
      Attention Deficit Hyperactivity Disorder . . . . Page   15
      Autistic Spectrum Disorder . . . . Page   31

Anxiety Disorders . . . . Page   61
      Generalized Anxiety Disorder . . . . Page   61
      Panic Disorder . . . . Page   63
      Agoraphobia . . . . Page   65
      Social Anxiety Disorder . . . . Page   67
      Specific Phobias . . . . Page   68
      General Etiology of Anxiety . . . . Page   71

Obsessive Compulsive and Related Disorders . . . . Page   83

Somatic Symptom Disorders . . . . Page   91
      Somatic Symptom Disorder . . . . Page   92
      Illness Anxiety Disorder . . . . Page   94
      Conversion Disorder . . . . Page   95
      Psychological Factors Affecting Other Medical Conditions . . . . Page   99
      Factitious Disorder . . . . Page 100

Dissociative Disorders . . . . Page 107
      Dissociative Identity Disorder . . . . Page 108
      Derealization/Depersonalization Disorder . . . . Page 117

Depressive Disorders, Bipolar and Related Disorders . . . . Page 129
      Depressive Disorders . . . . Page 129
      Bipolar and Other Disorders . . . . Page 133

Schizophrenia Spectrum and Other Psychotic Disorders . . . . Page 151

Psychology 2AP3: Abnormal Psychology - Major Disorders
Course Outline, Jan. - Apr. 2015

Time: **Mon., Wed. 2:30; Friday 4:30**
Classroom: **MDCL-1305**
Web site: **http://intropsych.mcmaster.ca/psych2ap3**
and on Avenue to Learn

Instructor: **Dick Day**
Office: Psych Bldg Room 404
Phone: 525-9140 ext. 23006
Email: dayrich@mcmaster.ca

Course Objectives

This course discusses the issues and controversies surrounding the meaning and categorization of psychological abnormality. We will also describe the major symptoms, hypothesized or suggested causes, and accepted treatments for major categories of mental disorder as described in the Diagnostic and Statistical Manual (DSM) of the American Psychiatric Association, version 5, always keeping in mind the criticisms of this categorization system.

The goals of the course include a deeper understanding of the nature, causes of, and current treatments for, psychopathology, and, more importantly, an appreciation for the tentative and incomplete nature of our understanding of mental illness.

Required Text: Barlow, Durand, Stewart & Lalumiere. (2015). *Abnormal Psychology: An Integrative Approach.* (4th Canadian Edition). Nelson Education

Recommended Text: Day, R.B. **Abnormal Psychology 2AP3 Handbook. 2014-15 Term 1**. McMaster Custom Courseware, 2014. (The book that you have in your hand.)

Course Outline:

The table below shows the topics we will be covering, and the order in which we will be covering them. The dates when each topic will be discussed are **approximate.**

Week of:	Topic	Text Readings
Jan. 5 Jan. 12	Introduction to Abnormal Psychology	Chapters 1 and 2
Jan. 11 Jan. 19 Jan. 27	Neurodevelopmental Disorders: ADHD; Autism Spectrum Disorder	Chapter 14, pp. 499-521
Jan. 27 Feb. 2 * Feb. 9	Anxiety Disorders & Obsessive-Compulsive Disorders: Generalized Anxiety Disorder; Panic Disorder; Phobias, OCD	Chapter 5
Feb. 16	Break Week	
Feb. 23 Mar. 2	Somatoform & Dissociative Disorders: Conversion; Amnesia; Dissociative Identity Disorder	Chapter 6
Mar. 9 * Mar. 16 Mar. 23	Mood Disorders: Major Depression; Bipolar Disorders	Chapter 7

Mar. 23 Mar. 30 Apr. 6	Schizophrenia	Chapter 13
	Classes end Wednesday, April 8th	

Evaluation: There will be two in-class tests, worth 30% each, and a final exam worth 40%. Each in-class test will consist of approximately 40 multiple-choice questions. You will have the first 60 minutes of the class period to complete each test. The midterms are non-cumulative, so the second midterm covered different material from the first midterm, though some questions may assume knowledge covered on the fisrt midterm.

The final exam will consist of 80 multiple-choice questions. You will have two hours for this test, which will take place during the December examination period. The final exam is cumulative with respect to lecture material, but NOT with respect to text readings.

The **tentative dates** for the in-class tests are as follows (and are marked on the course outline with an asterisk next to the date):

In-class Test #1: Wednesday, February 11th
In-class Test #2: Wednesday, March 18th

The **actual** dates of the in-class tests will depend on the availability of additional testing rooms (if required), and will be announced in class - and posted on the course website - **at least 10 days** prior to the actual test date. **IT IS YOUR RESPONSIBILITY TO MAKE SURE THAT YOU GET THIS INFORMATION.**

Missed Work: If you miss one of the in-class tests for documented medical or compassionate reasons, you should complete a Missed Work form in the office of the Associate Dean (Studies) of your Faculty. **Once your Associate Dean has accepted your reason for absence, the remaining in-class test and the final exam will be reweighted (40%, 60%, respectively) to cover the missed in-class test.** This is the only accommodation for missed midterms.

Discretionary notes will generally not be accommodated. Note also that the online student absence form (MSAF) can only be used once per term, only for medical absences, and only for assignments worth less than 30%. That means that **an MSAF will not excuse you from either of the midterm tests in this course.**

If you miss either midterm test WITHOUT a reason acceptable to the office of your Faculty's Associate Dean, I will weight that missed midterm as 10% of your final course grade (scored as a mark of 0%), and reweight the remaining midterm 35%, and the final exam as 55% of your final course grade. This reduces your maximum average in the course from 100% to 90%..

Final Grade Calculation and Adjustment: The final mark in Psychology 2AP3 will be computed by applying the following formula to the percentage scores on Test1, Test2, and Final Exam:

(Test1% x .30) + (Test2% x .30) + (Exam% x .40) = Final Course Percentage

Apart from excused or unexcused absences from an in-class test, every student will be assessed using the weighting formula shown above - with one exception:

In assigning final letter grades for the course I look at the pattern of performance over the two in-class tests and the final exam. If the overall average, as calculated by the formula above, is on the borderline of the next higher letter grade (e.g. 49%, 66%, or 84%) and if the marks on BOTH the final exam AND one in-class test are at the next higher level (e.g., D-, C+, A), then I will assign the next higher letter grade than the one indicated by your average (e.g., D-, C+, A).

Apart from this one final adjustment, final course grades in this course will not be changed unless they have been calculated incorrectly. I do not respond to phone, email or in-person requests to increase correctly-calculated grades in this course.

Note that although midterm and exam marks, and final course averages are posted on Avenue as well as on the intropsych Grades Lookup, **ONLY THE NUMERICAL POSTINGS ON THE GRADES LOOKUP REFLECT THE CORRECT CALCULATION OF YOUR MARKS AND FINAL AVERAGE**. The <u>letter</u> grades posted on Avenue and the Grades Lookup will be identical, and equally correct.

Academic Integrity and Academic Dishonesty: Academic dishonesty consists of misrepresentation by deception or by other fraudulent means and can result in serious consequences, e.g. the grade of zero on an assignment, loss of credit with a notation on the transcript (notation reads: "Grade of F assigned for academic dishonesty"), and/or suspension or expulsion from the university.

It is your responsibility to understand what constitutes academic dishonesty. For information on the various kinds of a academic dishonesty please refer to the Academic Integrity Policy, specifically Appendix 3, located at
http://www.mcmaster.ca/senate/academic/ac_integrity.htm

The following illustrates only three forms of academic dishonesty:
1. **Copying or using unauthorized aids on tests and examinations**.
2. Plagiarism, e.g. the submission of work that is not one's own or for which other credit has been obtained.
3. Improper collaboration in group work.

Grading in <u>Psychology 2AP3</u>

The final mark in Psychology 2AP3 will be computed by applying the following formula to the percentage scores on Test1, Test2, and Final Exam:

(Test1% x .30) + (Test2% x .30) + (Exam% x .40) = Final Course Percentage

The Final Course Percentage will be translated into a letter grade according to the following table of equivalence:

% Score	Letter	% Score	Letter	% Score	Letter
90 - 100	A+	70 - 72	B-	53 - 56	D
85 - 89	A	67 - 69	C+	50 - 52	D-
80 - 84	A-	63 - 66	C	0 - 49	F
77 - 79	B+	60 - 62	C-		
73 - 76	B	57 - 59	D+		

Using This Handbook and Other Course Materials

This Handbook

This Handbook contains the gist (and sometimes much more than the gist) of the notes I work from during lectures - at least the version of those notes that was current when the Handbook was printed. I provide a Handbook for my courses for several reasons.

First, I want to make sure that you do not have to be constantly scribbling (or typing) in notes during the lecture, but can spend most of your time thinking about the material we are covering. It makes little sense to me to have you taking dictation from material that I already have in digital form, and the best way to master the material in any course is to stay engaged with it for as long as possible.

Second, I want to make sure that you don't miss anything, either because you were unable to attend a particular lecture, or because you forgot or were unable to get everything down as I was rattling on.

Just a few more words about this Handbook. Keep in mind that **THIS HANDBOOK IS NOT THE OFFICIAL CONTENT OF THE COURSE**. The official course content is whatever we talk about in lecture. You will often find that there is material in this Handbook that is not mentioned in lecture. Any material in the Handbook that is not mentioned in lecture **IS NOT PART OF THE COURSE CONTENT THIS TERM**.

On the other hand, new information relevant to Abnormal Psychology is constantly being published, and now and again I will mention in lecture a new study or theory that does **NOT** appear anywhere in this Handbook. Any such material **IS** part of the official course content, and may appear on midterm tests and/or the final exam.

In particular, information provided by the guest speakers in this course **IS DEFINITELY PART OF THE COURSE CONTENT**, even though none of it appears in this Handbook, or in the online lecture recordings.

Course Website

Copies of the course outline, together with a number of other course materials, can be found on the two course websites:

The first is http://intropsych.mcmaster.ca/psych2ap3, (abbreviated below as "intro2AP3").

The second course website is on McMaster's learning management system, **Avenue to Learn** (abbreviated below as "A2L"). Information about the contents of the course website(s) can be found below.

Course Outline

There are links on the course home page (on both course website) to copies of the course outline, sometimes in HTML, sometimes in PDF format. I will not be providing paper copies of the outline in class. If changes are made to the course outline, those changes will be announced in class, and will appear shortly thereafter on both versions of the posted course outline.

If changes to the outline are announced, make sure to consult and/or download the outlines posted on the web to make sure you have the updated version. This is especially important for in-class test dates, which will not be known for certain until a few weeks into the course.

2AP3 Forum

On the A2L 2AP3 home page there is a tab or menu item for "Discussions". This is where all important announcements about the course will be posted (on the "Course Info and Instructor Announcements" section), and where you can post any questions or comments about the course on the "Comments and Questions" section. You should check the Forum for relevant postings at least once per week.

I also often post important course information as news items on the home page of the A2L 2AP3 site. Keep an eye out for these.

Lecture Materials

On the A2L site, and sometimes on the intro2AP3 site, you will find updated copies of the PowerPoint slides that I use in lecture under the link "Lecture Materials". The slides are posted in both PowerPoint 2003 (.PPT) format, and as a much larger Adobe Acrobat (.PDF) file.

I use the slides both to illustrate material from the lectures, and to remind me of what I want to say next so I won't wander too far off course during lectures. **The PowerPoint slides do NOT provide a full and accurate summary of the material in the lecture**. There will be a number of important points in lecture that will not appear on the slides, either because these points do not lend themselves to graphic illustration or because I don't want the slides to be overcrowded with text.

There may also be slides on which not all the points are of equal importance. What I want to stress is that **you should not use the posted PowerPoint slides as a substitute for your notes, or the material in this Handbook, as a way of mastering the course material.** The slides are a general guide to the course material, and usually (but not always) contain a mention or illustration of the most important points. To be sure that you have learned everything you need to know, compare your knowledge with the content of your class notes, or with the content of the lecture recordings.

PDF copies of the midterm tests will be posted on A2L under "Test Copies" a few days after each test has been marked, and the results posted.

Grades Lookup

On the intro2AP3 site, the "Grades Lookup" link provides access to a complete list of your marks in the course once you enter your student ID number. It will also show the answers you selected on each of the midterm tests, and allow you to compare your answers with the correct answers for each test.

Note that **ANYONE** who knows your ID number can get access to your course marks and final grade through this page. If you are concerned that this might happen, and do not want your course marks posted online, email me at any time and let me know. I will arrange to have your marks information removed from the online grades database. If your marks are not posted on intro2AP3, you will still be able to get them from the "Grades" section of A2L site, though you will not be able to compare your midterm answers with the master on A2L. Generally, midterm and exam marks are posted first on the intro2AP3 Grades Lookup, and only a few days later on A2L.

Once marks for each midterm are posted, be sure to check for yours. Sometimes (though rarely), midterm scans are misplaced, and the more time that passes before I am alerted to look for a missing scan, the less likely it is that I will find it.

Online Sample Quiz

This link on the intro2AP3 home page provides access to a sample quiz containing multiple-choice questions similar or identical to those that will appear on the in-class midterm tests and on the final exam. You can select questions specific to any content area(s) of the course, and choose how many questions (3, 5, or 10) will be shown per page. Once you have chosen and submitted your answers, you will be given feedback on whether your answers were correct.

Please note the caution on the main quiz page: "The sample quiz is **NOT** a study guide; it should be used only **AFTER** you have studied the material covered by the quiz questions, as a way of assessing your understanding of the material, and identifying content areas where you need to spend a bit more time. Trying to memorize the answers to all the questions in the hopes that they will show up on the in-class tests or final exam won't help you at all."

Several other cautions about using the online quiz:

As the quiz page indicates, about 1% of this time the quiz messes up and provides wrong or meaningless feedback about the accuracy of your answers. When this happens, you should log out (using the "Log Out" button on top of each quiz page) and start again. **DO NOT RELY ON THE QUIZ TO PROVIDE CORRECT ANSWERS TO THE QUESTIONS. ALWAYS RELY ON YOUR CLASS NOTES OR THIS HANDBOOK** to determine the correct answers to online quiz questions.

Note also that the online quiz does not contain any questions from the assigned readings in the text.

Because the material content of the course changes a bit from term to term, the online quiz may contain questions about material that is **NOT** part of this term's course content. Simply ignore those questions.

Since the recent publication of the American Psychiatric Association's Diagnostic and Statistical Manual of Mental Disorders, Fifth Edition (DSM-5), some quiz questions may make reference to DSM-IV terms, categories, and diagnostic criteria, though I am trying to update those questions as rapidly as I can. You can ignore any questions that refer to DSM-IV, unless their content is still relevant to DSM-5.

2AP3 Links

This page on the intro2AP3 site contains any useful or interesting links to external sites. I haven't updated this page recently, and there isn't much on it at the moment. If you find any sites that you think merit mention, let me know.

Search the Site

This page on the intro2AP3 site allows you to search for any text on the site. Because much of the content of the site is located in PowerPoint or PDF files, this isn't as useful as it might be otherwise, but give it a try if you're looking for something specific.

Contact Me

This link on the intro2AP3 home page takes you to a list of my office hours for the current month, and a link to my office cam so you can see whether I am in or not. I sometimes make changes to my office hours during the month, so if you are planning a visit to my office, check here first to make sure I will be available when you stop by.

On the A2L site, there will be a link (under News Items) to the intro2AP3 Contact Me page.

Lecture Recordings

Recordings of all course lectures will be posted on both course websites, typically within a day or two of their delivery. Audio-only recordings are posted in both MP3 and WMA formats, and audio-video recordings (ECHO recordings, combining slides and audio) will be posted on A2L only as MPEG (MP4) files.

On the intro2AP3 site, the audio recordings can be found through the "Lecture Recordings" links at the bottom of the page. On A2L, the audio and Audio-video recordings can be found under "Content".

On rare occasions, I forget to bring my recorder to class, or there is a technical glitch that results in a missed audio recording, and sometimes the Echo system that creates the audio-video recordings fails to work. So don't count on there always being a class recording available!

When we have guest speakers who are describing their experiences with mental disorder, their talks are **NOT RECORDED** in order to protect their privacy. You should therefore make sure to attend any such talks, as the midterm tests and final exam will contain questions about any guest presentations that take place during the course.

Getting Listed References

The contains a list of references at the end of each section, in the event that you would like to read a particular paper yourself, or would like more information on a topic we are covering. The McMaster Library has an excellent and extensive collection of Psychology journals available online, and many of them provide downloadable PDF copies of the full text of the research and theoretical articles I mention during lecture. I strongly urge you to get familiar with this resource, and learn how to access it. You will find this very helpful in many of your other courses, including courses outside psychology.

The place to start is here: http://library.mcmaster.ca/. If you are on campus, or already connected to the McMaster network, you can then simply type in the key words of the journal you are looking for (e.g., "journal abnormal psychology", as in Figure 1) making sure that you are searching for "Title keyword(s)", and then click "GO".

You will then see the list of journals whose titles contain those key words (see Figure 2). Scroll down to find the journal you are looking for; we'll take the Journal of Abnormal Psychology.

In this case (Figure 3), you will see that there are two sources for PDF copies of the full text of articles: the Scholars Portal provides access to full-text articles from 1988 to the current issue, and CSA PsycArticles provides full text PDFs from 1970 until the current issue. You can click on either one of these to locate the journal article you are interested in. It is hard to imagine an easier way to do searches.

Both the library web pages and the good folks in the library itself are superb resources for anyone looking for information. Don't hesitate to ask anyone there for help, since the opportunity to get you the resources you need is what they live for - seriously!

If you are off-campus, you can still get access to these resources using your MacID. Just begin by clicking "Login to LibAccess" link that you see at the bottom left

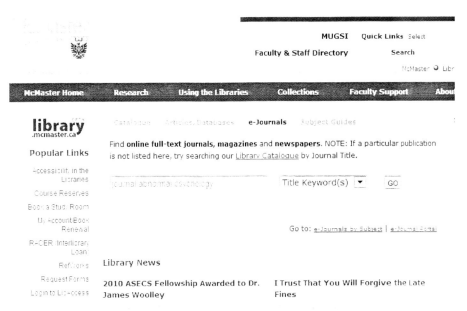

Figure 1: Library Main Page

of Figure 1, enter your MacID, and continue on as if you were on campus.

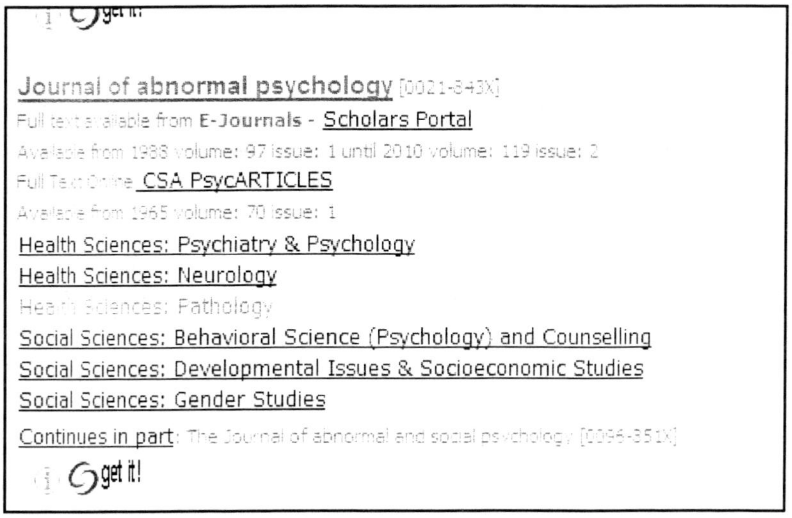

Figure 2: Journal of Abnormal Psychology listing

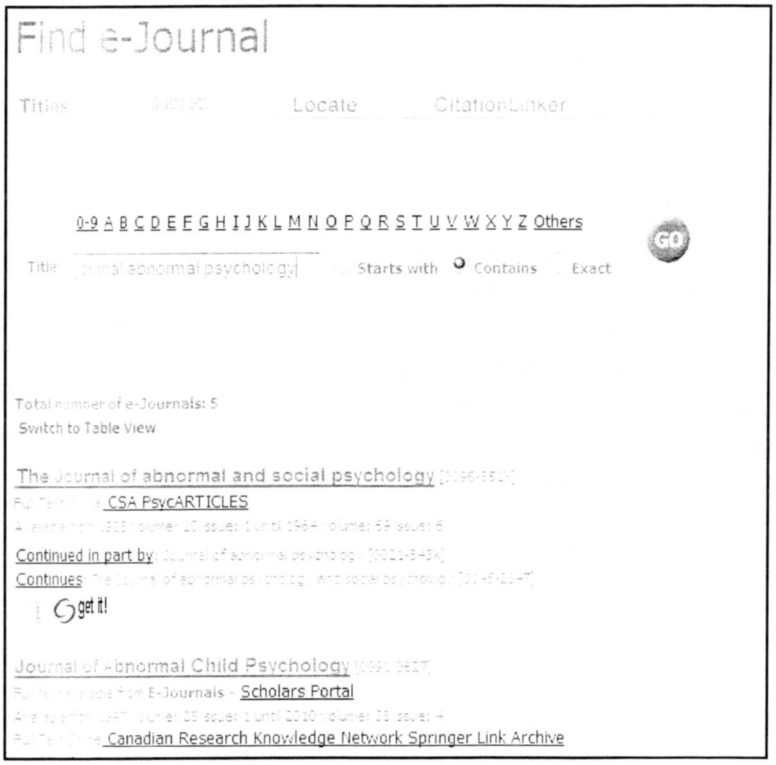

Figure 3: journal search results

If you are interested in keeping up with the growing literature in the area of abnormal and clinical psychology - or any other area of science for that matter, I recommend the Science Daily website (http://www.sciencedaily.com/). Be sure to check the "Health & Medicine" and "Mind & Brain" sections of the home page. You can also sign up for one or more of their daily new updates through links lower down on the home page.

Introduction to Abnormal Psychology

I. Introduction:

    A. There are a number of areas in psychology that have wide appeal to non-psychologists as well as to psychologists. Courses in these areas are always among the most popular at university. One of those is this course, **Abnormal Psychology** 2AP3.
        1. Abnormal psychology fascinates us in part because while we can imagine most forms of human thought and behavior, we often have trouble imagining what it would feel like to experience life as those with mental disorders do.
        2. Still less do we understand what might lead someone to develop these symptoms.

    B. What this course will **NOT** do:
        1. This is **not** a course in clinical psychology, so while we will talk about the ways in which we are now treating mental disorders, we will not be focusing on this area of psychological practice.
        2. This course will not make you a skilled or expert diagnostician. Indeed, as we will see, there is considerable question as to whether sorting symptoms into our current diagnostic categories (of the DSM or ICD) is really very useful.
            a. Note that inter-rater diagnostic reliability may actually decrease with increasing experience.

    C. What are the goals of this course?
        1. A primary goal is to help you understand what we currently think or believe we know about how and why mental disorders arise - **etiology**.
        2. A second goal is to help you gain an appreciation of how difficult investigating etiology is, both because of its complexity, and because of the ethical restraints that we necessarily put on research with people - and especially with people who are psychologically troubled or vulnerable.
        3. A third goal is to increase your ability to understand and appreciate the personal experiences of those who develop the symptoms of mental disorder.

II. Challenges of the course:

    A. The ideas, concepts, data, hypotheses and theories covered in this course are not always easy to organize or make sense of.
        1. To come away from this course with a real understanding of this area, you have to come a way a bit confused and perplexed.
        2. An educated person should always be perplexed to a certain degree, because perplexity is an accurate description of our current level of understanding.

B. Because of its content, no way to make this course completely objective and independent of the views and biases of the instructor. Each person who presents this material must do so in a way that reflects his or her beliefs, biases, pet hypotheses and so on.
   1. The problem of objectivity shows up immediately in the words we use to talk about the content of this course, and about the symptoms we will be describing and trying to understand.
      a. Almost every way of describing our subject matter reflects a particular point of view, a particular model or theory about abnormal psychology. All of us have preconceptions and implicit hypotheses or theories about **abnormal psychology**, (which is like calling medicine 'abnormal physiology) or **mental illness**, or **behavioral disorders**. We'll talk about the assumptions behind these terms later on.
      b. When we talk about psychological disorders, we often describe them as though they were an integral part of who the person is: Was talk about an individual as being 'a schizophrenic', or 'an antisocial personality', or 'a paranoid', or 'an alcoholic'. We only rarely do that with purely physical disorders, and almost always for a condition that cannot be cured:
         (1) a diabetic; a hemiplegic, an asthmatic, (though that can disappear too); but we don't talk about someone as 'an arthritic', even though arthritis is a permanent condition.
         (2) So we treat physical ailments as though they were imposed on the individual, but mental disorders as though they are intrinsic to the individual. Why?
      c. Perhaps it's because mental disorders often - perhaps generally - alter the nature of the self, or personality of the individual, while purely physical ailments do not.

C. Metalessons:
   1. Every course has content - things that we learn:
      a. Facts or observations.
      b. Theories that attempt to explain and make sense of those observations.
      c. General perspectives - ways of looking at issues and content.
   2. Most courses also carry with them **metalessons**: Things we come to understand even though they may not be among the central content of the course. Usually understanding these metalessons is our most important achievement in the course, even if the understanding is not something that appears on the tests or exam. That is certainly true of this course.
   3. One of the metalessons from abnormal is about the extent of our ignorance concerning the etiology of mental illness, or psychopathology. In virtually every case, every disorder we discuss, the bottom line with respect to causality will be - 'We're not sure.'

III. What is the nature of abnormality?

   A. The behavior of individuals ranges from shy, introverted and withdrawn to extroverted free-spending egoists; from peace-loving Quakers to violent political extremists.

   B. We consider most behavior to be normal, or at least the product of a sound mind. However, we call some people "crazy" or "mentally ill". What do we mean by that? When is behavior sufficiently abnormal, or "crazy" that we consider the individual as someone needing treatment?

C. Most personality theorists and mental health professionals argue that the there is no clear dividing line between normal and pathological - it is instead a continuum.

D. What we are really asking is what is abnormal to the point that we as a society, or we as scientists, or we as psychotherapists and psychiatrists think that a label should be attached to the individual's symptoms, and treatment recommended?

IV. **Criteria of Abnormality or Psychopathology**: What symptoms would you look for in deciding whether a person is disordered, or whether his behavior is the product of a disordered mind?

A. **Impairment Criterion**: We can consider someone mentally ill who shows disability or impairment in some important domain of interpersonal functioning, such as school, workplace, interpersonal relationships, etc. In fact, this criterion of impairment (or personal distress) is part of most defining criteria in the DSM-5, as it was in DSM-IV. But what about symptoms that only have the POTENTIAL to lead to impairment or disability?

B. **Personal Distress Criterion**: We describe as a mental disorder any symptom, or set of symptoms, that lead the individual to be concerned or distressed by his or her behavior, thoughts, or emotions.
1. But what about those who exhibit extraordinarily deranged behavior, loss of contact with reality, but who do not think they are in trouble?
2. What does this imply about homosexuality? What about shyness, inability to say the right thing to members of the opposite sex? Inability to assert oneself? We may be bothered by these things, but they are not considered psychological disorders.

C. Normally, we use a combination of both these criteria (and occasionally other criteria) to determine whether an individual's behavior, thoughts, or emotions merit some psychiatric label and treatment.

D. Ultimately, abnormality is whatever psychiatrists and psychologists agree that it is. That shared agreement (which changes every few years) is expressed in the DSM (and in the World Health Organization's International Classification of Diseases, which is still the official coding and description of mental and physical disorders.) See http://www.who.int/classifications/icd/en/

V. **Just What IS Psychopathology and What are Its Causes?** (mental illness, abnormal behavior, etc.) Everyone has a model of how we should understand or conceptualize this thing we call "mental disorder". Each model of causality makes assumptions about what mental disorder is, how it comes about and how it should be treated or ameliorated.

   A. **The Biomedical model**: This model argues that a mental disorder is really a physical disorder, a physical problem with the brain or nervous system, that leads to the psychological symptoms we identify as criteria of the disorder.
   1. This idea arose from the observation that certain mental disturbances occurred from syphilitic infection (tertiary syphilis); or mercury poisoning in the case of 'madness' among hatters.
   2. Chemical imbalance hypothesis of depression, schizophrenia is an example of the application of this model.
   3. This model is the source of much commonly used terminology with respect to psychopathology: a person is "sick", "mental illness", etc.
   4. A person is a schizophrenic in the same way that we say that someone is diabetic. Just as diabetes does not define the person who has it, neither does schizophrenia.
   5. Suggests purely physical/pharmacological treatment of all disorders.
   6. Schizophrenia, Depression, and the Neurodevelopmental disorders (e.g., ADHD, ASD) are considered leading candidates for this type of etiology.
   7. Problems associated with this now-dominant model (e.g., Deacon, 2013):
      a. No purely biological cause has been found for any mental disorder described in the DSM.
      b. There are no biological tests that allow mental disorders to be diagnosed.
      c. Despite the development of many new psychotropic drugs over the past 30 years, the prevalence and severity of mental disorder has not decreases, it has increased.

   B. **The Psychodynamic model**: This model argues that the symptoms we call mental disorder do not result from any physical or physiological problem in the brain or nervous system, but have purely psychological causes. Specifically, the symptoms of mental disorder result from maladaptive psychological responses to an internal, unconscious conflict.
   1. Internal conflict is translated into some external behavior pattern that is maladaptive, inappropriate, or destructive of normal functioning.
   2. One important assumption of the psychodynamic model - not usually shared by the medical model - is that the processes that lead to disorder are the same processes that produce or maintain order in our lives. They are not qualitatively different.
   3. Treatment involves bringing buried conflict into consciousness, where more rational means can be used to deal with it.
   4. Prime candidates are Anxiety Disorders, Somatic Symptom Disorders, Dissociative Disorders.

   C. **Behavioral model**: This model argues that the symptoms we call mental disorder are just behaviors that have been learned through the usual processes of reward, punishment, and generalization. There is no internal problem, no physical disorder, just behavior that is inappropriate, maladaptive, dangerous, or self-destructive.
   1. Abnormal behavior is learned, then generalized to situations in which it is not appropriate.

2. As in the psychodynamic model, the processes that lead to abnormality are the same as those that maintain normality.
3. Treatment involves changing the conditions of learning, and schedules of reward, to modify behavior.
4. Prime candidates are phobias (and other anxiety disorders), obsessive-compulsive disorders.

D. **Socio-Cultural model**: This model argues that abnormal behavior, and even internal emotional symptoms, result from stresses placed on the individual by his or her environment, and are therefore in an important sense caused by the society or culture in which the individual lives.
   1. This model helps account for the observation that there is more psychopathology in lower socioeconomic strata than in higher, and that maladaptive and criminal behavior increase in difficult economic times, and under the pressures of environmental stress, (e.g., high temperatures).
   2. This model is not as popular today, perhaps partly because it requires a change in the environment that is global and cannot be effected by therapists, and partly because of the noticeable conservative turn of political and social views in recent decades.
   3. But certainly there is evidence of a relationship between early social environment and brain functioning, and perhaps mental illness:
      a. **Burt (2009)** reports meta-analytic evidence from twin and adoption studies for significant contribution of shared environmental variance to a number of disorders, including conduct disorder, anxiety, oppositional defiant disorder, depression, etc. (But not ADHD)
   4. Also evidence for epigenetic effects on health related to socio-cultural situations:
      a. **Schreier & Chen. (2010)** found that parents' childhood socioeconomic status (SES) predicted blood pressure (BP) in 11-15 year olds over the course of a year.
         (1) Low parental childhood SES predicted increasing BP, while higher parental childhood SES predicted greater decreases in BP over that same period.
         (2) Effects apparent even when controlling for current SES, child health behaviors, parent psychosocial characteristics, general family functioning, and parent physiology.
      b. **Miller & Chen (2007)** found that early-life SES (home ownership) predicted later activity of two genes (GR and TLR4) regulating inflammation in adolescent females.
         (1) found that parental home ownership between ages 2 and 3 of children predicted higher GR and lower TLR4 during adolescence, suggesting better regulation of inflammatory responses.
         (2) These effects were still present when current SES, life stress, or health practices controlled for. These effects not reversed by changes in SES during later years.
         (3) Concluded unfavorable SES in early life predicts higher inflammatory responses in adolescence.
      c. **Yee & Prendergast (2010)** found that conditions of housing (Alone or in Groups) influenced responses to simulated bacterial infection in rats.
         (1) found that Group housing worsened inflammatory responses and sickness behaviors in females, but improved them in males.
   5. We will see later that the immune system has been implicated in the causal chain of several important mental disorders, including autism and schizophrenia.

E. **Cognitive model**: argues that abnormal behaviors, thoughts, and emotions result from maladaptive or incorrect ways of selecting information or interpreting events around us.
   1. Maladaptive modes of thinking are learned, consistent with the behavioral model.
   2. Treatment involves training individuals to think differently about themselves, and their situation.
   3. Now among the most popular and successful forms of treatment.
   4. Prime candidates are anxiety disorders, depression.

VI. Our Trip Through the Classification System

A. For the rest of this course, we will be looking at a variety of mental disorders, and we will follow the description and classification system of the American Psychiatric Association, as embodied in the American Psychiatric Association's Diagnostic and Statistical Manual of Mental Disorders, Fifth Edition - or just DSM-5.

B. Before we start this journey, we need to think about what these descriptions and classifications really mean - what they are and are not.

C. All systems of classification intend to bring things together that have some quality in common, and separate them from others that have something different in common.
   1. For mental disorders, the current classification is based on similarity and grouping of symptoms.
   2. The hope is that this classification also brings us closer to a classification on the basis of causes - and we'll say more about 'causes' later.

D. Most North American psychiatrists use the classification system for psychopathology: the Diagnostic and Statistical Manual (DSM) of the American Psychiatric Association (APA). The DSM discriminates different mental disorders on the basis of similarity in symptom patterns.

E. A brief history of the APA's DSM:
   1. **DSM-I**; 1952. A variant of ICD-6, first listing of accepted categories for diagnosis, together with a description of the characteristics of each category. Strongly biased toward psychodynamic interpretations of disorders, and first manual to emphasize clinical utility rather than simple statistical categorization. Contained **106** categories in its 130 pages.
   2. **DSM-II**; 1968. Tried to remove the psychodynamic theoretical bias from DSM-I. Made diagnosis more objective. Listed **182** disorders in its 134 pages. Like DSM-I, categorized disorders broadly as neuroses (anxiety disorders without loss of contact with reality) vs psychoses (loss of contact with reality as evidenced by hallucinations, delusions.)
   3. **DSM-III**; 1980; Moved even more in the direction of atheoretical description. Designed to be more compatible with the ICD. Tried to base categorization strictly on description

of symptoms rather than on assumptions about causes. The psychodynamic view abandoned, more leaning toward biomedical model. Listed **265** diagnostic categories in its 494 pages.
4. **DSM III-R**; 1987. Revision of DSM III. Some categories dropped, others added. Contained **292** diagnoses in 567 pages.
5. **DSM-IV**; 1994: Lists **297** disorders in 886 pages.
6. **DSM-IV-TR**; 2000. Diagnostic categories and most specific diagnostic criteria unchanged, but descriptive text updated, and some diagnostic codes modified to maintain consistency with ICD.
7. **DSM-V**; 2013. About 900 pages; Number of diagnostic categories: Again about 300, not including subcategory codes, but including some conditions that may be a focus of clinical attention.
   a. Organizes its description of mental disorders in lifespan order, with symptoms first diagnosed in early life described first, and symptoms most common in later life described last.
   b. DSM-5 also includes (in Section III) a description of conditions not coded for in DSM-5, but worthy of future study. These include (but are not limited to):
      (1) Persistent Complex Bereavement Disorder
      (2) Caffeine Use Disorder
      (3) Internet Gaming Disorder
      (4) Neurobehavioral Disorder Associate with Prenatal Alcohol Exposure (Fetal Alcohol Syndrome)

F. What does DSM-5 mean by "mental disorder"?
   1. "A mental disorder is a syndrome characterized by clinically significant disturbance in an individual's cognition, emotion regulation, or behavior that reflects a dysfunction in the psychological, biological, or developmental processes underlying mental functioning. Mental disorders are usually associated with significant distress or disability in social, occupational, or other important activities. An expectable or culturally approved response to a common stressor or loss, such as the death of a loved one, is not a mental disorder. Socially deviant behavior (e.g., political, religious, or sexual) and conflicts that are primarily between the individual and society are not mental disorders unless the deviance or conflict results from a dysfunction in the individual, as described above." (DSM-5, p. 20)
   2. DSM-5 also recognizes explicitly that there is a thin line between normal and pathological, delineated by the presence of stress or impairment: "...in the absence of clear biological markers or clinically useful measurement of severity for many mental disorders, it has not been possible to completely separate normal and pathological symptom expressions contained in diagnostic criteria. This gap in information is particularly problematic in clinical situations in which the patient's symptoms presentation by itself (particularly in mild forms) is not inherently pathological and may be encountered in individuals for whom a diagnosis of 'mental disorder' would be inappropriate. Therefore a generic diagnostic criterion requiring distress or disability has been used to establish disorder thresholds, usually worded 'the disturbance causes **clinically significant** distress or impairment in social, occupational, or other important areas of functioning'. (DSM-5, p. 21)
   3. But there is no accepted definition of "clinically significant", so there is a lot of

subjectivity here.
4. The DSM is not a cookbook: "Diagnostic criteria are offered as guidelines for making diagnoses, and their use should be informed by clinical judgment..."

G. What the DSM 5 is, and is not.
1. The DSM 5 is a set of diagnostic labels or categories which are used by clinicians to describe and classify the problems that their patients present.
2. Purpose of these labels and categories is to help clinicians decide which treatment options are appropriate for their patients, and a descriptive shortcut that clarifies communication between professionals.
3. The DSM 5 categories are **not** (necessarily) indicative of etiological relationships between disorders. Note that between DSM II and DSM III, and between DSM-IV and DSM-5, changes were made in major category in which many disorders fall.
   a. "The current classification of psychiatric disorders reflects clinical syndromes with largely unknown etiology and is based on historical descriptions provided by prominent clinicians over the last 125 years." (Lee, Ripke, Neale et al, 2013; p. 984)
4. It is also hoped that eventually, the DSM categories will better reflect the causal (etiological) relationships between disorders.
5. Note that the labels in the DSM are applied to the **SYMPTOMS** an individual experiences, **NOT** to the individuals themselves even though we often, and wrongly, apply them to individuals in ordinary (and sometimes even in professional) conversions: e.g., "she is obsessive-compulsive", "he is schizophrenic", etc.

H. What do categories mean to DSM 5?
1. Identifies a dysfunction based on personal distress, impaired functioning, or an increased risk of suffering impaired functioning.
2. Given the nature of disorder criteria, it is possible in a number of cases for two people with very different symptoms to meet the criteria for the same disorder.
3. Must be used with sensitivity to different cultural practices.

VII. Criticisms of classification, and of DSM in particular; and DSM-5 especially

A. Many people argue that classification using symptom categories like those in DSM is misguided; that categorization assumes similar symptoms mean similar disorders, or existence of disease process or common mechanism of etiology. Not necessarily so.
1. Critics point out that classifications change with clinical experience over the years: DSM-IV is not the same as DSM-III-R, which was not the same as DSM-II, and DSM-V is coming.
2. Critics also note that there are 'trends' and 'fads' in classification. Certain diagnoses become popular or unpopular.
   a. Once, N. American diagnosticians classified as schizophrenic patients that U.K. diagnosticians would classify as manic-depressive.
   b. During 1980s and 1990s, MPD became more common diagnosis than at any previous time.
   c. Borderline personality disorder now much more common diagnosis.

3. Categorization can label individual, even if diagnosis was inappropriate. Later diagnoses and treatment biased by label. Social stigma also attached to label.
4. Some (psychodynamic theorists) would like to classify according to underlying mechanisms of symptom formation.
5. Others would like to forego categorization altogether in favor of simple description.

B. See disorders as entities rather than as points on a continuum - this has been a focus of criticism in the long runup to DSM-IV. Especially since DSM makes clear there are no clear boundaries between disorders, or no disorder.

C. Some 'disorders' seem very out of place in a classification of mental disorders:
1. Learning Disorders in childhood (math, etc.)
2. Conduct Disorder; Oppositional Defiant Disorder
3. Motor disorders in childhood
4. Substance-related disorders
5. Sleep Disorders
6. Medication-Induced Movement Disorders
7. Mental Retardation - genetic, and no treatment; is it a 'disorder'?
8. Factitious Disorders

D. Critics argue that the DSM, and DSM-5 in particular because of its broad and inclusive diagnostic criteria, makes ordinary experiences of life, like depressed mood and grief, into mental disorders, putting many normal individuals at risk of being diagnosed and medicated.
1. A number of psychological associations have criticized the DSM-5 for expanding the range of otherwise normal behaviors and emotions that now could fall under a diagnostic category as a mental illness.
2. Several especially contentious changes:
   a. Normal bereavement can now be diagnosed as major, since the exception for bereavement that was present in DSM-IV has been removed from DSM-5.
   b. Extreme childhood temper tantrums now have a new diagnostic label: "disruptive mood dysregulation disorder". The APA argues that this will save children from being misdiagnosed as having childhood bipolar disorder, but critics argue that normal tantrums will become a mental illness.
   c. Typical 'senior moments' now also can receive a diagnostic label: "mild neurocognitive disorder."
   d. Excessive (and who decides?) thoughts or feelings about pain or discomfort now qualify for a diagnostic label (somatic symptom disorder). Critics argue that this makes normal reactions to a disease into mental illness."
   e. The new category of binge eating applies to any case of "Adding binge eating as a new category for overeating that occurs at least once a week for at least three months. It could apply to people who sometimes gulp down a pint of ice cream when they're alone and then feel guilty about it."

E. Proponents of diagnostic classification argue that:
1. Useful because it gives clinicians a common language or shorthand in which to describe or discuss cases. Label conveys information quickly.
2. In many cases, similar symptoms may actually indicate similar underlying disease or dynamic processes of etiology.

3. In many cases, similar symptoms respond to similar treatments.
4. Without trying to classify we cannot make first steps toward understanding disorders.

VIII. What will we cover in the DSM, and why?

A. Given the size of DSM-5 (about 300 disorders described in 900 plus pages) we obviously can discuss only a small fraction of them.

B. How did I choose the disorder categories and disorders that we will discuss? Several criteria employed; not all at the same time.
1. Some disorders chosen for discussion because they are common, are therefore frequently seen in clinical settings, and should be understood: E.g., anxiety disorders, depression.
2. Some disorders chosen because can be extremely debilitating, and have bee an important focus of research and clinical attention for a long time: E.g., depression, bipolar disorder, schizophrenia.
3. Some disorders chosen because they are interesting, and/or promise once understood to illuminate a number of aspects of general psychological functioning: E.g., dissociative disorders, somatic symptom disorders.
4. Some disorders chosen because they have often been or have recently become, the focus of public and research attention: ADHD, Autism.
5. Some disorders chosen because they are areas of controversy: E.g., DID.

C. In almost every case, we will look at these disorders from several perspectives:
1. Description and DSM 5 diagnostic criteria.
2. Epidemiology: Who gets the disorder, how commonly? How does it progress?
3. Etiology: What are the causes of the disorder?
4. Briefly (in most cases) Mention current treatments.

IX. Etiology: Causes and Explanations

A. What do we mean by a 'cause'?
1. If A always produces B, we can say that A is a **sufficient** cause of effect B.
2. If B never happens unless A is present, we can say that A is a **necessary and sufficient** cause of B.
3. But we almost never find this situation psychology - and certainly not in abnormal psychology.

B. Consider the question 'What is the cause of fire?'
1. It takes three factors ('causes') to produce a file: Fuel; heat, and oxygen.
2. All three are necessary, but no one or two is sufficient: Remove any one and the fire goes out (or won't start).

C. This is how the diathesis-stress model of mental illness works:
1. A **diathesis** is a predisposition, a readiness. It can be genetic, neurochemical, or structural (caused

by e.g., prenatal or perinatal trauma).
2. A **stress** is a precipitating condition, generally thought of as environmental or experiential.
   a. Could be personal illness, educational failure
   b. Could be unemployment, demotion, criticism at work
   c. Could be relationship loss or change
3. In the presence of the diathesis, the stress triggers the disordered symptoms.
4. So while we would like a simple causal chain that leads from a single gene through some affected brain structure or neurochemical deficit, to a psychological process, to a symptom, things are never that simple.

D. **Belsky & Pluess (2009)**. The environmental sensitivity hypothesis. Argue that we should think differently about diathesis-stress. Rather than susceptibility to negative environmental events, as diathesis-stress hypothesis proposes, some genes confer differential susceptibility to environmental influences, both positive and negative. (See also Ellis et al, 2011)
   1. Perhaps "those putatively 'vulnerable' individuals most adversely affected by many kinds of stressors may be the very same ones who reap the most benefit from environmental support and enrichment, including the absence of adversity." (**Belsky & Pluess, 2009**, p. 886)
   2. Examples:
      a. **Lengua et al (2000)** found that highly impulsive children showed fewest depressive symptoms when mothers provided consistent discipline, but most symptoms when discipline highly inconsistent. The relationship between parenting and depression was strongest in the most impulsive children, absent in the least impulsive.
      b. **Foley et al. (2004)**: found that adolescent boys with low-MAO-A-activity allele **more** likely to have conduct disorder if exposed to higher levels of childhood adversity, but **less** likely to have conduct disorder if exposed to lower levels of adversity.
      c. **Caspi et al. (2003)** demonstrated that alleles of the serotonin receptor promoter region (5-HTTLPR) moderates effects of life stress during early adulthood on depressive symptoms, as well as on probability of suicide ideation/attempts and of major depression episode at age 26 years.
         (1) Individuals with two short (s) alleles most adversely affected, whereas effects on l/l genotypes were weaker or entirely absent. Carriers of s/s allele scored best on outcomes when life stresses absent.
         (2) A number of studies indicate that individuals carrying short alleles (s/s, s/l) not only functioned most poorly when exposed to many stressors but functioned best when they encountered few or none.
         (3) **Taylor et al. (2006)**: young adults with two short alleles (s/s) showed more depressive symptoms than those with other allele combinations when exposed to early adversity (i.e., problematic child-rearing history), and many recent negative life events, but showed fewest symptoms when they had experienced a supportive early environment or recent positive experiences. (B&P, p. 897)
      d. Same result for 5-HTTLPR in moderating environmental influences with respect to anxiety (**Gunthert et al., 2007; Stein, Schork, & Gelernter, 2008**) and ADHD.

E. The cascade of reductionistic 'causes':
   1. We start with presenting symptoms.
   2. Assume they reflect (are 'caused' by) problems/dysfunction on one or more psychological functions or systems (e.g., attention, memory, perception, self-regulation, attribution, etc.).

3. We assume those psychological dysfunction 'caused' by abnormality in brain chemistry or structure.
4. This can be caused by: Drugs, traumatic brain injury, prenatal teratogens, bacterial or viral infections, or - a favorite candidate - genetic abnormality.
5. But socio-cultural factors like learning and experience can also affect brain chemistry and structure (in the case of learning, at least).
6. So what is 'the cause'?

F. What we accept as a sufficient cause or satisfactory explanation for a physical disorder depends in part on our own theoretical orientation or explanatory perspective. An internist, a psychiatrist, a social worker, and the national development office would see the 'causes' and remedies of this case differently. Who would be 'correct'?

G. The question of causation is a complex and multi-faceted one. There is an important sense in which all of the 'explanations' we just advanced for test anxiety are true - each at a different level of analysis, or each within the context of a different construct system for understanding psychopathology.

H. Example of depression and its relation to low levels of neurotransmitter activity
1. Because we find an associate between depression and low levels of neurotransmitter activity (esp. serotonin) in the brain, the tendency is to see the neurotransmitter deficit as the cause of the disordered thinking and the depressed affect.
2. This seems even more likely when we discover that drugs that increase neurotransmitter activity often (though not always) result in alleviated depression.
3. But if we give cognitive therapy, also get alleviated depression AND same changes in neurotransmitter activity induced by drugs. PLUS, drug-induced alleviation occurs days or weeks after neurotransmitter activity has returned to normal.
4. So what caused what?

I. EEG and behavior therapy: **Miskovic et al (2011)** reported that EEG in individuals with social anxiety changed to normal after behavioral therapy. so how can we attribute the social anxiety to abnormalities in brain wave activity, if a purely psychological intervention can change those brain waves?

References

Beardon, C.E., Jasinska, A.J. & Freimer, N.B. (2009). Methodological Issues in Molecular Genetic Studies of Mental Disorders. *Annual Review of Clinical Psychology*, 5:49–69.

Belsky, J. & Pluess, M. (2009a). Beyond Diathesis Stress: Differential Susceptibility to Environmental Influences. *Psychological Bulletin*, 135 (6), 885-908.

Belsky, J. & Pluess, M. (2009b). The Nature (and Nurture?) of Plasticity in Early Human Development. *Perspectives on Psychological Science*, 4(4), 345-351.

Belsky, J., Jonassaint, C., Pluess, M., Stanton, M., Brummett, B. & Williams, R. (2009). Vulnerability genes or plasticity genes?. *Molecular Psychiatry*, 14, 746-754.

Blatt, S. (2008). *Polarities of Experience*. Washington, DC: American Psychological Association.

Brown, T.A. & Barlow, D.H. (2005). Dimensional versus categorical classification of mental disorders in the fifth edition of the *Diagnostic and Statistical Manual of Mental Disorders* and beyond: Comments on the Special Section. *Journal of Abnormal Psychology*, 114, 551-556.

Caspi, A., Sugden, K., Moffitt, T. E., Taylor, A., Craig, I.W., Harrington, H., et al. (2003). Influence of life stress on depression: Moderation by a polymorphism in the 5 HTT gene. *Science*, 301, 386–389.

Charney, D.S. & Babich, K.S.. (2002). Foundation for the NIMH strategic plan for mood disorders research. *Biological Psychiatry*, 52, pp. 455–56.

Deacon, B. J. (2013). The biomedical model of mental disorder: A critical analysis of its validity, utility, and effects on psychotherapy research. *Clinical Psychology Review*, 33, 846-861.

Ellis, B. J., Boyce, W.T., Belsky, J., Bakermans-Kranenburg, M.J. & van Ijzendoorn, M.H. (2011). Differential susceptibility to the environment: An evolutionary-neurodevelopmental theory. *Development and Psychopathology*, 23, 7-28.

Foley, D. L., Eaves, L. J., Wormley, B., Silberg, J. L., Maes, H. H., Kuhn, J., & Riley, B. (2004). Childhood adversity, monoamine oxidase a genotype, and risk for conduct disorder. *Archives of General Psychiatry*, 61, 738–744.

Frances, Allen (2013). *Essentials of Psychiatric Diagnosis: Responding to the Challenge of DSM-5*. Guilford Press.

Frances, Allen. (2013) Saving Normal: *An Insider's Revolt Against Out-of-Control Psychiatric Diagnosis, DSM-5, Big Pharma, and the Medicalization of Ordinary Life*. William Morrow.

Gunthert, K. C., Conner, T. S., Armeli, S., Tennen, H., Covault, J., & Kranzler, H. R. (2007). Serotonin transporter gene polymorphism (5- HTTLPR) and anxiety reactivity in daily life: A daily process approach to gene– environment interaction. *Psychosomatic Medicine*, 69, 762– 768.

Hyman S. 2007. Can neuroscience be integrated into the DSM-V? *Nature Review, Neuroscience.* 8:725–32.

Lengua, L. J., Wolchik, S. A., Sandler, I. N., & West, S. G. (2000). The additive and interactive effects of parenting and temperament in predicting adjustment problems of children of divorce. *Journal of Clinical Child Psychology*, 29, 232–244.

Luyten, P. (2006). Psychopathology: A simple twist of fate or a meaningful distortion of normal development? Toward an etiologically based alternative to the DSM approach. *Psychoanalytic Inquiry*, 26, 521-535.

Luyten, P. & Blatt, S.J. (2007). Looking back toward the future: Is it time to change the DSM approach to psychiatric disorders? The case of depression. *Psychiatry: Interpersonal and Biological Processes*, 70, 85-99.

Stein, M. B., Schork, N. J., & Gelernter, J. (2008). Gene-by-environment (serotonin transporter and childhood maltreatment) interaction for anxiety sensitivity, an intermediate phenotype for anxiety disorders. *Neuropsychopharmacology*, 33, 312–319.

Taylor, S., Way, B., Welch, W., Hilmert, C., Lehman, B.,&Eisenberger, N. (2006). Early Family Environment, Current Adversity, the Serotonin Transporter Promoter Polymorphism, and Depressive Symptomatology. *Biological Psychiatry*, 60(7), 671-676.

Widiger, T.A. & Trull, T.J. (2007). Plate tectonics in the classification of personality disorder. *American Psychologist*, 62, 71-93.

Neurodevelopmental Disorders:
Attention Deficit/Hyperactivity Disorder (ADHD)

I. Introduction to Neurodevelopmental Disorders

    A. What are the disorders in this category?
        1. Intellectual Disabilities:
            a. Intellectual Disability (Intellectual Development Disorder).
        2. Communication Disorders:
            a. Language Disorders.
            b. Speech Sound Disorder.
            c. Childhood-Onset Fluency Disorder (Stuttering).
            d. Social (Pragmatic Communication Disorder.
            e. Unspecified Communication Disorder.
        3. Autism Spectrum Disorder.
        4. Attention-Deficit/Hyperactivity Disorder:
            a. Combined Presentation.
            b. Predominantly Inattentive Presentation.
            c. Predominantly hyperactive/impulsive presentation.
            d. Other Specified Attention-Deficit/Hyperactivity Disorder.
            e. Unspecified Attention-Deficit/Hyperactivity Disorder.
        5. Specific Learning Disorder
            a. Specifiers:
                (1) with impairment in reading.
                (2) with impairment in written expression.
                (3) with impairment in mathematics.
            b. Specify if Mild, Moderate, Severe.
        6. Motor Disorders:
            a. Development Coordination Disorder.
            b. Stereotypic Movement Disorder.
            c. Tourette's Disorder.
            d. Persistent (chronic) Motor or Vocal Tic Disorder.
            e. Provisional Tic Disorder.
            f. Other Specified Tic Disorder.
            g. Unspecified Tic Disorder.
        7. Other Neurodevelopmental Disorders:
            a. Other Specified Neurodevelopmental Disorder.
            b. Unspecified Neurodevelopmental Disorder.

II. Attention-Deficit/Hyperactivity Disorder;

A. First described in 1902 by English physician Dr. George Still, and has since become most studied developmental disorder in childhood. **Nigg, (2006)** calculates that ca 2,700 journal articles or book chapters on ADHD published from 2001 - 2005 alone.

B. Changes in name over the years:
1. In 1960s, often known as minimal brain dysfunction.
2. Term ADD introduced in the U.S., for children with and without hyperactivity; AD + H with hyperactivity, AD - H for those without.
3. In late 1980s, ADHD introduced to describe those with hyperactivity and/or impulsivity; ADD used to describe those with inattention.
4. In DSM-IV (1994) ADHD used for all cases, with three subcategories.
5. Same in DSM-5.

III. Description: The name given the disorder says it all:

A. Has difficulty paying attention, and/or is excessively active physically.
1. Easily distracted by events or stimuli around him or her, and so fails to complete tasks or assignments, loses things that are necessary for his activities, or wanders off to something else.
2. Quickly forgets and does not heed or follow information or instructions.

B. Is excessively active, physically:
1. Constantly moving, climbing, running, fidgeting even when sitting.
2. Often talks excessively, blurting out answers before questions have been completed.
3. Has trouble awaiting turn, and often butts into conversations, games. or other activities inappropriately.

C. Impulsive:
1. Difficulty postponing gratification and working for long-term goal.
2. Take risks that other children would not, and as a result are accident-prone.
3. Often damage or destroy their toys - including those they like the best - as well as others' property.

D. Social clumsiness:
1. Egocentric; tactless; unawares of image.
2. Insensitive to convention.
3. Over-talkative.
4. Difficulty reading facial expressions.
5. Aggressive tendencies.
6. Lack of judgment; poor understanding of group dynamics.

E. Most often detected and reported in school settings.

IV. DSM-5 Diagnostic Criteria

A. Two sets of criteria; The first describes the **Predominantly Inattentive** type
   1. Criterion 1: "At least six of the following nine symptoms of inattention. Symptoms must persist for at least 6 months, and to a degree that is inconsistent with developmental level, and have negative effect on social and academic or occupational functioning. " All quotations are from DSM-5, page 59-61:
      a. The individual "often fails to give close attention to details or makes careless mistakes in schoolwork, at work, or during other activities".
      b. The individual "often has difficulty sustaining attention in tasks or play activities".
      c. The individual "often does not seem to listen when spoken to directly".
      d. The individual "often does not follow through on instructions and fails to finish school-work, chores, or duties in the workplace". Not due to a failure to understand instructions, or to oppositional behavior.
      e. The individual "often has difficulty organizing tasks and activities".
      f. The individual "often avoids, dislikes, or is reluctant to engage in tasks that require sustained mental effort (such as schoolwork or homework)".
      g. The individual "often loses things necessary for tasks or activities (e.g., toys, school assignments, pencils, books, or tools)".
      h. The individual is "often easily distracted by extraneous stimuli".
      i. The individual is "often forgetful in daily activities".
   2. Criterion 2: This set describes the **Predominantly Hyperactive-Impulsive Type**. Six ore more of the following symptoms of hyperactivity-impulsivity. Symptoms must persist for at least 6 months "to a degree that is maladaptive and inconsistent with developmental level:" (note the frequent reference to school-based activities).
      a. The individual "often fidgets with or taps hands or feet or squirms in seat".
      b. The individual "often leaves seat in situations where remaining seated is expected".
      c. The individual "often runs about or climbs excessively in situations in which it is inappropriate (in adolescents or adults, may be limited to subjective feelings of restlessness)".
      d. The individual "often unable to play or engage in leisure activities quietly".
      e. The individual "is often 'on the go' or often acts as if 'driven by a motor".
      f. The individual "often talks excessively"
      g. The individual "often blurts out answers before questions have been completed"
      h. The individual "often has difficulty awaiting his or her turn".
      i. The individual "often interrupts or intrudes on others (e.g., butts into conversations or games)".
   3. Note the use of "often" in all these criteria - who decides what 'often' is? And how do we distinguish any of these symptoms from the normal behaviors of young (especially male) children?

B. 'Several' of these symptoms (and how many is 'several') appeared before the age of 12 years. (An expansion of the criteria from DSM-IV, where they had to appear before 7 years of age.)

C. 'Several' of these symptoms appear in at least two settings "(e.g., at home, school, or work; with friends or relatives, in other activities)."

D. "There is clear evidence that the symptoms interfere with, or reduce the quality of, social, academic, or occupational functioning."

E. The symptoms do not occur only in the context of schizophrenia or another psychotic disorder, and they "are not better explained by another mental disorder (e.g., mood disorder, anxiety disorder, dissociative disorder, personality disorder, substance intoxication or withdrawal)."

F. Clinician specifies whether the symptoms are:
 1. A combination of features from both (1) and (2).
 2. Predominantly inattentive (from criterion 1).
 3. Predominantly hyperactive/impulsive (criterion 2).

G. Clinician specifies the current severity of symptoms:
 1. **Mild**: Few or no symptoms beyond those required to meet the diagnostic criteria, and there is only minor impairment in social or occupational functioning.
 2. **Moderate**: "Symptoms or functional impairment between "mild" and "severe" are present."
 3. **Severe**: There are many more symptoms than are required to meet the diagnostic criteria, OR several particularly severe symptoms are present, OR there is "marked impairment" in social or occupational functioning. (P. 61)

V. Epidemiology: How many people have it; who gets it most, and when?

 A. Most common measures of how common a disorder is are **prevalence** and **incidence**:
  1. **Incidence** measures how many new cases of a disorder occur in a time period
  2. **Prevalence** is a measure of how many people have the disorder.
   a. Point prevalence (not sensible if incidence is high).
   b. Annual (or other) prevalence.
   c. Lifetime prevalence.

 B. How do we assess prevalence and incidence?
  1. **Clinical estimates**: How many people appear in clinics, hospitals, with the disorder?
  2. Community estimates:

 C. Prevalence estimates for ADHD range from 3% to about 8%
  1. APA (2013): Estimates 5% or children and 2.5% of adults affected.
  2. Kessler et al (2005b): 410/10,000 (4.1%)
  3. Nigg (2006): 700/10,000 (7%)
  4. CDC (2008) 500/10,000 (5%)

5. Parent or teacher survey data often yield prevalence estimates in the double digits (as high as 20% in at least one study).
6. DSM-IV criteria yield higher prevalence estimates than those of DSM-III.
7. Rates also change with development, so prevalence probably lower in adolescence than in childhood, though rates of diagnosis higher in adolescence than in childhood.

D. General Epidemiology:
1. Hyperactive-impulsive type typically has onset in nursery or primary school, and is more common in boys than girls.
2. Inattentive type typically has onset in primary or high school, and equally common in boys and girls
3. Overall, diagnosis twice as common among boys as girls, and more common among adolescents and teens than younger children.
4. Less common among Hispanic children than among whites or African-American children.
5. Accounts for 30-50% of childhood psychiatric outpatients; 40-70% of childhood psychiatric inpatients.
6. CDC reported 3% mean annual increase in ADHD diagnoses from 1997 to 2006.

VI. Disorders concurrent with ADHD (comorbidity)

A. In clinical settings, about 70% of ADHD patients have Conduct Disorder (or Oppositional Defiant Disorder)
1. Children comorbid for Conduct Disorder tend to have earlier age of ADHD onset, a greater number of antisocial behaviors, and show more physical aggression.
2. Only ADHD children comorbid for Conduct Disorder are at risk for antisocial behavior or drug use in adulthood.

B. Mood disorder: About 50% of lithium-responsive bipolar children are hyperactive

C. A number of other disorders at lesser rate:
1. Tourette's disorder (20-60% of male Tourette's patients have ADHD)
2. Anxiety disorder, including OCD
3. Schizophrenia
4. Autism and PDD
5. Antisocial personality disorder: Found in 25% of adults with ADHD
6. Essentially, ADHD over-represented in many Axis I and Axis II disorders

VII. Etiology: Psychological Systems and Functions:

A. **Attention** is obvious problem, but ADHD child can play video games for hours but not focus on homework for 5 minutes; may not be able to pay attention even in area they like and want to do well in.
   1. **Selective attention**: Filtering stimuli to focus on important ones; sustained attention. **NOT** a problem in ADHD.
   2. **Attentional orienting in space**: Turning to sight or sound, both automatic and strategic: **NOT** a problem in ADHD.
   3. **Arousal (alerting) and vigilance**: Remaining prepared to attend. Uses brainstem and other norepinephrine projections ending in right frontal cortex, and other cortico-cortical circuits. Arousal and vigilance are **IMPAIRED** in ADHD-C.
      a. Higher rates of low-frequency, slow-wave brain activity in resting EEG.
      b. **Nigg (2006)**: "underarousal, poor alertness, and low vigilance are characteristic of samples of children with ADHD." (p. 96),
      c. Arousal and sleep in ADHD: ADHD children more physically active during sleep; shorter REM latency, and more REM cycles in ADHD.
      d. The data are consistent with cortical underarousal.

B. Executive Functioning or Cognitive Control:
   1. **Response Inhibition (response suppression)**: Response suppression and shifting response set (right inferior prefrontal cortex, caudate) ; set shifting response set (prefrontal cortex, possibly cerebellar loop in some tasks). **IMPAIRED in ADHD**:
      a. Go/No-Go tasks: S makes response in one context (e.g., capital letter) but not in another (lowercase letter). 'Go' response set established by high proportion of 'Go' trials; suppression on rare No-Go trials assessed. Imaging data indicate preferential involvement of inferior region of dorsolateral prefrontal cortex on no-go as opposed to Go trials. Strong evidence for ADHD deficit in this case.
      b. Stop task: S makes different responses to two stimuli. On some fraction of trials (e.g., 25%) tone indicates that S should not respond. Timing of tone varied to determine how much warning S needs to stop. Clearly an ADHD deficit on this task.
      c. Set shifting needs further study: Modest impairment in Wisconsin Card Sorting Task (WCST).
   2. **Working memory**: Verbal working memory, visuo-spatial working memory Planning sequence of actions (dorsolateral prefrontal cortex). **IMPAIRED** in ADHD (see **Martinussen et al, 2005; Willcutt et al, 2005b** for meta-analysis of studies since 1995).
      a. Small to medium effect on verbal working memory; substantial deficit in spatial working memory: but may be accounted for by deficit in spatial short-term memory

VIII. Major neuroimaging and brain wave findings in ADHD

A. EEG/ERP:
   1. 20% of ADHD children have abnormal EEG findings (vs 15% generally).

2. Reduced right>left asymmetry in prefrontal cortices, with relatively smaller right side activity.
3. Many EEG/ERP studies suggest ADHD associated with excess slow wave activity consistent with cortical under arousal; weaker evoked potentials to stimuli and repose cues, consistent with poor alerting (as well as poor response mobilization).

B. Imaging:
1. 93% of children with right cortical lesions show ADHD (**Voeller, 1986**).
2. PET scans (**Lou et al, 1984**) of 11 ADHD children after xenon-133 inhalation:
    a. High blood flow in primary sensory regions of occipital and temporal cortices.
    b. All children showed hypoperfusion of frontal lobes (especially white matter).
    c. Majority (7/11) had hypoperfusion of caudate nuclei in basal ganglia.
    d. Psychostimulant medication increased blood flow in mesencephalon and basal ganglia, and decreased flow in primary sensory and motor cortexes.

IX. Etiology: Physiology: Four brain regions implicated in ADHD:

A. Prefrontal cortex, especially right prefrontal cortex:
1. Prefrontal areas are among last brain areas to mature; they continue to undergo synaptic pruning and myelination into adolescence, and even into early adulthood. (**Benes, 2001**)
2. In ADHD, best replicated findings involve **right inferior prefrontal cortex**, which seems to be related to problems with response inhibition and other cognitive control operations. (see **Rubia et al, 1999, 2003**)

B. The **corpus callosum** (in particular the genu; the anterior part):
1. Imaging evidence suggests that parts of the CC may be smaller in ADHD than in controls, but studies disagree as to which part is smaller.

C. The **basal ganglia**: (caudate, putamen, subthalamic nucleus, substantia nigra)
1. Caudate and putamen most often mentioned in connection with ADHD. Hypoactivation of caudate during executive task performance.
2. These structures closely interconnected with prefrontal regions, and work with them "to control unwanted response tendencies and to monitor whether current actions are moving toward the expected goal."

D. The **cerebellum:** (in particular the cerebellar vermis)
1. Multiple projections to basal ganglia and prefrontal cortices.
2. Appears to be involved in wide range of timing and temporal information processing, including detecting when expected consequences should occur.
3. Reports cerebellar vermis smaller in ADHD than in control children (a finding also reported for autism and schizophrenia), though the exact cerebellar regions involved *may* be specific to ADHD.

X. Etiology: Neurochemistry:

   A. Interest raised in several neurotransmitters:
      1. Dopamine - in the limbic or caudate regions.
      2. Norepinephrine - in the reticular formation.
      3. Serotonin - often elevation in blood in ADHD children.

XI. Etiology: Genetic Terms and Concepts

   A. We will be talking about genetic contributions to mental disorders frequently, and need to introduce several concepts and terms before we do this for the first time. Some may be familiar already, but the review won't hurt.
      1. Two questions or issues:
         a. How do we find out whether genes play a role in mental disorder (or anything, for that matter)?
         b. How do we measure or express the extent of that contribution?

   B. How do we find out whether genes play a role?
      1. Basic terminology and concepts:
         a. **Phenotype vs genotype**: Phenotype is an individual's observable or measurable characteristics.
         b. Genes have their effects in several ways:
            (1) **Additive effects**: Operations of individual genes sum together to produce final phenotypic result (e.g., genes for intelligence?)
            (2) **Non-Additive effects**:
               (a) **dominant-recessive** relationships: Effect of one allele (copy) of a gene on the other allele.
               (b) **epistatic effects**: Effect of one gene on a completely different gene.
      2. New wrinkles in genetics:
         a. **Epigenetics**: The epigenome is a set of chemical markers (generally methyl groups) attached to the DNA of the genes, that regulates gene expression. A methylated gene is not expressed, and is therefore functionally absent from the genome, even though it is physically present. There are several remarkable features of the epigenome:
            (1) **Environmental determination**: An individual's epigenome is affected by both prenatal and postnatal experience. Genes can be silenced or activated by our personal experience.
            (2) **Multi-generational inheritance**: Any alternations made in an individual's epigenome through experience can be passed on to that individual's offspring, even as far as the third generation.

- (3) **Parental imprinting**: Some copies (alleles) of a gene are active only if they came from the father, while the copy that came from the mother is epigenetically silences. Other genes are active only if they came from the mother, with the copy inherited from the father being silenced.
3. Basic determination of genetic contribution is to compare the similarity in phenotypes of individuals whose genetic relatedness is known.
    a. Because mental disorder is a binary situation (you have the disorder or not), some mathematical techniques for comparison are not easily available in this case.
    b. So we look at **concordance rates** (the presence of shared disorder) between individuals of different degrees of relatedness, especially twins.
    c. Two types of twins:
        (1) **monozygotic** (identical) twins: Share 100% of their genes and gene effects in common. (But we have to keep in mind that even MZ twins are not 100% identical in their genetic effects because of differences in their epigenomes.)
        (2) **dizygotic** (non-identical or fraternal) twins: Share 50% of their genome, and 25% of the non-additive genetic effects - same as any two siblings.
    d. If a disorder is 100% determined by gene effects, then the concordance rate for MZ twins will be 100%, and for DZ twins about 50%.
        (1) no disorder we know of show that pattern - there has never been a report of 100% MZ concordance rate for any disorder.
        (2) though concordance rates may be high for some disorders (as we will see), something else is always required - some condition in or input from the environment - hence the diathesis-stress model of mental disorder.
    e. One challenge in using MZ twins to determine concordance and genetic involvement is that many disorders occur at such low rates that finding any twin who has the disorder is difficult, let alone finding a sample large enough to draw conclusions from. Several Scandinavian countries (Sweden, Denmark) have very complete population data, including twin registries, that makes them popular places to conduct any behavioral genetics research.
    f. If we can't find twins, we can still look at the concordance rate between parents and children, between siblings, or between index cases and other relatives. We would expect that high genetic involvement would be indicated by higher concordance rates for closer relatives.

C. How do we measure or express the extent of that contribution?
1. **Concordance rates**, of course, especially for MZ and DZ twins.
2. **Heritability coefficient** (h^2): Calculated from concordance rates vis the formula $h2 = 2(cMZ - cDZ)$, it assesses the proportion of variability in some phenotypic characteristic that is accounted for by genetic variation between people.
    a. More widely reported in other areas of psychology (e.g., personality, intelligence) than in abnormal psychology because abnormality is not a continuous variable like (e.g.) IQ or extraversion.
    b. We will see heritability coefficients a few times in this course - including today.
    c. Keep in mind several things:
        (1) **heritability coefficients are about populations, not about individuals**: If the heritability coefficient for I.Q. is .50, that does **NOT** mean that half your I.Q. is

due to genes and half to the environment. It means that of all the variability in the population in I.Q., half can be attributed to genetic variations between individuals.

(2) **heritability coefficients are not constants**: They are different in different populations, and may (and do) change over time in any given population.
  (a) if genetic variation in population is low (e.g., as in many Asian countries), heritability for anything will be lower than in a population (e.g., like Canada's) where genetic variability is high.
  (b) heritability will be lower in populations with large amount of environmental variation (e.g., developing or under-developed countries) than in populations where there is a much more even distribution of resources and life situations.

D. Heritability of ADHD
1. ADHD does show tendency to run in families, though girls with ADHD have stronger family history of ADHD than do ADHD boys. (Vandenberg et al, 1986)
2. Findings in behavioral genetic studies of ADHD using parent ratings of behavior:
   a. Heritability estimates range from .60 to .90 (e.g., Thapar et al, 2000; Faraone et al, 2001a). Somewhat lower when teacher ratings of ADHD symptoms used.
   b. Nonshared environmental effects are modest to small; shared environment effects are practically nonexistent.

E. Apart from general estimates of genetic influence,. How do we locate individual genes that might be involved in a disorder?
1. **Candidate-gene approach**: Most widely used approach; involves a focus on polymorphism in genes of theoretical interest.
2. **Whole-genome scan**:
   a. Only recently possible.
   b. Search entire genome for 'hot spots' that are associated with a disorder. Then search those regions more intensively for individual genes.

F. The search for endophenotypes:
1. Traditionally, we looked for genetic basis for disorder by finding an association between some gene (or chromosomal region) and the phenotypic symptoms - i.e., the disorder itself.
2. But that means we have to compare a sample of individuals with the disorder to a matched sample without it, and that can be a problem if the disorder is infrequent - as most are.
3. A relatively recently idea has been to look for a link between genes and underlying aspects of disorders: The problematic psychological functions, or structures or neurochemistry of the disorder. The is the search for **endophenotypes** of the disorder.
   a. This allows us to work with any individuals who share the underlying Endophenotypes, even if they do not meet the criteria for the disorder.
   b. It also makes sense if the disorder is determined by several different genes in combination, or if not all individuals with the disorder share the same underlying functional problems or structural/chemical defects.
   c. It is also useful if several disorders share some underlying functional problems in

common - we would then be able to say something about all such disorders rather than just about one.

G. Developmental pathways built on early temperamental precursors. Three major traits and their relationship to ADHD:
1. **Extraversion**, approach, or positive affect:
   a. thought to be mediated by dopaminergic circuitry.
   b. consistent with dysfunctional reward circuitry in ADHD.
2. **Neuroticism**, withdrawal, or negative affect:
   a. though to be related to limbic reactivity to stress.
   b. related to a range of psychopathologies.
3. **Conscientiousness**, or constraint (or effortful control, in children):
   a. related to concept of cognitive control, or executive functioning.
   b. related to functioning and development of anterior cortical neural circuitry.

XII. Etiology: Genetics

A. Molecular genetic findings: Many genes with small effects
1. Two whole-genome scans for ADHD identify different areas of the genome:
   (1) **Fisher et al (2002)**: 5p12; 10q26; 12q23; 16p13
   (2) **Bakker et al (2003)**: 7p13; 9q33; 13q33; 15q15
2. Candidate genes:
   a. Dopaminergic neurotransmission system: DAT1, DRD4, DRD5, DBH, DDC.
      (1) DAT1 (also called SLC6A3), a dopamine transporter gene on chromosome 5
      (2) DRD4, a dopamine D4 receptor gene, on chromosome 11; a receptor expressed mostly in the prefrontal regions
   b. Noradrenergic system: NET1, ADRA2A, ADRA2C).
   c. Serotonergic system: 5-HTT, HTR1B, HTR2A, TPH2..
   d. Neurotransmission and neuronal plasticity: SNAP25, CHRNA4, NMDA, BDNF, NGF, NTF3, NTF4/5, GDNF.
3. But these genes do not have major effects: Odds ratios of 1.2 - 1.4, meaning allele increases risk of ADHD by 20-40%
4. The high-risk alleles found in over half the population; so multi-gene influence must exist.

XIII. Etiology: Environmental

A. **Low birth weight**: Appears to explain a small proportion of ADHD cases, especially those involving motor problems

B. **Prenatal alcohol exposure**: Not clear whether it leads to ADHD specifically or to other types of learning and developmental delays

C. **Natal or perinatal hypoxia**: (Getahun et al, 2012)

D. **Maternal diabetes mellitus**: Nomura et al (2012) found that mean inattention score at baseline (age 3-4) for offspring exposed to mother's DM significantly higher than for offspring unexposed, but no difference in hyperactivity/impulsivity scores between the two groups.

E. **Exposure to toxic substances**: Lead (pre- and postnatal); mercury; manganese

F. **Family SES**:
   1. **Nomura et al (2012)**: Children in low SES families, compared to high SES families, had greater inattention and hyperactivity/impulsivity scores. There was also a two-fold increased risk for ADHD at baseline and at age 6 years among children in low SES families.
   2. **Larson et al (2013)**: Studied records of over 800,000 Swedish individuals born between 1992-2000. Looked at family income during first 5 years of life for individuals diagnosed with ADHD. Found that low family income in early childhood associated with increased risk of ADHD, even after controlling for unmeasured selection factors.

G. No clear evidence that psychological trauma, early parental deprivation, or attachment problems play a causal role

H. **Harold et al (2013)** found significant relationship between risk of ADHD symptoms in adopted-at-birth children and rearing mother ADHD symptoms, and hostile parenting behavior.

XIV. The Bottom Line on Etiology:

A. Neuropsychological models alone will not explain all of ADHD; there are undoubtedly several different developmental pathways.

B. "ADHD denotes a grouping of multi factorially determined syndromes without an established causal etiology and with fuzzy boundaries." (**Nigg, 2006**, p. 46)

XV. Treatment:

A. Psychopharmacological treatment:
1. **Nigg (2006)**: methylphenidate (Ritalin) use in U.S. nearly doubled from 1981 to 1987, leveled off for several years in the late 1980s, they doubled again from 1990 to 1995.
2. Estimate is that 3% of U.S. children are on some form of medication for ADHD.
3. **Stimulants**: methylphenidate (Ritalin); dextroamphetamine (Dexedrine), and pemoline (Cylert) are most commonly used medications.
   a. 75% of ADHD children respond to psychostimulants (D-amphetamine; methylphenidate, the ingredient in Ritalin) or antidepressants (tricyclic or MAO inhibitors).
   b. One theory: Stimulants channel/reduce excessive, poorly synchronized variability in various dimensions of arousal and reactivity. (Evans et al, 1986)
4. ADHD children respond with increased excitability and hyperactivity to sedatives. (benzodiazepines, barbiturates) (See Rapport et al, 1980)
5. **Tricyclic antidepressants**:
   a. generally considered when stimulants exacerbate tics of Tourette's Disorder; when stimulants are ineffective, or when stimulant side effects are intolerable.
   b. not a first choice because of safety and side-effect considerations.

B. Supportive psychotherapy:
1. Behavior modification.
2. CBT or problem-solving therapy.
3. At recent meeting of Experimental Biologists, there seemed to be a consensus that behavioral/cognitive therapies intended to reduce impulsivity and reinforce positive habits might replace the high doses of stimulants given to both children and young adults with ADHD.
4. Other approaches:
   a. **Taylor & Kuo (2011)** found that children with ADHD benefitted from ongoing exposure to green space. ADHD children who regularly play in green settings have milder symptoms than children who play in built outdoor and indoor settings, regardless of sex of child or income of parents.
   b. Training in executive functions, like working memory: But **Rapport et al (2013)** found no evidence in a meta-analysis that such computer-based training regimes helped.

References

American Psychiatric Association (2000). *Diagnostic and Statistical Manual of Mental Disorders*, 4th Edition, text revised. Washington, D.C.

CDC (2008). Diagnosed Attention Deficit Hyperactivity Disorder and Learning Disability: United States, 2004-2006. Vital and Health Statistics; July 2008; Series 10, Number 237.

CDC (2009). Summary Health Statistics for U.S. Children: National Health Interview Survey, 2008.

Bakker, S.C., van der Meulen, E.M., Buitelaar, J.K., Sandkuijl, L.A., Pauls, D.L et al (2003). A whole-genome scan in 164 Dutch sib pairs with attention-deficit/hyperactivity disorder: Suggestive evidence for linkage on chromosomes 7p and 15q. *American Journal of Human Genetics*, 72, 1251-1260.

Beardon, C.E., Jasinska, AJ. & Freimer, N.B. (2009). Methodological Issues in Molecular Genetic Studies of Mental Disorders. *Annual Review of Clinical Psychology*, 5, 49-69.

Bellgrove et al (2008). Spatial Attentional Bias as a Marker of Genetic Risk, Symptom Severity, and Stimulant Response in ADHD. *Neuropsychopharmacology*, 33, 2536–2545.

Benes, F.M. (2001). The development of prefrontal cortex: The maturation of neurotransmitter systems and their interaction. In C.A. Nelson & M. Luciana (Eds.) *Handbook of Developmental Cognitive Neuroscience*. Cambridge, MA: MIT Press.

Campbell, S.B. (1985). Hyperactivity in preschoolers: Correlates and prognostic implications. *Clinical Psychology Review*, 5, 405-428.

Evans, R.W., Gualtieri, C.T. & Hicks, R.E. (1986). A neuropathic substrate for stimulant drug effects in hyperactive children. *Clinical Neuropharmacology*, 9, 264-281.

Faraone, S.V., Biederman, J., Friedman, D. (2000). Validity of DSM-IV subtypes of attention deficit/hyperactivity disorder: A family study perspective. *Journal of the American Academy of Child and Adolescent Psychiatry*, 39, 300-309.

Fisher, S.E., Franks, C., McCracken, J.T., McGough, J.J., Marlow, A.J., MacPhie, I.L. et al (2002). A genomewide scan for loci involved in attention deficit hyperactivity disorder. *American Journal of Human Genetics*, 70, 1183-1196.

Harold, G.T., Leve, L.D., Barrett, B., Elam, K., Neiderhiser, J.M., Natsuaki, M.N., Shaw, D.S., Reiss, D. & Thapar, A. (2013). Biological and rearing mother influences on child ADHD symptoms: revisiting the developmental interface between nature and nurture. *Journal of Child Psychology and Psychiatry*, 54:10, pp 1038-1046.

Kessler, R.C., Berglund, P.A., Demler, O., Jin, R. & Walters, E.E. (2005a). Lifetime prevalence and age-of-onset distributions of DSM-IV disorders in the National Comorbidity Survey Replication (NCS-R). *Archives of General Psychiatry*, 62(6), 593-602.

Kessler; R.C., Chiu, W.T., Demler, O. & Walters, E.E. (2005b). Prevalence, Severity, and Comorbidity of 12-Month DSM-IV Disorders in the National Comorbidity Survey Replication. *Archives of General Psychiatry*, 62, 617-627.

Larson, H., Sariaslan, A., Angstrom, N., D'Onofrio, B. & Liechtenstein, P. (2013). Family income in early childhood and subsequent attention deficit/hyperactivity disorder: A quasi-experimental study. *Journal of Child Psychology and Psychiatry*, **:* (2013), pp **-**

Lou, H.C., Hendriksen, L. & Bruhn, P. (1984). Focal cerebral hypoperfusion in children with dysphasia and/or attention deficit disorder. *Archives of Neurology*, 41, 825-829.

Martinussen, R., Hayden, J., Hogg-Johnson, S. & Tannock, R. (2005). A meta-analysis of working memory impairments in children with attention deficit/hyperactivity disorder. *Journal of the American Academy of Child and Adolescent Psychiatry*, 44, 377-384.

Nigg, J.T. (2006). *What Causes ADHD? Understanding What Goes Wrong and Why*. Guilford Press.

Rapport, M.D., Orban, S.A., Kohler, M.J. & Friedman, L.M. (2013). Do programs designed to train working memory, other executive functions, and attention benefit children with ADHD? A meta-analytic review of cognitive, academic, and behavioral outcomes. *Clinical Psychology Review*, 33, 1237-1252.

Rubia, K., Overmeyer, S., Taylor, E., Brammer, M., Williams, S.C.R., Simmons, A. et al (1999). Hypofrontality in attention deficit hyperactivity disorder during higher order motor control: A study with functional MRI. *American Journal of Psychiatry*, 156, 891-896.

Rubia, K., Smith, A.B., Brammer, M.J., Taylor, E. (2003). Right inferior prefrontal cortex mediates response inhibition while mesial frontal cortex is responsible for error detection. *NeuroImage*, 20, 351-358.

Scarr, S. & McCartney, K. (1983). How people make their own environments: A theory of genotype greater than environmental effects. *Child Development*, 54, 425-435.

Seng, W-L. & Shur-Fen Gau, S. (2013). Executive function as a mediator in the link between attention-deficit/hyperactivity disorder and social problems. *Journal of Child Psychology and Psychiatry*, 54(9), pp 996-1004.

Thapar, A., Harrington, R., Ross, K., McGuffin, P. (2000). Does the definition of ADHD affect heritability? *Journal of the American Academy of Child and Adolescent Psychiatry*, 39(12), 1528-1536.

Tye, C., Rijsdijk, F., Greven, C. U., Kuntsi, J., Asherson, P. and McLoughlin, G. (2012), Shared genetic influences on ADHD symptoms and very low-frequency EEG activity: a twin study. *Journal of Child Psychology and Psychiatry*, 53: 706-715.

Voeller, K. K. S. (1986). Right-hemisphere deficit syndrome in children. American Journal of Psychiatry, 143, 1004-1009. Voeller, K. K. S. (1991). Toward a neurobiologic nosology of attention deficit hyperactivity disorder. *Journal of Clinical Neurology*, 6 S, S2-S8.

Willcutt, E.G., Doyle, A.E., Nigg, J.T., Faraone, S.V. & Bennington, B.F. (2005). Validity of the executive function theory of attention deficit hyperactivity disorder: A meta-analytic review. *Biological Psychiatry*, 57(11), 1336-1346.

Williams, L.M.; Hermens, D.F.; Palmer, D.; Kohn, M.; Clarke, S.; Keage, H.; Clark, C.R.; Gordon, E. (2008). Misinterpreting Emotional Expressions in Attention-Deficit/Hyperactivity Disorder: Evidence for a Neural Marker and Stimulant Effects. *Biological Psychiatry*, 63(10), 917-926.

Neurodevelopmental Disorders: Autism Spectrum Disorder

I. Introduction

    A. First described in 1943 by Dr. Leo Kanner (1894-1981) of John Hopkins University, describing behavior of 11 children. Described one as follows: "He seems to be self-satisfied. He has no apparent affection when petted. He does not observe the fact that anyone comes or goes, and never seems glad to see father or mother or any playmate. He seems almost to draw into his shell and live within himself."

    B. Between Kanner in 1943 and 1989, nearly 3,000 articles published on autism; between 1990 and 2004, 3,700 published; nearly 3,000 since 1994.

    C. Children and adolescents with autism (and mental retardation) not aware they have disorder, able adolescents and adults are concerned about being described as 'disordered', 'abnormal', and prefer to see themselves as neurologically atypical. They label others as 'neurologically typical' (or NT). Some members of research community thus refer to 'Autism Spectrum Condition' (ASC) rather than Autism Spectrum Disorder (ASD).

II. Diagnostic criteria in DSM-5: (quotations from DSM-5, pp. 50-51)

    A. "Persistent deficits in social communication and social interaction across multiple contexts, as manifested by the following":
        1. "**Deficits in social-emotional reciprocity**, ranging ... from abnormal social approach and failure of normal back-and-forth conversation; to reduced sharing of interests, emotions, or affect; to failure to initiate or respond to social interactions."
            a. Infants fail to cuddle, or show indifference or aversion to affection or physical contact.
            b. Little or no interest in establishing relationships.
            c. Lack of eye contact, failure to respond to parents' voices, or to their names
            d. Often unaware of needs, emotions of others, who are treated mechanically, as objects.
            e. Prefer solitary activities.
        2. "**Deficits in nonverbal communication behaviors** used for social interaction, ranging, for example, from poorly integrated verbal and nonverbal communication; to abnormalities in eye contact and body language or deficits in understanding and use of gestures; to a total lack of facial expression and nonverbal communication."
            a. No use of posture, facial expression, gestures, to regulate social interactions.
            b. Absence of pointing, showing, or bringing favorite objects to others.
        3. "**Deficits in developing, maintaining and understanding relations**, ranging, for example, from difficulties adjusting behavior to suit various social contexts,; to difficulties in sharing imaginative play or in making friends; to absence of interest in peers."
        4. "Specify current severity"

a. "Requiring very substantial support"
b. "Requiring substantial support"
c. "Requiring support:"

B. **"Restricted, repetitive patterns of behavior, interests, or activities**, as manifested by at least two of the following:"
   1. "Stereotyped or repetitive motor movements, use of objects, or speech (e.g. simple motor stereotypes, lining up toys or flipping objects, echolalia, idiosyncratic phrases.)"
   2. "Insistence on sameness, inflexible adherence to routines, or ritualized patterns of verbal or nonverbal behavior (e.g., extreme distress at small changes, difficulties with transitions, rigid thinking patterns, greeting rituals, need to take same route or eat same food every day.)"
   3. "Highly restricted, fixated interests that are abnormal in intensity or focus (e.g., strong attachment to or preoccupation with unusual objects, excessively circumscribed or perseverative interests.)"
   4. "Hyper- or hyporeactivity to sensory input or unusual interests in sensory aspects of the environment (e.g., apparent indifference to pain/temperature, adverse response to specific sounds or textures, excessive smelling or touching of objects, visual fascination with lights or movement.)"
   5. Specify current severity:
      a. "Requiring very substantial support"
      b. "Requiring substantial support"
      c. "Requiring support:"

C. The symptoms must be present early in development, though they may not be fully apparent until "social demands exceed limited capacity, or may be masked by learned strategies later in life.)"

D. The symptoms must cause "clinically significant impairment in social, occupational, or other important areas of current functioning."

E. The symptoms are not better explained by other disorders, such as intellectual development disorder. Intellectual disability and ASD frequently occur together, so to apply both diagnosis "social communication should be below that expected for general developmental level."

F. Note: The DSM-IV criterion requiring that there be deficits in verbal as well as non-verbal communication has been eliminated, since Autism Spectrum Disorder now includes what would have been described as Asperger's Syndrome, in which verbal language skills are generally unimpaired.

G. Associated descriptive features and mental disorders:
   1. 75% of cases comorbid for Mental Retardation (generally moderate IQ 35-50)
   2. Cognitive skills development uneven - some young children with Autism can read
   3. In higher functioning cases, receptive language may be less developed than expressive language.

III. Epidemiology

   A. Prevalence: Controversial: Many different estimates, ranging from <1 to 70 per 10,000
      1. **APA (2013)** - DSM-5: "In recent years, reported frequencies for ASD across U.S. and non-U.S. countries have approached 1% of the population, with similar estimates in child and adult samples. It remains unclear whether higher rates reflect an expansion of the diagnostic criteria in DSM-IV to include subthreshold cases, increased awareness, difference in study methodology, or a true increase in the frequency of ASD." (P. 55)
      2. DSM-IV estimates prevalence from epidemiological studies at 2-5 cases per 10,000
      3. **Volkmar (2007):** Estimated **35/10,000**, but recent studies yield higher rates.
      4. **Yeargin-Allsopp et al (2003)**: CDC survey reports 34-36 per 10 000 for ASD, but
      5. Autism Society of Canada estimates prevalence of 50 in 10,000 for ASD.
      6. CDC (http://www.cdc.gov/ncbddd/autism/overview.htm) : " CDC's Autism and Developmental Disabilities Monitoring (ADDM) Network (2007): 67/10,000 of 8-year-old children in U.S. had ASD.

   B. Increase in prevalence:
      1. 18 surveys between 1966-1993, median prevalence was 5/10,000; 18 surveys between 1994-2004, median prevalence was 13/10,000 (**Fombonne, 2003b**).
      2. MIND study finds 273% increase in autism cases in California between 1987 and 1998.
      3. Why the increase?
         a. Increased awareness of the disorder.
         b. Earlier diagnosis.
         c. Changes in diagnostic practice.
         d. Diagnostic substitution' (i.e., choosing to use a label of autism as opposed to a label of mental retardation for educational purposes; especially when investigators use educational case records (**Wing & Potter, 2002; Fombonne, 2001; Croen, Grether, & Selvin, 2002b**).
      4. No indication that incidence increasing in successive birth cohorts.

   C. More males than females overall (4-5/1), highest male:female ratios found in normal range on cognitive assessment; lowest male:female ratios in individuals with autism and profound mental retardation (**Lord et al., 1982**). Reason for difference unclear.

   D. Comorbidity:
      1. 75% of cases comorbid for Mental Retardation (generally moderate IQ 35-50).
      2. Considerable comorbidity with ADHD. Estimates are that about 50% of children with ASD also meet the criteria for ADHD.
      3. Gastrointestinal abnormalities.
      4. **Leyfer, O.T. et al (2006)**: Examined comorbidity in a sample of 1009 children from Boston, Mass. and Salt Lake City, Utah. Ranging in age from 5 to 17 years.
         a. Specific Phibia (44%)
         b. Obsessive-Compulsive Disorder (37%)
         c. Other anxiety disorders (23%)
         d. Mood disorders (21% comorbidity)
      5. **Simonoff et al (2008)**. Evaluated comoribidity in a 112-child sample in the U.K. diagnosed with Autism.

      a. 71% met criteria for some other DSM-IV diagnostic category.
      b. 63% met criteria for a "main" disorder (ADHD; oppositional and conduct disorders; any emotional disorder)
      c. ADHD (28%)
      d. Anxiety or phobic disorder (42%)
        (1) Social Anxiety Disorder (29%)
        (2) GAD (13%)
        (3) Panic Disorder (10%)
      e. OCD (8%)
      f. ODD (28%)

IV. Etiology: Psychological function:

  A. **General intellectual functioning**:
    1. Large proportion of children with autism (~75%) also have concurrent diagnosis of mental retardation, but recent studies suggest IQs above 70 may be more common, perhaps due to failure to include milder forms of ASD in earlier samples.
    2. Intellectual skills scattered in autism:
      a. Worse on tasks requiring language, abstract reasoning, integration and sequencing.
      b. Better on tasks requiring visuo-spatial processing, attention to detail, and rote memory
    3. Asperger's pattern of skills different, but not all studies replicate this finding.

  B. **Splinter or savant abilities**:
    1. Autistic savants (term coined by Rimland, 1978) mirror similar earlier findings in mentally retarded (about 1 in 2,000). Rimland reported that about 10% of individuals with autism showed some such ability.
    2. **Rimland (1978)** posited that most common were: musical, memory, artistic, mathematical (especially rapid calculation), geographical knowledge (e.g., maps, routes, etc.), and pseudo verbal (knowing spelling and pronunciation but not meaning)
    3. Other reported talents include: mechanical ability; calendrical calculations.
    4. Most cases showed ability by age 4, and reached peak of ability by age 10.
    5. Autistic savants usually functioning in intellectually disabled IQ range. (but see **Pring et al, 1995**)

  C. **Motor development**:
    1. 60% show dysdiadochokinesia (inability to perform rapid, alternating movements)
    2. 33% have difficulties with gait or postural positioning (balance)
    3. 15% have abnormal muscle tone
    4. 5% have problems with their reflex status:
    5. 5% have abnormal extrapyramidal signs:
      a. Extrapyramidal motor system involved in coordination of movement. Called "extrapyramidal" to distinguish tracts that travel through "pyramids" of medulla. Pyramidal pathways directly innervate motor neurons of spinal cord or brainstem;

extrapyramidal system modulates and regulates anterior horn cells.
		b. E.g., Impaired finger tapping, Impaired heel tapping, unpaired rapid tongue. movements, Hypomimia, Flexed posture, Slow or shuffling gait, Body bradykinesia, Rigidity in arms, Action tremor in arms; Rest tremor in arms.
	6. Clumsiness does not seem to differentiate Asperger's from classic autism. (**Prior, 2003**)

D. **Theory of mind** theory (ToM):
	1. Theory of mind: Our understanding of the mental activity and expressed emotions of others. Understanding from their expression, behavior, tone of voice, etc., what other people are thinking. Understanding from their behavior what they know and believe.
	2. Many theorists argue that autism involves a deficit in Theory of Mind (ToM) such that individuals with autism have difficulty understanding mental states, including difficulty in emotion recognition. (e.g., **Mitchell, 1997**)
	3. Suggests children with autism do not understand that others have mental states (e.g., thoughts, beliefs, feelings, intentions) that influence actions; and do not understand that they must take these mental states into account in dealing with others. Cannot provide 'mentalistic' explanations for behavior, and cannot predict others' behavior.
	4. Children with autism have specific difficulties in understanding states of mind in others:
		a. **States of ignorance or knowledge**: Understanding when others know or do not know something, or when their beliefs are false.
			(1) E.g.: Children asked what absent child would think if presented with package of smarties ("There are Smarties in there"). Then Smarties replaced with pencils, and child asked what absent child would think was in the box. Autistic children above the age of 4 more likely to answer 'pencils'
		b. **Pretense, lying deceiving, cheating**: Are problematic because understanding them required understanding emotion and motivation in others, and understanding that others have a theory of your mind.
		c. **Jokes, irony, sarcasm also a problem**: Jokes problematic because they involve understanding what other people believe. When what people say is not what they really mean, and the real meaning must be determined bu their tone, and by and awareness of what they must be thinking or feeling. (e.g., **Happé, 1994**)
	5. Issues and problems with ToM: While some theorists argue that ToM problems can account for most autistic symptoms, others point out (or argue) that:
		a. Social impairments emerge before precursors of theory of mind. **Leekam (1993)**
		b. ToM and communicative ability develop independently in parallel; not causally related.
		c. High-functioning autistic children and Asperger's often do well on ToM tasks (but others suggest they solve such problems differently from typical children).
		d. ToM deficits also appear in mental retardation.

E. **Face and Emotion perception**:
	1. We typically judge an individual's emotion from his or her facial expression.
	2. Eye-tracking and behavioral studies indicate that there are deficits in face perception in autism (See **Dalton et al, 2005**; **Joseph & Tanaka, 2003**).
	3. **Weeks & Hobson (1987)** found that autistic children preferred to sort faces by non-motional attributes such as hairstyles and accessories rather than by emotional expression. When required to do so, performance impaired.

4. **Dawson et al (2002)**: Children with autism showed usual difference in ERPs to familiar vs unfamiliar **objects**, but not to mother's face vs unfamiliar face.
5. **Baron-Cohen et al (1999)**: Used fMRI to examine differences in brain activation during face processing. Ps looked at pictures of eyes and tried to determine what **emotion** the eyes conveyed. Found controls very active in amygdala and frontal lobes, high-functioning autism and Asperger autism group used frontal lobes much less, and did not activate amygdala at all, but used **superior temporal gyrus**.
6. **Schultz et al (2000); Grelotti et al (2005)**: Areas of brain that are active when typicals process *objects* (i.e., structures in the **inferior temporal gyrus**) active in individuals with autism when they processed *faces*. Lateral fusiform gyrus, active when typicals process faces, but not in autism.
7. Some studies find autistic children in normal range recognizing facial expression of emotion, perhaps especially when controls matched for verbal ability.
8. Perhaps involuntary, automatic processing of emotional expression is deficient in autism, and/or autistic children use different means for decoding emotional expression (e.g., **Adolphs et al, 2001**).
9. But how should we understand the deficit?
    a. Is it a problem with social perception of emotion?
    b. Or is it a problem with general perception of faces?

F. **Social perception**
   1. Eye-tracking studies find individuals with autism shown filmed social interaction look at mouths (and at random objects in scene) rather than eyes.
   2. Klin (2000): Ss presented with **Heider & Simmel (1944)** animations in which geometric forms move and act like people.
      a. Non-autistic viewers "recognize the social nature of the cartoon and make social attributions". (p. 73)
      b. Autistic viewers tend to make attributions of physical causation. E.g., 38-year old male with high normative IQ and autism: "The cartoon starts when a small equilateral triangle breaks out of a square. A small sphere or circle appears and slides down the broken rectangle. The triangles were either equilateral or isosceles. Later the small, I think, isosceles triangle and sphere bounce around each other, maybe because of a magnetic field." (P. 72)

G. **Extreme Male Brain Theory** (Simon **Baron-Cohen, 2002**)
   1. Male female brain differences:
      a. Males have stronger drive to systemize, which involves identifying rules that govern how a system works. Knowing the rules, you can control the system or predict its behavior.
      b. Females have a stronger drive to empathize, "which involves recognizing what another person may be feeling or thinking, and responding to those feelings with an appropriate emotion of one's own."
   2. People with autism have exaggerated male profile, with strong drive to systemize and weak drive to empathize.
      a. When adults with Asperger's syndrome (a subgroup on the autistic spectrum) took the same questionnaires given to non-autistic adults, they exhibited extreme Type S brains. Psychological tests reveal a similar pattern.

3. This explains social disability in autism, because empathy difficulties make it harder to make and maintain relationships with others.
4. Also explains the "islets of ability" that people with autism display in subjects like math or music or drawing - all skills that benefit from systemizing.
5. The obsessions sometimes developed by people with autism reflect very intense systemizing. In severe autism, child might express obsessions by bouncing constantly on a trampoline or spinning around and around, because motion is lawful and predictable.
6. Hypothesize that genetically, autism results from assortative mating between parents who are strong systemizers. Evidence of this:
    a. Parents of autistic children faster on complete embedded figures test than males/females in general.
    b. Parents of autistic children more likely to have fathers who are talented systemizers (engineers, for example).
    c. FMRI data show that males and females show different patterns while performing empathizing or systemizing tasks. Both mothers and fathers of children with autism show strong male patterns of brain activity.
    d. Parents of autistic children above average on questionnaire measuring how many autistic traits one has. These results suggest that both parents contribute genes that ultimately relate to a mind with an affinity for systematic thinking.
7. **Scott et al (2014)** assessed possible correlated effects of androgen exposure on the development of facial features associated with masculinity. Created composite images of faces that captured statistical regularities associated with high and low Autism-Spectrum Quotient (AQ) scores. Assessed correlations between perceived facial masculinity and AQ scores.
    a. Expt. 1: Observers rated high-AQ males as more masculine.
    b. Expt. 2: Same result as Expt. 1, with different photographs, composite-image methods, and observers.
    c. No association of masculinity and AQ scores for female faces in either study.
    d. Expt. 3: Created high- and low-AQ male composites from the five AQ subscales. High-AQ images rated more masculine on each subscale.

H. **Intense World Theory: (Markram et al, 2007)**
1. Builds on the assumption that the strong response to sensory stimulation that is a characteristic (though not a defining one) of autism is at the root of the entire autism spectrum.
2. Also based on neurohistological and neuroanatomical work both in autopsy of autistic individuals, and on the VPA rat model of autism.
    a. About 10% of children whose mothers took valproic acid (VPA) as a mood stabilizer and anticonvulsant during pregnancy have symptoms on the autism spectrum.
        (1) Recent study (**Bromley et al, 2008**) reports children whose mothers were taking Valproate during pregnancy were 7x more likely (6.3%) to develop symptoms on the autism spectrum as children whose mothers were not taking Valproate (.9%)
    b. Rats treated *in utero* to VPA have damage to brainstem, and show withdrawn social behavior and hyper-reactivity to stimuli similar to that in autism.
    c. VPA rats also have more cells in cortex and more abundant intro- and extra-cortical

connections.
3. Hypothesis is that autistic brain is similar, with too many connections and hyper reactivity to stimuli so external world is overwhelming.
4. Seeks to explain most of the symptoms of autism as withdrawal from, and increased organization of, this overwhelming and fragmented external world.
   a. Social withdrawal also leads to reduced exposure to, and acquisition of, language.
   b. Repetition and stereotypy are attempts to regulate the chaos.
   c. Face perception problems are difficulties in organizing the sensory/perceptual chaos.
5. Changes in amygdala lead to ready, rapid, and memorable conditioning of fear, leading to withdrawal from world.
6. Makes autism resemble extreme introversion - might explain why major tranquilizers are the most common pharmacological therapy for autism.
7. Still **VERY** new theory, much testing remains

I. **Empathy Imbalance Hypothesis (Smith, 2009)**
   1. Distinguishes between:
      a. **Cognitive Empathy** (CE), the ability to understand and predict behavior of others by understanding mental states, especially mental states such as believing, knowing, pretending, and guessing (essentially the same as Theory of Mind).
      b. **Emotional Empathy** (EE) an emotional response based on and the same as, the emotional state of another.
   2. Theory argues that children with autism have weak CE, but heightened EE, and develop a cognitive-behavioral style (whether seen as weak central cohesion, executive dysfunction, or high systemizing ability) to protect themselves from others' emotions. "Avoidance behavior, obsessive interests, and insistence on routines may regulate the stress that stems from living among people whose behavior is difficult to comprehend but whose emotions are all too readily sensed. Low CE ability may reduce salience of social stimuli and render the social world unpredictable and confusing. High EE sensitivity may compound this and act as a deterrent to attending to social world. In normal development, people use CE to regulate and resolve EE responses; people with autism may try to control and narrow their attention in an attempt to regulate EE." (Smith, 2009, p. 495)
   3. Evidence for EIH:
      a. Children with autism show more facial affect than typically developing children in empathy paradigm study.
      b. Faces of adults with autism show heightened electromyographic responsiveness to other people's expressions of happiness and fear.
      c. Children with autism show appropriate electrodermal responses to images of distressed people and sometimes refuse to look at such images.
      d. Adults with Asperger syndrome report high levels of personal distress in response to others' suffering.
      e. Results from eye-tracking and physiological studies are consistent with the claim by people with autism that it is painful for them to make eye contact with others
      f. Practitioners and caregivers perceive some people with autism as being highly sensitive to the emotions of others.
   4. Suggest that CE and EE more separable in males than females, so empathy imbalance disorders more likely in males.
      a. **Kylliainen & Hietanen (2006)** suggest people with autism avoid eye contact to

decrease arousal.
b. **Dalton et al. (2005)** report evidence of intense emotional response in individuals with autism associated with direct gaze, and propose that "face-processing deficits in autism arise from hyperactivation in the central circuitry of emotion that produces heightened sensitivity to social stimuli" (p. 524).
5. Intense world hypothesis also suggests hypersensitive EE.
6. EIH related to extreme-male-brain theory (EMB) of autism:
   a. EIH and EMB both incorporate TOM hypothesis, but empathic imbalance seems incompatible with EMB.
   b. EMB sees CE and EE as single dimension, with male brains not good at either.
   c. EIH sees males as at greater risk of empathic imbalance. "Children with autism may find it difficult to engage emotionally with others because their capacity for EE is excessive and not complemented by commensurate CE." (Smith, 2009, p. 494)

V. Etiology, Physiology and Brain Function:

A. Introduction:
   1. We have identified at least three basic functional deficits in autism:
      a. **Social cognition**, including face and emotion recognition (which may or may not be causally related to ToM, and/or executive functions).
      b. **Language**, which also has a social component, because language development depends on attending to the language spoken around the child.
      c. **Motor behavior and motor coordination.**
   2. In looking at the brain structures and activities that underlie these, we will see corresponding anomalies.

B. What are the structures underlying these functions?
   1. **Motor behavior and motor coordination**:
      a. The motor cortex
      b. The premotor cortex (we'll talk about this again)
      c. The cerebellum
   2. **Language**:
      a. Broca's area (frontal lobe)
      b. Wernicke's area (parietal/temporal)
   3. **Executive functions**: Prefrontal lobe
   4. **Social cognition**: Various areas, collectively referred to as the **social brain** (identified by functional neuroimaging, e.g., **Brothers, 1990**). Among these structures are:
      a. Amygdala
      b. Anterior cingulate
      c. Parts of the prefrontal cortex
      d. Superior temporal sulcus (STS)
      e. FFA - on inferior surface of temporal lobe
   5. And a very special set of neurons in the premotor cortex, called **mirror neurons**:

a. Cells first identified in macaque monkeys in early 1990s that fire when monkey performs action, and when it observes another (monkey or human) perform same action.
   b. Cannot directly verify presence in humans (would require implanted electrodes), but indirect brain-imaging measures, including EEG, confirm presence of mirror neurons in humans. (http://www.sciencedaily.com/releases/2005/04/050411204511.htm)

C. **Structural and functional abnormalities** in these areas:
   1. **Language areas**:
      a. Reduced functional connectivity between Wernicke's and Broca's area during language processing in autism. (**Just et al, 2004**)
      b. Generally low functional connectivity between frontal and parietal areas. (**Just et al, 2007**)
   2. **Amygdala**:
      a. Reduced density, cell size, and dendritic arborization (Bauman, 1996; Kemper, & Bauman, 1998).
      b. **Kleinhans et al (2011)**: Found lower activation during face perception in ASD compared with matched controls. While both groups showed activation in bilateral fusiform gyri, controls had significantly higher responses in right and left amygdalas, among other areas. Study concluded that ASD individuals made less or little use of subcortical brain regions involved in face detection and automatic emotional face processing.
   3. **Cerebellum**:
      a. Reduced density, cell size, and dendritic arborization (Bauman, 1996; Kemper, & Bauman, 1998; **Allen & Courchesne, 2003**). Link with autism symptoms unclear, but nature of abnormalities suggest prenatal origin.
   4. **Cingulate and prefrontal cortices**:
      a. Reduced density, cell size, and dendritic arborization (**Bauman, 1996; Kemper & Bauman, 1998**).
      b. FMRI (and older classic) studies find lower blood flow in **frontal and prefrontal areas**, mostly bilateral, but more pronounced in left hemisphere.
      c. **Ernst, Zametkin, Matochik, Pascualvaca, & Cohen (1997)**: PET study found lower dopaminergic activity in **medial prefrontal cortex** in autism.
      d. Dorsomedial prefrontal cortex (DPFC) critical for 'social cognition', i.e., for thinking about others' thoughts, feelings, and intentions (**Castelli et al., 2000; Schultz et al., 2003**), and for working memory, executive functions. fMRI (**Luna et al, 2002**) found decreased task-related activity here.
      e. **Schultz et al (2003)**: Abnormal fMRI activation for frontotemporal regions (and amygdala) for perception of emotions from eye expression.
      f. **Wicker (2008)**: fMRI finds lower activity in high-functioning autism and Asperger's than in typical controls in dorso-medial and right lateral prefrontal cortex.
   5. **Temporal lobe and FFA**:
      a. STS involved in perception of facial expressions, social gestures, interpretation of direction of eye gaze) (**Allison, Puce, & McCarthy, 2000; Schultz et al., 2003**).
      b. Also engaged by ToM tasks (**Castelli et al., 2000; Martin & Weisberg, 2003; Schultz et al., 2003**)
      c. Voxel-based morphometry suggests fewer cells in inferior temporal area

d. FFA hypoactive in autism (e.g., **Pierce et al., 2001**; **Schultz et al., 2000**), with degree of hypoactivation correlated with degree of social disability.
  6. **Mirror neurons**:
     a. (See **Fecteau et al, 2006**; **Oberman et al, 2005**):
     b. **Williams et al (2001)**: Connection between autism and dysfunction of the mirror neurons. Several studies provide evidence for this theory. (see **Ramachandran & Oberman, 2006**)
     c. In autism, seems that mirror neurons only fire when individual acts, not when another person seen acting.
  7. Note that reduced activity in area could be due to something intrinsic to that area, or to reduced activation from other areas, or failure in communication. Present studies cannot determine which (if either) is the case. Could be effect rather than cause.

D. **Other structural and functional abnormalities**:
  1. Studies report reduced **corpus callosum** size, but where this reduction is on CC not clear, since findings inconsistent.
  2. By early adulthood, 25-30% of individuals with autism have seizures; females more frequently than males.
  3. In most EEG studies, more than 50% of autistic Ps have abnormalities, even without seizures. All regions of the cortex, mostly bilateral, involved
  4. Brain as much as 10% larger by volume in toddlers with autism (**Courchesne et al., 2001**; **Sparks et al., 2002**); differences smaller, less consistently found in adolescence and adulthood. (e.g., **Aylward et al., 2002**; **Herbert et al., 2003**)
  5. **Piven et al (1995)**: fMRI of 22 male autistic individuals find total brain volume, total brain tissue, total lateral ventricle volume higher than in controls.
  6. Head circumference larger, regardless of age, but not at birth. (e.g., **Lainhart et al., 1997**
  7. **Courchesne et al (2003)** argue that autism associated with neuronal overgrowth in childhood plus with slower growth later, and/or reduced neuronal pruning.

E. **Uddin et al. (2011):** Reported that it was possible to use MRI scans to distinguish between children and adolescents with Autism and a matched sample of neurotypical controls with 90% accuracy based on differences in "gray matter in the posterior cingulate cortex, medial prefrontal cortex, and bilateral medial temporal lobes - regions within the default mode network" Concluded that multiple brain regions exhibit abnormal structural organization in autism.

VI. Etiology, Neurochemistry:.

A. Interest in dopaminergic systems based on role in movement problems and of dopamine-blocking agents in the treatment of autism (**Anderson & Hoshino, 1997**), but no consistent results from studies of both dopaminergic and catecholaminergic systems in autism.

B. Serotonin:
 1. Elevated blood serotonin in about 33% of autistic subjects. (e.g., **Anderson & Hoshino, 1997**)
 2. Serotonin synthesis normally declines by age 5 years. In autism, between 2 and 15 years rises to a value 1.5 times the normal adult level.

VII. Etiology: Autoimmune Factors

A. A growing body of evidence suggests that viral attack on the brain, taking place during gestation, may be involved in as many as 25% of cases of autism.

B. **Goines & Van de Water (2010)**: Reviewed recent research on possible involvement of immune system dysfunction in autism. Note the discovery of autoantibodies targeting brain proteins in both children with autism and their mothers.
 1. Research suggests maternal autoantibodies directed toward fetal brain proteins are "highly specific for autism".
 2. Also note that date re cellular immune system in children with autism a defect in signaling pathways shared by immune system and central nervous systems.

C. **Heuer et al (2008)**: Reported reduced levels of plasm immunoglobulin (Ig) in children with autism compared with typically-developing controls. Also found that children with greatest reduction in Ig showed most behavioral symptoms.

D. **Vargas et al (2005)**: Studied brain tissues and cerebrospinal fluid (CSF) from autistic patients and determined magnitude of neuroglial and inflammatory reactions and their cytokine expression profiles. Found an active neuroinflammatory process in the cerebral cortex, white matter, and notably in cerebellum of deceased autistic patients. Also found marked activation of microglia and astroglia, and cytokine profiling indicated macrophage chemoattractant protein (MCP)-1 and tumor growth factor-☺1, derived from neuroglia, were most prevalent cytokines in brain tissues. CSF showed a unique proinflammatory profile of cytokines, including a marked increase in MCP-1. "Our findings indicate that innate neuroimmune reactions play a pathogenic role in an undefined proportion of autistic patients..."

E. **Zimmerman et al. (2007)**: Found that the blood of children with autism and their mothers for immune reactivity to rat brain protein, and compared that reactivity to that of control mothers without autistic children.
 1. Found similar patterns of reactivity to rat brain proteins in autistic children, their mothers, and children with other neurodevelopmental disorders, that differed from the reactivity of mothers of typically-developing children, and from the normal siblings of children with autism and normal child controls.
 2. The maternal patterns of antibody reactivity were present in autism mothers from 2 to 18 years after the birth of their affected children and were unrelated to birth order.
 3. Suggested that these maternal serum antibodies could cross the placenta and alter fetal brain development.

F. **Braunschweig et al (2008)**: Maternal plasma antibodies against human fetal and adult brain proteins analyzed in mothers of children with autistic disorder and matched controls.
   1. Found reactivity to two protein bands from 11.5% mothers of children with autism (AU) against fetal but not adult brain, which was not noted in controls. The presence of reactivity to these two bands was associated with parent report of behavioral regression in AU children when compared to control children.
   2. "The presence of these antibodies in the plasma of some mothers of children with autism, as well as the differential findings between mothers of children with early onset and regressive autism may suggest an association between the transfer of IgG autoantibodies during early neurodevelopment and the risk of developing of autism in some children."

G. **Braunschweig et al. (2012)**: "profiled fetal-brain reactive autoantibodies of large cohort of mothers of children with autism and controls, finding significant associations between presence of IgG reactivity to fetal brain proteins at 37 and 73 kDa and childhood diagnosis of full autism, which also correlated with lower expressive language scores.
   1. Also found reactivity to proteins at 39 and 73 kDa that correlated with broader diagnosis of ASD and increased irritability on the Aberrant Behavioral Checklist. This provides evidence of "multiple patterns of reactivity to fetal brain proteins by maternal antibodies associated with ASD and specific childhood behavioral outcomes."

H. **Braunschweig et al (2013)**. Identify seven specific proteins attacked by maternal autoantibodies in autism mothers, cases they described as Maternally Autoimmune-Related autism (MAR autism):
   1. lactate dehydrogenase A and B (LDH A and B).
   2. Cypin.
   3. Stress-induced phosphoprotein 1 (STIP1).
   4. Collapsin response mediator proteins 1 and 2 (CRMP1, CRMP2).
   5. Y-box-binding protein.
   6. "Exclusive reactivity to specific antigen combinations noted in 23% of mothers of ASD children and only 1% of controls.
   7. ASD children from mothers with specific reactivity to LDH, STIP1 and CRMP1 and/or cypin (7% vs 0% in controls) had elevated stereotypical behaviors compared with ASD children from mothers lacking these antibodies.
   8. Report that these biomarkers have over 99% specificity for autism risk thereby advancing our understanding of the etiologic mechanisms and therapeutic possibilities for MAR autism.

VIII. Etiology; Genetic Factors:

A. Here is what the DSM-5 says about this: (p. 57) "Heritability estimates fir ASD have ranged from 37% to higher than 90%, based on twin concordance rates. Currently, as many as 15% of cases of ASD appear to be associated with a known genetic mutation, with different de novo copy number variants or de novo mutations in specific genes associated with the disorder in different families. However, even when an autism spectrum disorder is associated with a known genetic mutation, it does not appear to be fully penetrant [i.e., not all individuals with the mutation will develop the symptoms associated with ASD]. Risk for the remainder of cases appears to be polygenic, with perhaps hundreds of genetic loci making relatively small contributions." (P. 57)

B. Currently, autism considered "one of the most heritable of all psychiatric conditions, more so than bipolar disorder or schizophrenia, and much more so than alcoholism or antisocial behavior." (P. 157)

C. Among MZ twins, 65-75% concordance rate for autism; 3-10% for dizygotic twins.
   1. Parents who have a child with an ASD have 2%–8% chance of having a second child who is also affected. (**Boyle et al, 2004**; **Muhle et al, 2004**; **Smalley et al (1988)** (compared with .3% overall; 1500% increase in risk)

D. Heritability estimates based on concordance data all over 90%.

E. ASDs occurs more often than expected with other medical conditions that have genetic components:
   1. Fragile X syndrome (problem with too many repeats of the FMR-1 gene on the X-chromosome).
   2. tuberous sclerosis (tumor growth on brain, other organs).
   3. congenital rubella syndrome.
   4. phenylketonuria (PKU). (Inability to metabolize phenylalanine into tyrosine; leads to mental retardation).
   5. duplication of chromosome 15.
   6. neurofibromatosis (growth of nerve tumors; harmless or damaging).

F. Whatever genes are involved they seem to make individuals who do not have full-fledged autism susceptible to milder or incomplete version of autism (**variable expressivity**):
   1. Co-twins of MZ autistic probands may have atypical autism or Asperger's syndrome. (**Folstein & Rutter, 1997**)
   2. 20% of siblings of autistic probands had social or communication impairments, or a restricted pattern of interests, compared with 3% of sibs of Down's controls. (**Bolton et al., 1994**):

G. Whatever genes involved affect several traits, and dispose individual to other, non-autism disorders (**pleiotropy**) (e.g., **Folstein & Piven, 1991**; **Smalley et al., 1995**). Rates of psychiatric disorders in parents of autistic children and parents of Down's children:
   1. Anxiety disorders (23.5% autistic; 2.9% Down's controls)
   2. major depression (32.3% autism; 11.1% controls)

3. social phobia (20.2% vs 2.4%)
4. substance abuse (22.1% vs 0%)

H. Evidence suggests that autism is both etiologically and genetically heterogeneous:
   1. **Etiological heterogeneity**: Disorder may be caused by both genetic and environmental etiologies.
   2. **Genetic heterogeneity**: Disorder may be caused by several different alleles of same gene, and/or by several different genes

I. Polygenic model: Autism/ASD caused by many genes each of which has a small effect, either additive or multiplicative (epistatic)
   1. Epidemiological, twin and family studies suggest vast majority of ASD cases arise from complex genetic predisposition, perhaps involving interactions between 3–4 loci, and perhaps as many as 10 loci (**Pickles et al., 1995**).
   2. But if this model correct, looking for additional genes pointless, since each would only contribute a small bit to autism

J. Candidate genes:
   1. Promising candidate is chromosome 15, where frequent chromosome duplications documented. Recent reports suggest that UBE3A locus or a subset of GABA genes in that region may be involved. (See **Glessner et al., 2009**)
   2. Another candidate is somewhere on chromosome 7, in the 7q31-33 region. (**International Molecular Genetic Study of Autism Consortium, 1998**)
   3. Other linkages reported on chromosomes 3, 13, 18, and 19 (**Pericak-Vance, 2003**)
   4. Also candidate gene is serotonin transporter gene (5-HTT) - also of interest in anxiety, as we shall see.
   5. **Wang et al (2009)**: Found common genetic variants on 5p14.1 associates with autism spectrum disorders. This region is between two genes, cadherin 9 (CDH9) and cadherin 10 (CDH10), that produce neuronal cell-adhesion molecules that affect how nerve cells communicate with each other. Authors suggest that these variants may be involved in up to 15 percent of ASD cases.
   6. Copy number variations in gene regions implicated in autism spectrum disorders (from **Glessner et al., 2009**):
      a. Chromosome 2: gene area NRXN1
      b. Chromosome 3: gene area CNTN4
      c. Chromosome 7: gene area AUTS2
      d. Chromosome 15: gene area UBE3A
      e. Chromosome 16: area 16p11.2
      f. Chromosome 22: areas 22q.11.21 and SHANK3
      g. **Berkel et al (2010)**: Identified new copy number variations in SHANK2 synaptic scaffolding gene (chromosome 11) in two unrelated individuals with autism-spectrum disorder (ASD) and mental retardation. DNA sequencing of SHANK2 in 396 individuals with ASD, 184 individuals with mental retardation and 659 unaffected individuals (controls) revealed additional variants specific to ASD and mental retardation cases, including a new nonsense mutation and seven rare inherited changes."

7. **Weiss et al. (2009)**: Found linkage of autism to three regions of human genome including parts of chromosomes 6 and 20,. Also found SNP in chromosome 5 near a gene known as semaphorin 5A, which is thought to help guide the growth of neurons and their long projections called axons. Expression of this gene appears to be reduced in brains of autism patients compared to controls.

IX. Etiology, Environmental Factors: Risk of autism associated with many different factors:
   A. Mother smoking daily in early pregnancy
   B. Caesarian delivery
   C. Baby being small for gestational age
   D. Threefold increase in risk for mothers born outside Europe or North America (probably related to lack of immunity to viral infections during pregnancy or selective migration of mothers with genetic vulnerability to autism)
   E. Congenital malformations
   F. **Bilder et al. (2009)**: Children with autism spectrum disorders 1.8 times to be first-borns compared with matched controls. Also 1.7 times more likely to have mothers over the age of 35 (compared with mothers 20-24), and to have experienced a breech birth.

X. Treatment:

   A. Psychosocial and educational interventions
      1. Applied Behavioral Analysis (ABA) and EIBI (Early Individualized Behavioral Intervention) - same thing:
         a. Ivar Lovaas: Applied B.F. Skinner's experimental behavior analysis to people with autism. Limited success at first, but refocused efforts on children under 5, placed implementation of treatment in child's own home and increased intensity to about 40 hours weekly. In one study, 47% of the children (9 children) made progress to the point of becoming "recovered", while further 42% (8 children) made significant improvements. Only 11% made little to no gains. In 2002, Lovaas wrote, *Teaching Individuals With Developmental Delays: Basic Intervention Techniques.*
         b. Several research groups find very high parent satisfaction with ABA, though studies not able to replicate the amount of progress previously reported (**Bibby, Eikeseth, Martin, Mudford, & Reeves, 2002; Boyd & Corley, 2001; Smith et al., 2000**) in modified versions of behavioral interventions.
      2. Teaching social skills, usually from later preschool through school age and in adolescents and adults - a major theme of the treatment literature in the past few years.
      3. **Smith et al. (2000) and National Research Council Committee (2001)** argue that number of treatment hours, and training of therapists/teachers important. Allowing for individual differences in abilities, and needs necessary for success in any approach (**Anderson & Romancyzk, 1999**)." (P. 152)

B. Environmental enrichment:
1. **Woo & Leon (2013).** Reported that when 3-12 year-old children with autism were assigned to a sensorimotor enrichment group that received daily olfactory/tactile stimulation along with exercises that stimulated other paired sensory modalities, they showed significant improvements in cognitive performance and autism severity after 6 months.
   a. 42% of enriched group and only 7% of the control group had clinically significant improvement.
   b. On Leiter-R Visualization and Reasoning test, change in mean scores for enriched group was 11.3 points higher than for control group.
   c. 69% of parents in enriched group and 31% of parents in control group reported improvement in their child over the 6-month study.

C. Pharmacological interventions:
1. Tranquilizers (neuroleptics) and antidepressants most common approach. Older 'typical' neuroleptics include chlorpromazine (Thorazine); trifluoperazine (Stelazine):
   a. **Campbell & Cueva (1995); Campbell et al (1997)**: Found neuroleptics reduced stereotyped and other problematic behaviors and increased engagement. But side effects (e.g., sedation, withdrawal, tardive dyskinesia) limited usefulness.
   b. **McDougle et al. (2000)**: Newer, atypical neuroleptics (e.g., risperidone (Risperdal), clozapine (Clozaril), olanzapine(Zyprexa, Lanzac)) have fewer side-effects (e.g., reduced risk of tardive dyskinesia), and have largely replaced first-generation neuroleptics for treatment of severe agitation or stereotyped movements, self-injury, severe behavior problems.
2. Antidepressants:
   a. Clomipramine (tricyclic antidepressant) inhibits norepinephrine and serotonin reuptake, while other agents in this group more selective for serotonin. Not yet extensively studied, but commonly used to treat behavioral difficulties, particularly repetitive behaviors, stereotyped mannerisms, and difficulties with anxiety and dealing with change (**Martin et al., 1999**).
   b. Serotonin reuptake inhibitors (SRIs) are of interest given observation of high peripheral serotonin levels in autism and the observation that these agents may help with the repetitive behaviors reminiscent of obsessive compulsive disorder (**McDougle, 1997**).
3. Several new pharmacological treatments being tested:
   a. **Hardan, et al. (2012)**: Treatment of children with oral doses of N-Acetylcysteine, which modulates glutaminergic neurons, led to symptoms improvement compared with controls.
   b. **Naviaux et al (2013)**: Study done with mouse model of autism, based on hypothesis that one common factor in many cases of autism is mitochondria-based extracellular signalling that affects and over-activates the puraminergic signaling system.
      (1) Drugs that counteract and reduce puraminergic signaling were found to reduce 16 autism-related deficits in the mouse model of autism.
      (2) "These included correction of the core social deficits and sensorimotor coordination abnormalities, prevention of cerebellar Purkinje cell loss, correction of the ultrastructural synaptic dysmorphology, and correction of the

hypothermia, metabolic, mitochondrial, P2Y2 and P2X7 purinergic receptor expression, and ERK1/2 and CAMKII signal transduction abnormalities."

References

Adolphs, R., Sears, L. & Piven, J. (2001). Abnormal processing of social information from faces in autism. *Journal of Cognitive Neuroscience*, 13, 232-240.

Allen, G. & Courchesne, E. (2003). Differential effects of developmental cerebellar abnormality on cognitive and motor functions in the cerebellum: An fMRI study of autism. American Journal of Psychiatry, 160(2), 262-273.

Allison, T., Puce, A., & McCarthy, G. (2000). Social perception from visual cues: Role of the STS region. *Trends in Cognitive Science*, 4, 267-278.

Anderson, G.M. & Hoshino, Y. (1997) Neurochemical studies of autism. In: Cohen DJ, Volkmar FR (Eds) *Handbook of Autism and Pervasive Developmental Disorders*, 2nd ed. John Wiley, New York, pp 325–343.

Anderson, S.R. & Romanczyk, R.G. (1999). Early Intervention for Young Children with Autism: Continuum-Based Behavioral Models. *Journal of the Association for Persons with Severe Handicaps*, 24(3), 162-173.

Aylward, E.H., Mindshew, N.J., Field, K., Sparks, B.F. & Singh, N. (2002). Effects of age on brain volume and head circumference in autism. *Neurology*, 59(2), 175-183.

Baird G, Chairman T, Baron-Cohen S, et al. A screening instrument for autism at 18 months of age: a 6 year follow-up study. J Am Acad Child Adolesc Psychiatry. 2000;39:694-702.

Baron-Cohen, S., Ring, H.A., Wheelwright, S. Et al (1999). Social intelligence in the normal and autistic brain: An fMRI study. *European Journal of Neuroscience*, 11(6), 1891-1898.

Bauman, M. L. (1996). Neuroanatomic observations of the brain in pervasive developmental disorders. *Journal of Autism and Developmental Disorders*, 26, 199-203.

Berkel, S., Marshall, C.R., Weiss, B. Et al. (2010). Mutations in the SHANK2 synaptic scaffolding gene in autism spectrum disorder and mental retardation. *Nature Genetics*, 42, 489–491.

Bertrand J, Mars A, Boyle C, Bove F, Yeargin-Allsopp M, Decoufle P. Prevalence of autism in a United States population: the Brick Township, New Jersey, investigation. Pediatrics. 2001;108:1155-1161.

Bibby P., Eikeseth S., Martin N., Mudford O., and Reeves D. (2002). Progress and outcomes for children with autism receiving parent-managed intensive interventions. *Research in Developmental Disabilities*, 23 81-104.

Bilder, D., Pinborough-Zimmerman, J., Miller, J. & McMahon, W. (2009). Prenatal, Perinatal, and Neonatal Factors Associated With Autism Spectrum Disorders. Pediatrics, 123(5), pp.

Bolton, P., McDonald, H., Pickles, A. et al (1994). A case-control family history study of autism. *Journal of Child Psychology and Psychiatry*, 35, 877-900.

Boyd, R., & Corley, M. (2001). Outcome survey of intensive behavioural intervention for young children with autism in a community setting. *Autism*, 5, 430-441.

Boyle C, Van Naarden Braun K, Yeargin-Allsopp M. (2004) The Prevalence and the Genetic Epidemiology of Developmental Disabilities. In: *Genetics of Developmental Disabilities*. Merlin Butler and John Meany eds., p. 716-717.

Brambilla, P., Hardan, A., di Nemi, S.U., Perez, J., Soares, J.C. & Barale, F. et al, (2003). Brain anatomy and development in autism: Review of structural MRI studies. *Brain Research Bulletin*, 61(6), 557-569.

Braunschweig, D., Ashwood, P., Krakowiak, P., Hertz-Picciotto, I., Hansen, R., Croen, L.A. et al. (2008). Autism: maternally derived antibodies specific for fetal brain proteins. *Neurotoxicology*, 29: 226-231.

Braunschweig, D., Duncanson, P., Boyce, R., Hansen, R., Ashwood, P., Pessah, I.N. et al. (2012). Behavioral correlates of maternal antibody status among children with autism. *Journal of Autism and Developmental Disorders*, 42(7): 1435-1445.

Braunschweig et al (2013). Autism-specific maternal autoantibodies recognize critical proteins in developing brain. *Translational Psychiatry* 3, e277.(published online, July 2013)

Bromley, et al, (2008). Autism spectrum disorders following in utero exposure to antiepileptic drugs. *Neurology*, 71, 1923-1924.

Brosnan, M., Scott, F., Fox, S. & Pye, J. (2004). Gestalt processing in autism: Failure to process perceptual relationships and the implications for contextual understanding. *Journal of Child Psychology and Psychiatry*, 45, 459-469.

Brothers, L. (1990). The social brain: A project for integrating primate behavior and neurophysiology in a new domain. *Concepts Neuroscience*, 1, 27-151.

Campbell, M. & Cueva, J.E. (1995). Psychopharmacology in child and adolescent psychiatry: A review of the past seven years. Part II. *Journal of the American Academy of Child and Adolescent Psychiatry*, 34(10), 1262-

Campbell, M., Armenteros, J. L., Malone, R. P., Adams, P. B., Eisenberg, Z. W., & Overall, J. E. (1997). Neuroleptic-related dyskinesias in autistic children: A prospective, longitudinal study. *Journal of the American Academy of Child and Adolescent Psychiatry*, 36, 835-843.

Carter, A.S., Volkmar, F.R., Sparrow, S.S., Wang, J., Lord, C., Dawson, G., Fombonne, E., Loveland, K., Meisbov, G., and Schopler, E., (1998). "The Vineland Adaptive Behavior Scales: Supplementary norms for individuals with autism," *Journal of Autism and Developmental Disorders*, 28, 4, pp. 287-302.

Castelli, Happe, Frith & Frith (2000). Movement and Mind: A Functional Imaging Study of Perception and Interpretation of Complex Intentional Movement Patterns. *NeuroImage* 12, 314-325.

Castelli, Frith, Happe, & Frith, U. (2002). Autism, Asperger syndrome, and brain mechanisms for the attribution of mental states to animates shapes. *Brain*, 125, 1839-1849.

Centers for Disease Control and Prevention, National Center on Birth Defects and Developmental Disabilities, Autism and Developmental Disabilities Monitoring Network. Available at: http://www.cdc.gov/ncbddd/dd/aic/states/default.htm#addm.

Chakrabarti S, Fombonne E. Pervasive developmental disorders in preschool children. *JAMA*. 2001;285:3093-3099.

Christian, S.L.; Brune, C.W.; Sudi, J.; Kumar, R.A.; Liu, S.; Karamohamed, S.; Badner, J.A.; Matsui, S.; et. al. (2008). Novel Submicroscopic Chromosomal Abnormalities Detected in Autism Spectrum Disorder. Biological Psychiatry, 63(12), 1111-1117.

Courchesne, E., Karns, C.M., Davis, B.S. et al (2001). Unusual brain growth patterns in early life in patients with autistic disorder: An MRI study. *Neurology*, 57, 245-254.

Courchesne, E., Carper, R., Akshoomoff, N. (2003). Evidence of Brain overgrowth in the First Year of Life in Autism. *JAMA*, 290, 337-344.

Croen LA, Grether JK, Hoogstrate J, Selvin S. The changing prevalence of autism in California. J Autism Dev Disord. 2002;32:207-215.

Dalton, K.M., Nacewicz, B.M., Johnstone, T. et al. (2005). Gaze fixation and the neural circuitry of face processing in autism. *Nature Neuroscience*, 8, 519-526.

Dawson, G., Webb, S., Schellenberg, G.D., Dager, S., Friedman, S. Aylward, E. et al. (2002). Defining the broader phenotype of autism: Genetic, brain, and behavioral perspectives. *Developmental Psychopathology*, 14, 581-611.

Department of Developmental Services. Changes in the population of persons with autism and pervasive developmental disorders in California's Developmental Services System: 1987 through 1998. Report to the Legislature March 1, 1999:1-19. Available at: http://www.dds.ca.gov:1999. Accessed December 11, 2003.

Ernst, M., Zametkin, A. J., Matochik, J. A., Pascualvaca, D., & Cohen, R. M. (1997). Low medial prefrontal dopaminergic activity in autistic children. *Lancet*, 350, 638.

Fecteau, S.; Lepage, J.F.; Théoret, H. (2006). Autism Spectrum Disorder: Seeing Is Not Understanding. *Current Biology*, 16(4), pp. R131-R133.

Folstein & Piven (1991). Etiology of autism: Genetic influences. *Pediatrics*, 87, 767-773.

Folstein, S. & Rutter, M. (1977). Infantile autism: A genetic study of 21 twin pairs. *Journal of Child Psychology and Psychiatry*, 18, 297-321

Fombonne, E. (2003). Modern Views of Autism, *Can. J. Psychiatry*, 48:503-505.

Fombonne, E. (2003b). Epidemiology of autism and other pervasive developmental disorders: an update. *J. Autism. Dev. Disord.* 33:365-381

Fombonne E. (2002). Epidemiological trends in rates of autism. *Molecular Psychiatry*. 7(suppl 2): S4-S6.

Fombonne E. (2001). Is there an epidemic of autism? *Pediatrics*. 2001;107:411-413.

Fombonne E, Chakrabarti S. No evidence for a new variant of measles-mumps-rubella-induced autism. Pediatrics. 2001;108:E58.

Frith, U. (1989). *Autism: Explaining the enigma.* Oxford, UK: Basil Blackwell.

Frith, U. (2003). *Autism: Explaining the enigma, (second edition).* Oxford, UK: Basil Blackwell

Frith, C.D. & Frith, U. (2006). The neural basis of mentalizing. *Neuron*, 50(4), 531-534.

Frye, D., Zelazo, P.D., Palfai, T. (1995). Theory of mind and rule-based reasoning. *Cognitive Development*, 10, 483-527.

Glessner et al. (2009). Autism genome-wide copy number variation reveals ubiquitin and neuronal genes. Nature 459, pp. 569-573.

Goines P, & Van de Water J. (2010). The immune system's role in the biology of autism. *Current Opinion in Neurology*, 23: 111-117.

Grelotti, D.J., Klin, A., Gauthier, L. Skudlarski, P., Cohen, D.J., Gore J.C. et al (2005). FMRI activation of the fusiform gyrus and amygdala to cartoon characters but not to faces in a boy with autism. *Neuropsychologia*, 43(3), 373-385.

Happé, F. (1994). Wechsler IQ profile and theory of mind in autism: A research note. *Journal of Child Psychology and Psychiatry*, 35, 1461-1471.

Happé, F. & Frith, U. (2006). The weak coherence account: Detailed focused cognitive style in autistic spectrum disorders. *Journal of Autism and Developmental Disorders*, 36, 5-25.

Hardan, A.Y. et al (2012). A Randomized Controlled Pilot Trial of Oral N-Acetylcysteine in Children with Autism. *Biological Psychiatry*, 71:956–961.

Heider, F. & Simmel, M. (1944). An experimental study of apparent behavior. *The American Journal of Psychology*, 57(2), 243-259.

Herbert, M.R., Ziegler, D.A., Deutsch, C.K., O'Brien, M., Lange, N., Bakardjiev, A., Hodgson, J., Adrien, K.T., Steele, S., Makris, N., Kennedy, D., Harris, G.J., & Caviness, V.S. Jr. (2003). Dissociations of cerebral cortex, subcortical and cerebral white matter volumes in autistic boys. *Brain*, 126, 1182-1192.

Heuer L, Ashwood P, Schauer J, Goines P, Krakowiak P, Hertz-Picciotto I et al. (2008). Reduced levels of immunoglobulin in children with autism correlates with behavioral symptoms. *Autism Research*, 1: 275-283.

International Molecular Genetic Study of Autism Consortium. (1998). A full genome screen for autism with evidence for linkage to a region on chromosome 7q. *Human Molecular Genetics*, 7(3), 571-8.

Joseph, R.M. & Tanaka, J. (2003). Holistic and part based face recognition in children with autism. *Journal of Child Psychology and Psychiatry*, 44, 529-542.

Just, M.A., Cherkassky, V.L., Keller, T.A. & Minshew, N. (2004). Cortical activation and synchronization during sentence comprehension in high-functioning autism: Evidence of underconnectivity. *Brain*, 127, 1811-1821.

Just, M.A., Cherkassky, V., Keller, T., Kana, R. & Minshew, N. (2007). Functional and anatomical cortical under connectivity in autism: Evidence from an fMRI study of an executive function task and corpus callosum morphometry. *Cerebral Cortex*, 17(4), 951-961.

Kanner L. Autistic disturbances of affective contact. Nervous Child. 1943;2:217-250.

Kemper, T.L. & Bauman, M. (1998). Neuropathology of infantile autism. *Journal of Neuropathology and Experimental Neurology*, 57, 645-652.

Kemper, T. L., & Bauman, M. L. (1993). The contribution of neuropathologic studies to the understanding of autism. *Neurologic Clinics*, 11, 175-187.

Kleinhans, N.M., Richards, T., Johnson, C., Weaver, K.E., Greenson, J., Dawson, G., & Aylward, E. (2011). fMRI evidence of neural abnormalities in the subcortical face processing system in ASD. *Neuroimage*. 54(1): 697-704.

Klin, A. (2000). Attributing social meaning to ambiguous visual stimuli in higher functioning autism and Asperger syndrome: The Social Attribution Task. *Journal of Child Psychology and Psychiatry*, 41, 831-846.

Kylliäinen, A., & Hietanen, J. K. (2006). Skin conductance responses to another person's gaze direction in children with autism. *Journal of Autism and Developmental Disorders*, 36, 517-525.

Lainhart, J.E., Piven, J., Wzorek, M., Landa, R., Santangelo, S., Coon, H., and Folstein, S. (1997) Macrocephaly in children and adults with autism. *Journal of the American Academy of Child and Adolescent Psychiatry*, 36:282-290.

Leekam, S.R. (1993). Children's understanding of mind. In M. Bennett, (Ed.). *The Child as Psychologist*. London: Harvester Wheatsheaf, pp. 26-61.

Leyfer, O.T. et al (2006). Comorbid Psychiatric Disorders in Children with Autism - Interview Development and Rates of Disorders. *Journal of Autism and Developmental Disorders*. 36:849–861.

Lord, C., Schopler, E., & Revecki, D. (1982). Sex differences in autism. *Journal of Autism and Developmental Disorders*, 12, 317-330.

Luna, B., Minshew, N.J., Garver, K.E., Lazar, N.A. et al (2002). Neocortical system abnormalities in autism: An fMRI study of spatial working memory *Neurology*, 59:834-840

Madsen KM, Hviid A, Vestergaard M, et al. A population-based study of measles, mumps, and rubella vaccination and autism. N Engl J Med. 2002;347:1477-1482.

Markram, H., Rinaldi, T. & Markram, K. (2007). The intense world syndrome - an alternative hypothesis for autism. *Frontiers in Neuroscience*, 1(1), 77-96.

Martin, A., Koenig, K., Scahill, L. Bregman, J. (1999). Open label quetapine in the treatment of children and adolescents with autistic disorder. *Journal of Child and Adolescent Psychopharmacology*, 9, 99-107.

McDougle, C.J. (1997). Update on pharmacologic management of OCD: Agents and augmentation. *Journal of Clinical Psychiatry*, 58 (suppl. 12), 11-17.

McDougle, C.J., Kresch, L.E. & Posey, D.J. (2000). Repetitive thoughts and behavior in pervasive developmental disorders: Treatment with serotonin reuptake inhibitors. *Autism & Developmental Disorders*, 30, 427-435.

Martin, A. & Weisberg, J. (2003). Neural Foundations For Understanding Social And Mechanical Concepts. *Cognitive Neuropsychology*, 20, (3-6), 575-587.

Mitchell, P. (1997). *Introduction to theory of mind: Children, autism, and apes.* London, UK: Edward Arnold Publishers.

Morrow, E.M., Yoo, S-Y, Flavell, S.W., Kim, T-K., Lin, Y., Hill, R.S., et al. (2008). Identifying Autism Loci and Genes by Tracing Recent Shared Ancestry. *Science*, 321, 218-223.

Morton, J. (2004). *Understanding developmental disorders: A causal modeling approach.* Oxford, UK: Blackwell.

Mosconi, M., Zweigenbaum, L. & Piven, J. (2006). Structural MRI in autism: Findings and future directions. *Clinical Neuroscience Research*, 6(3-4), 135-144.

Mottron, L. & Burack, J. (2001). Enhanced perceptual functioning in the development of autism. In J. Burack, T. Charman, N. Yirmiya & P. Zelazo (Eds.) *The development of autism: Perspectives from theory and research.* Mahwah, NJ: Lawrence Erlbaum Associates.

Mottron, L., Dawson, M., Soulières, I. Hubert, B. & Burack, J. (2006). Enhanced perceptual functioning in autism: An update and eight principles of autistic perception. *Journal of Autism and Development Disorders,* 36(1), 27-43.

Muhle, R, Trentacoste V, & Rapin I. (2004). The Genetics of Autism. *Pediatrics,* 113, 472-486.

National Research, C. (2001). *Educating young children with autism.* Washington, DC: National Academy Press.

Naviaux et al (2013): Antipurinergic Therapy Corrects the Autism-Like Features in the Poly(IC) Mouse Model. *PLoS ONE* 8(3): e57380.

Navon, D. (1977). Forest before trees: The precedence of global features in visual perception. *Cognitive Psychology,* 9, 353-383.

Oberman, L.M., Edward, T., Hubbards, M., McCleery, J.P., Altschuler, E.L., Ramachandra, V.S. & Piineda, J.A. (2005). EEG evidence for mirror neuron dysfunction in autism spectrum disorders. *Cognitive Brain Research,* 24, 190–198.

Ozonoff, S. & Jensen, J. (1999). Specific executive function profiles in three neurodevelopmental disorders. *Journal of Autism and Developmental Disorders,* 29(2), 171-177.

Ozonoff, S., Pennington, B.F. & Rogers, S.J. (1991). Executive functioning deficits in high-functioning autistic individuals: Relationship to theory of mind. *Journal of Child Psychology and Psychiatry,* 32, 1081-1106.

Pericak-Vance, M.A. (2003). The genetics of autism. In: Plomin R, DeFries J, Craig I, McGuffin P (Eds). *Behavioral genetics in the postgenomic era.* APA Books, Washington, DC.

Pinedad,e, J.A. (2005). EEG evidence for mirror neuron dysfunction in autism spectrum disorders. *Cognitive Brain Research,* 24, 190–198.

Penn, H. (2006). Neurobiological correlates of autism: A review of recent research. *Child Neuropsychology,* 12(1), 57-79.

Perner, J., & Lang, B. (2000). Theory of mind and executive function: Is there a developmental relationship? In S. Baron-Cohen, H. Tager-Flousberg & D. Cohen (Eds.) *Understanding other minds: Perspectives from developmental cognitive neuroscience.* Oxford, UK: Oxford University Press

Pichichero ME, Cernichiari E, Lopreiato J, Treanor J. (2002). Mercury concentrations and metabolism in infants receiving vaccines containing thiomersal: a descriptive study. *Lancet,* 360, 1737-1741.

Pickles, A., Bolton, P., Macdonald, H. et al., (1995). Latent-class analysis of recurrence risk for complex phenotypes with selection and measurement error: A twin and family history study of autism. *American Journal of Human Genetics*, 57, 717.

Pierce, K., Muller, R.A., Ambrose, J., Allen, G., & Courchesne, E. (2001). Face processing occurs outside the fusiform "face area" in autism: Evidence from function fMRI. *Brain*, 124(1)0, 2059-2073.

Piven, J., Arndt, S., Bailey, J. et al (1995). An MRI study of brain size in autism. *American Journal of Psychiatry*, 152, 1145-1149.

Plaisted, K. (2000). Aspects of autism that theory of mind cannot easily explain. In S. Baron-Cohen, H. Tager-Flusberg & D.J. Cohen (Eds.). *Understanding other minds: Perspectives from autism and cognitive neuroscience (2nd edition)*. Oxford, UK: Oxford University Press.

Plaisted, K. (2001). Reduced generalization in autism: An alternative to weak central coherence. In J. Burack, T. Charman, N. Yirmiya & P. Zelazo (Eds.) *The development of autism: Perspectives from theory and research*. Mahwah, NJ: Lawrence Erlbaum Associates.

Pring, L., Hermelin, B., & Heavey, L. (1995). Savants, segments, art, and autism. *Journal of Child Psychology and Psychiatry*, 36, 1065-1076.

Prior, M. (2003). What do we know and where should we go? In M. Prior (Ed.). *Learning and Behavior Problems in Asperger Syndrome*. New York: Guilford Press. Pp. 295-319.

Ramachandran, V.S. & Oberman, L.M. (2006). Broken mirrors - a theory of autism. *Scientific American*, 295(5), 62-69.

Report to the Legislature on the Principal Findings from the Epidemiology of Autism in California. A Comprehensive Pilot Study. Davis, Ca: M.I.N.D. Institute, University of California, Davis; October 17, 2002.

Rimland, B. (1978). Inside the mind of the autistic savant. *Psychology Today*, August, 69-80.

Rogers S. (1998) Empirically supported comprehensive treatments for young children with autism. *Journal of Clinical Child Psychology*, 27:168-179.

Rumsey, J.M. (1985). Conceptual problem solving in highly verbal, nonretarded autistic men. *Journal of Autism and Developmental Disorders*, 15, 23-36.

Russell, J. (2002). Cognitive theories of autism. In J.E. Harrison & A.M. Owen (Eds.) *Cognitive deficits in brain disorders*. London, UK: Martin Dunitz.

Russell, J. (Ed.) (1997). *Autism as an executive disorder*. Oxford, UK: Oxford University Press.

Russell, J., Mauthner, N., Sharpe, S., Tidswell, T. (1991). The "windows task" as a measure of strategic deception in preschoolers and autistic subjects. [Special issue: Perspectives on the child's theory of mind: II). *British Journal of Developmental Psychology*, 9, 331-349.

Rutter, M. (2013). Changing Concepts and Findings on Autism. *Journal of Autism and Developmental Disorders.* 43:1749–1757.

Schechter, R. & Grether. J.K. (2008). Continuing Increases in Autism Reported to California's Developmental Services System: Mercury in Retrograde. *Archives of General Psychiatry.* 2008;65(1):19-24.

Schultz, R.T., Gauthier, I., Klein, A., Fulbright, R., Anderson, A., Volkmar, F.R. et al (2000). Abnormal ventral temporal cortical activity among individuals with autism and Asperger syndrome during face discrimination. *Archives of General Psychiatry*, 57, 331-340.

Schultz, R.T., Gauthier, I., Klin, A. et al (2000). Abnormal ventral temporal cortical activity during face discrimination among individuals with autism and Asperger syndrome. *Archives of General Psychiatry*, 57, 331-340.

Schultz, R.T., Grelotti, D.J., Klin, A. Et al (2003). The role of the fusiform face area in social cognition: Implications for the pathobiology of autism. *Philosophical Transactions of the Royal Society of London - Series B: Biololgical Sciences.* 358(1430), 415-427.

Shah, A. & Frith, U. (1983). Why do autistic individuals show superior performance on the block design task? *Journal of Child Psychology and Psychiatry*, 24, 613-620.

Simonoff, E. et al. (2008). Psychiatric Disorders in Children With Autism Spectrum Disorders: Prevalence, Comorbidity, and Associated Factors in a Population-Derived Sample. Journal of the American Academy of Child and Adolescent Psychiatry. 47:8.

Smalley, S.L., Asarnow, R.F. & Spence, A. (1988). Autism and genetics: A decade of research. *Archives of General Psychiatry*, 45, 953-961.

Smalley, S.L., McCracken, J. & Tanguay, P. (1995). Autism, affective disorders, and social phobia. *American Journal of Medical Genetics*, 611, 19-26.

Smith, T., Buch, G.A., & Gamby, T.E. (2000). Parent directed, intensive early intervention for children with pervasive developmental disorder. *Research in Developmental Disabilities*, 21, 297–309.

Stratton, K, Gable, A., McCormick, M.C. (Eds.) (2001). *Immunization Safety Review Committee: Thimerosal-Containing Vaccines and Neurodevelopmental Disorders.* Washington, DC: National Academies, Institute of Medicine; 2001.

Taylor B, Miller E, Lingam R, Andrews N, Simmons A, Stowe J. (2002). Measles, mumps, and rubella vaccination and bowel problems or developmental regression in children with autism: population study. *British Medical Journal,* 324:393-396.

Uddin, L. Q., Menon, V., Young, C.B., Ryali, S., Chen, T., Khouzam, A., Minshew, N.J. & Hardan, A.Y. (2011). Multivariate Searchlight Classification of Structural Magnetic Resonance Imaging in Children and Adolescents with Autism. *Biological Psychiatry*, 70 (9), pg. 833-841.

Van Kooten, Imke A. J., Palmen, S. J. M. C., von Cappeln, P. Stein busch, H.W.M., Korr, H., Heinsen, H.., P.R., van Engeland, H. & Schlitz, C. (2008). Neurons in the fusiform gyrus are fewer and smaller in autism. *Brain*, 131(4), 987-999.

Vargas, D.L, Nascimbene, C., Krishnan, C., Zimmerman, A.W. & Pardo, C.A. (2005). Neuroglial activation and neuroinflammation in the brain of patients with autism. *Annals of Neurology*, 57: 67-81.

Volkmar, F.R. (Ed.) (2007). Autism and Pervasive Developmental Disorders (2nd Edition). Cambridge, UK: Cambridge University Press.

Volkmar, F., Lord, C., Bailey, A. Schultz, R. & Klin, A. (2004). Autism and pervasive developmental disorders. *Journal of Child Psychology and Psychiatry*, 45(1), 135-170.

Wang et al. Common genetic variants on 5p14.1 associate with autism spectrum disorders. *Nature*, online April 28, 2009 DOI: 10.1038/nature07999

Weeks, S.J. & Hobson, R.P. (1987). The salience of facial expression for autistic children. *Journal of Child Psychology and Psychiatry*, 28, 137-151.

Weiss et al (2009). A genome-wide linkage and association scan reveals novel loci for autism. *Nature*, 461(8), Oct. 9, 2009. Pp. 802-808.

Wicker, Bruno (2008). New insights from Neuroimaging into the emotional brain in autism. In MacGregor, E. Et al. *Autism: An integrated view from neurocognitive, clinical, and intervention research*. Malden, MA: Blackwell Publishing.

Williams, J., Whiten, A., Suddendorf, T. & Perrett, D. (2001). Imitation, mirror neurons and autism. *Neuroscience and Biobehavioral Reviews*, 25(4), 287-295. ***

Woo, C.C. & Leon, M. (2013). Environmental Enrichment as an Effective Treatment for Autism: A Randomized Controlled Trial. *Behavioral Neuroscience*, online first May 20 , 2013.

Yeargin-Allsopp M, Rice C, Karapurkan T, Doernberg N, Boyle C, Murphy C. (2003). Prevalence of autism in a US metropolitan area. *JAMA*. 2003;289:49-55.

Yrigollen, C.M.; Han, S.S.; Kochetkova, A.; Babitz, T.; Chang, J.T.; Volkmar, F.R.; Leckman, J.F.; et. al. (2008). Genes Controlling Affiliative Behavior as Candidate Genes for Autism. *Biological Psychiatry*, 63(10), 911-916.

Zimmerman, A.W., Connors, S.L., Matteson, K.J., Lee, L.C., Singer, H.S., Castaneda, J.A. et al. (2007). Maternal antibrain antibodies in autism. *Brain, Behavior & Immunity*, 21: 351-357.

Other Sources

Abrams, D.A. et al. (2013). Underconnectivity between voice-selective cortex and reward circuitry in children with autism. *Proceedings of the National Academy of Sciences*, (no pagination).

Boccuto, L., et al (2013). Decreased tryptophan metabolism in patients with autism spectrum disorders. *Molecular Autism*, 4:16.

Boyd, B.A. et al (2013). Comparative Efficacy of LEAP, TEACCH and Non-Model- Specific Special Education Programs for Preschoolers with Autism Spectrum Disorders. *Journal of Autism and Developmental Disorders*. (published online, June 2013.

Brown, A.S. et al (2013). Elevated maternal C-reactive protein and autism in a national birth cohort. *Molecular Psychiatry*, 1-6.

Cook, R., Brewer, R., Shah, P. & Bird, G. (2013). Alexithymia, Not Autism, Predicts Poor Recognition of Emotional Facial Expressions. *Psychological Science*, (published online 25 March 2013.)

Dougherty, J.D. et al (2013). The Disruption of Celf6, a Gene Identified by Translational Profiling of Serotonergic Neurons, Results in Autism-Related Behaviors. *The Journal of Neuroscience*, February 13, 2013 • 33(7):2732-2753.

Fein, D. et al (2013). Optimal outcome in individuals with a history of autism. *Journal of Child Psychology and Psychiatry*, 54:2, pp 195-205.

Frans, E.M. et al (2013). Autism Risk Across Generations A Population-Based Study of Advancing Grandpaternal and Paternal Age. *JAMA Psychiatry*, (Published online March 20, 2013.

Hoerder-Suabedissena, A. et al (2013). Expression profiling of mouse subplate reveals a dynamic gene network and disease association with autism and schizophrenia. *Proceedings of the National Academy of Sciences*, vol. 110(9), 3555-3560.

Jiang, X. et al (2013). A quantitative link between face discrimination deficits and neuronal selectivity for faces in autism. *NeuroImage: Clinical*, 2, 320-331.

Khana, S. et al (2012). Local and long-range functional connectivity is reduced in concert in autism spectrum disorders. *Proceedings of the National Academy of Sciences, (online 2012)*.

Movsas, T.E. et al (2013). Autism Spectrum Disorder Is Associated with Ventricular Enlargement in a Low Birth Weight Population. *Journal of Pediatrics*, (online).

Peters, J.M. et al (2013). Brain functional networks in syndromic and non-syndromic autism: a graph theoretical study of EEG connectivity. *BMC Medicine*, 11:54.

Rao, P.A. & Landa, R.J. (2013). Association between severity of behavioral phenotype and comorbid attention deficit hyperactivity disorder symptoms in children with autism spectrum disorders. *Autism*, published online 5 June 2013.

Roberts, A.L. et al (2013). Association of Maternal Exposure to Childhood Abuse With Elevated Risk for Autism in Offspring. *JAMA Psychiatry*, (Published online March 20, 2013.)

Scott, N.J., Jones, A.L., Kramer, R.S.S & Ward, R. (2014). Facial Dimorphism in Autistic Quotient Scores. *Clinical Psychological Science*, 1-12. Online July 15, 2014.

Smoller, J.W. et al (2013). Identification of risk loci with shared effects on five major psychiatric disorders: a genome-wide analysis. *Lancet*, 381: 1371-79.

Steinman, G. & Mankuta, D. (2013). Insulin-like growth factor and the etiology of autism. *Medical Hypotheses*, (online June, 2013; no pagination).

Wodka, E.l., Mathy, P. & Kalb, L. (2013). Predictors of Phrase and Fluent Speech in Children With Autism and Severe Language Delay. *Pediatrics*, 131;e1128; (originally published online March 4, 2013).

Anxiety Disorders

I. Introduction

    A. General list of disorders under this heading (DSM 5): topics in **bold** will be discussed
1. Separation Anxiety Disorder
2. Selective Mutism
3. **Specific Phobia**
4. **Social Anxiety Disorder** (Social Phobia)
5. **Panic disorder**
6. **Agoraphobia**
7. **Generalized anxiety disorder**
8. Substance/Medication Induced Anxiety Disorder
9. Anxiety disorder due to another medical condition
10. Other Specified Anxiety Disorder
11. Unspecified Anxiety Disorder

    B. Characteristic feature are symptoms of anxiety and avoidance behavior. Are the most frequently found in the general population, with specific phobias and social phobia being the most common. Panic disorder most common among people seeking treatment.

    C. 75% of individuals with an anxiety disorder will have their first episode by age 21.5.

Generalized Anxiety Disorder

I. Description:

    A. Symptoms include:
1. **Motor tension symptoms**: Trembling, shaking, muscle tension or aches and soreness, restlessness, fatigue.
2. **Autonomic hyperactivity symptoms**: Tachycardia, sweating, dizziness, nausea, or other GI complaints.
3. **Vigilance or scanning symptoms**: Exaggerated startle response, trouble concentrating, trouble falling asleep or staying asleep, irritability.
4. May be associated with mild depression, and impairment is usually only mild.

II. Definition and diagnostic criteria under DSM 5:

    A. "Excessive anxiety and worry (apprehensive expectation), occurring more days than not for at least 6 months, about a number of events or activities (such as work of school performance.)" p. 222.

B. "The person finds it difficult to control the worry."

C. "The anxiety and worry are associated with three (or more) of the following six symptoms (with at least some symptoms present for more days than not for the past 6 months). Note: Only one item is required in children."
   1. "restlessness or feeling keyed up or on edge"
   2. "being easily fatigued"
   3. "Difficulty concentrating or mind going blank"
   4. "Irritability"
   5. "Muscle tension"
   6. "Sleep disturbance (difficulty falling asleep or staying asleep, or restless unsatisfying sleep)"

D. The symptoms "cause clinically significant distress or impairment in social occupational or other important areas of functioning."

E. The symptoms are not due to the physiological effects of substance (e.g., a drug of abuse, a mediation) or to "another medical condition."

F. The symptoms are not better explained by another mental disorder.

III. Epidemiology:

A. Usually starts in 20s and 30s. Onset occurs in childhood or adolescent in sizeable proportion of cases. About equally common in all age groups.

B. Most common anxiety disorder among children and the elderly; one of the most common disorders in primary care (family physician) - second only to depression.

C. DSM-5 says:
   1. Annual prevalence in U.S. is .9% among adolescents, 3% among adults.
   2. U.S. lifetime prevalence is 9% (up from an estimate of 5% under DSM-IIIR criteria).
   3. Other countries, .4% to 3.5%.

D. About 67% of patients have another concurrent disorder.

E. Clinically, about 55-60% of those given the diagnosis are women. In epidemiologically studies, about 66% of those with the symptoms of the disorder are female.

F. Most people with the symptoms do not seek help, or wait a long time before doing so. Often seek help for a condition (e.g., depression) that is complicated by GAD.

Panic Disorder

I. Description and symptoms:

    A. Experience differs between individuals, but involve sudden, unexpected episodes of severe anxiety accompanied by strong somatic symptoms that lead the individual to want to escape as soon as possible.

    B. Symptoms:
        1. Tachycardia, chest pain, sweating, trembling or shaking.
        2. Sensations of shortness of breath (dyspnea) or smothering; feeling of choking.
        3. Dizziness, light-headedness.
        4. Chills or hot flushes.
        5. Nausea or other GI symptoms.
        6. Paresthesias (numbness or tingling sensations).
        7. Derealization (feelings of unreality) or depersonalization (being detached from oneself).
        8. Fear of losing control or going crazy; fear of dying.

    C. Peak very quickly (typically within 10 minutes), last up to 1 hour (though rarely that long), and can take place many times a day, or only once every few months or even years.

II. **Criteria under DSM5:**

    A. "Recurrent unexpected panic attacks. A panic attack is an abrupt surge of intense fear or intense discomfort that reaches a peak within minutes, and during which time four (or more) of the following symptoms occur:" (p. 208)
        1. Palpitations, pounding heart, accelerated heard rate [tachycardia]
        2. Sweating
        3. Trembling or shaking
        4. Sensations of shortness of breath or smothering
        5. Feeling of choking
        6. Chest pain or discomfort
        7. Nausea or abdominal distress
        8. Feeling dizzy, unsteady, light-headed, or faint
        9. Chills or heat sensations
        10. Paresthesias (numbness or tingling sensations)
        11. Derealization (feelings of unreality) or depersonalization (being detached from oneself)
        12. Fear of losing control or going crazy
        13. Fear of dying

    B. "At least one of the attacks has been followed by 1-month (or more) of one or both of the following:
        1. Persistent concern or worry about additional panic attacks or their consequences (e.g., losing control, Having a heart attack, 'going crazy'.)

2. a significant maladaptive change in behavior related to the attacks (e.g., behaviors designed to avoid having panic attacks, such as avoidance of exercise or unfamiliar situations.)"

C. "The disturbance is not attributable to the physiological effects of a substance (e.g., a drug of abuse, a medication) or another medical condition (e.g., hyperthyroidism, cardiopulmonary disorders)"

D. "The disturbance is not better explained by another mental disorder (e.g., ... social anxiety disorder, ... specific phobias, ... PTSD...)"

III. Epidemiology

A. DSM-5 estimates annual prevalence in U.S. and several European countries as 2-3% in adults and adolescents.

B. **Kessler et al. (2005ab)**: In U.S., 12-month prevalence Panic Disorder is 270/10,000 (2.7%); lifetime prevalence is 470/10,000 (4.7%). Other U.S. estimates of lifetime prevalence range from 1.7% - 3.5%.
   1. Estimated annual prevalence of panic attacks, not meeting the full criteria for PD, is about 11%, according to DSM-5.
   2. Panic attack prevalence in Europe much lower, ranging from approximately 2.5% to 3.5%.

C. Lifetime prevalence between 1.4% and 3% in various countries; much lower in Asian countries (40-150/10,000).

D. Average age of onset in U.S. according to DSM-5 is early 20s (22-23 years of age).

E. More common among women than men (1.5 - 2.5 to 1 in the population; 2.5 - 3 to 1 in the clinical population. Call it 2:1 females:males

F. High rates of comorbidity for:
   1. Anxiety disorders, especially agoraphobia.
   2. Major depression and bipolar disorder (10 - 50% estimated comorbidity).

G. Course variable, unpredictable. Several panic attacks per week or daily. Disorder generally last many years, but may be limited to several during period of weeks or months.

H. Estimates of outcome (Starcevic, 2005, p. 50):
   1. 30-35% recover nearly or completely without treatment.
   2. 50% have mild or occasional symptoms, with minor interference in functioning, and need for occasional or (rarely) prolonged treatment.
   3. 15-20% have continuous moderate to severe symptoms with continuous interference with functioning, and require continuous treatment.

Agoraphobia

I. DSM-5 diagnostic criteria: (p. 217-218)

   A. "Marked fear or anxiety about two (or more) of the following five situations:"
      1. Using public transportation (e.g., automobiles, buses, trains, ships, planes.)
      2. Being in open spaces (e.g., parking lots, marketplaces, bridges.)
      3. Being in enclosed places (e.g., shops, theaters, cinemas.)
      4. Standing in line or being in a crowd.
      5. Being outside of the home alone."

   B. "The individual fears or avoids these situations because of thoughts that escape might be difficult or help might not be available in the event of developing panic-like symptoms or other incapacitating or embarrassing symptoms (e.g., fear of falling in the elderly, fear of incontinence,)"

   C. "The agoraphobic situation almost always produces fear or anxiety."

   D. The agoraphobic situations are actively avoided, require the presence of a companion, or are endured with intense fear or anxiety."

   E. "The fear or anxiety is out or proportion to the actual danger posed by the agoraphobic situations and to the sociocultural context."

   F. "The fear, anxiety, or avoidance is persistent, typically lasting 6 months or more."

   G. "If another medical condition ... is present, the fear, anxiety or avoidance ids clearly excessive."

   H. "The fear, anxiety, or avoidance is not better explained by the symptoms of another mental disorder - for example [social anxiety disorder, specific phobia, PTSD, separation anxiety]."

II. Epidemiology

   A. According to DSM-5, the annual prevalence of agoraphobia in adolescents and adults is about 1.7%, with twice as many females diagnosed as males.

   B. **Kessler et al., (2005ab).** In U.S., 12-month prevalence of Agoraphobia w/o PD is 80/10,000 (0.8%); lifetime prevalence is 140/10,000 (1.4%).

   C. About 95% of individuals who present with Agoraphobia also have current or previous Panic Disorder.

III. Panic Disorder Etiology - biological factors:

A. Some studies show higher rate of panic disorder in relatives of diagnosed cases.
   1. **Starcevic (2005**, p. 55): 10-25% lifetime prevalence rate among first-degree relatives, compared with 1-3% in controls, but although several twin studies found higher concordance rate for MZ than for DZ twins, recent studies do not replicate this.
   2. Some evidence that tendency to hyperventilation associated with the disorder. Signs of hyperventilation disappear when panic disorder has been treated with anti-panic medication.
   3. Researchers report evidence of high catecholamine (norepinephrine, epinephrine, dopamine) levels in the urine of individuals with panic disorder.
      a. MAO (which catalyzes catecholamines) is also high, but cause-effect relationship between disorder and biochemistry is unclear.
      b. But normal subjects exposed to novel stress also show elevated plasma catecholamines.
   4. Others suggest that it results from massive stimulation of the beta-adrenergic nervous system (beta receptors respond to epinephrine and norepinephrine with the flight-or-flight response), since symptoms mimic autonomic hyperactivity, or activity of beta-adrenergic receptors. But no success in relieving panic attacks with beta blockers such as propranolol. (Talbott, p. 448)
   5. [drop this] **Gorman et al. (2000)**: Neuroanatomical hypothesis of panic disorder
      a. Evidence that cardiovascular and respiratory reactivity abnormal in panic disorder, suggesting brainstem involvement.
      b. Argues panic disorder involves same pathways as conditioned fear in animals
      c. A conditioned fear stimulus stimulates **central nucleus** of the amygdala, which then coordinates autonomic and behavioral responses. Central nucleus:
         (1) Stimulates increase in respiratory rate.
         (2) via the hypothalamus, activates autonomic arousal vis the sympathetic nervous system.
         (3) activates locus coeruleus, resulting in increased norepinephrine release, and increased blood pressure, heart rate, and behavioral fear response
         (4) activates **paraventricular nucleus** of hypothalamus, causing increase in release of stress hormones from the adrenal gland.
   6. The majority (ca 70%) of sufferers from panic attacks show attack when sodium lactate is infused into their blood. Only 5% of normals show this response. Not clear why this happens, or how it is chemically related to the disorder, but several hypotheses exist.
      a. Originally thought that increased blood levels of lactate or decreased levels of calcium were responsible somehow.
      b. Now argued that infusions produce large increase in NE in susceptibles.
      c. PET studies suggest several brain differences between lactate positives and normals or lactate negatives):
         (1) Higher overall levels of brain metabolism in patients with positive lactate infusion results (not normals or lactate negatives).
         (2) Higher activity in nondominant hippocampal area (again, only for positive lactates).
      d. Some PD patients have increased sympathetic tone, adapt more slowly to repeated stimuli, and have excessively ANS responses to moderate stimuli.
      e. Also a correlation between panic disorder and mitral valve prolapse. 50% of patients show this, but only 5% of general population. Produces mid-systolic click, and when normals are symptomatic, produce heart rate increases and respiratory changes similar to panic disorder, both thought to be genetic.

IV. Etiology - Psychodynamic approaches:

   A. Reoccurrence of earlier separation anxiety, an idea taken from Bowlby.
      1. 20-50% of adults with agoraphobia with panic attacks recall showing symptoms of pathological separation anxiety as children.
      2. Imipramine blocks distress vocalizations in dogs and monkeys when separated, and also is highly effective in eliminating panic attacks in humans.
      3. **Gittelman et al. (1971)** showed that children with school phobia (which is usually based on separation anxiety) respond well to imipramine treatment and return to school.
         a. Related to castration anxiety.

Social Anxiety Disorder (Social Phobia)

I. Description and DSM-5 diagnostic criteria: (DSM-5, pp. 202-203)

   A. "Marked fear or anxiety about one or more social situations in which the individual is exposed to possible scrutiny by others. Examples include social interactions (e.g., having a conversation, meeting unfamiliar people), being observed (e.g., eating or drinking), and performing in front of others (e.g., giving a speech.)"

   B. "The individual fears that he or she will act in a way or show anxiety symptoms that will be negatively evaluated (i.e., will be humiliating or embarrassing; will lead to rejection or offend others.)"

   C. "The social situations almost always provoke fear or anxiety."

   D. "The social situations are avoided or endured with intense fear or anxiety."

   E. "The fear or anxiety is out of proportion to the actual threat posed by the social situation and to the sociocultural context." [Note that unlike DSM-IV, this criterion does NOT specify that the individual him- or herself must recognize the excessiveness of the fear or anxiety.]

   F. "The fear, anxiety or avoidance is persistent, typically lasting for 6 months or more." [Note the addition of 'typically' to this criterion, suggesting that in especially intense cases, the duration could be less.]

   G. "The fear, anxiety or avoidance causes clinically significant distress or impairment in social, occupational, or other important areas of functioning."

   H. "The fear, anxiety or avoidance is not attributable to the physiological effects of a substance (e.g. a drug of abuse, a medication) or another medical condition."

I. "The fear, anxiety or avoidance is not better explained by the symptoms of another mental disorder such as panic disorder, body dysmorphic disorder, or ASD."

J. "If another medical condition .... is present, the fear, anxiety, or avoidance is clearly unrelated or is excessive."

II. Epidemiology:

A. DSM-5 says annual prevalence in U.S. is about 7% (much lower - .5% to 2% elsewhere in the world; 2.3% is median in Europe).

B. DSM-5 says higher rates of symptoms among females than males in the general population, but same (or slightly higher for males) in clinical populations: "it is assumed that gender roles and social expectations play a significant role in explaining the higher help-seeking behavior in male patients." (P. 204)

C. **Kessler et al. (2005ab)**: In U.S., 12-month prevalence of Social Phobia is 680/10,000 (6.8%); lifetime prevalence is 1200/10,000 (12.1%).

D. **Crake & Waters (2005)**: Claim on the basis of **Kessler et al. (1994)** that social phobia is the most prevalent of all the anxiety disorders, with a 1330/10,000 (13.3%) lifetime prevalence.

E. Disorder often begins in adolescence: DSM-5 lists 13 as median age of onset, with 75% of cases developing between 8 and 15 years of age.

F. DSM-5 notes that in community samples, about 30% of individuals experience remission of symptoms within 12 months, and 50% experience remission within a few years. "For approximately 60% of individuals without a specific treatment for social anxiety disorder, the course takes several years or longer." (P. 205)

Specific Phobias

I. Description and diagnostic criteria under DSM-5: (pp. 197-198)

A. "Marked fear or anxiety about a specific object or situation (e.g., flying, heights, animals, receiving and injection, seeing blood)."

B. "The phobic object or situation almost always provokes immediate fear or anxiety."

C. "The phobic object or situation isd actively avoided or endured with intense fear or anxiety."

D. "The fear or anxiety is out of proportion to the actual danger posed by the specific object or situation and to the sociocultural context." [Note the removal of the qualifier that the person recognizes that the fear is excessive or unreasonable, as in DSM-IV.]

E. "The fear, anxiety or avoidance is persistent, typically lasting for 6 months or more."

F. "The fear, anxiety or avoidance causes clinically significant distress or impairment in social, occupational, or other important areas of functioning."

G. "The disturbance is not better explained by the symptoms of another mental disorder..."

H. Code based on the phobic stimulus:
   1. **Animal** (e.g., spiders, insects, dogs.)
   2. **Natural environment** (e.g., storms heights, water) Generally has a childhood onset.
   3. **Blood-Injection-Injury type**: (needles, invasive medical procedure, etc.) "Highly familial, and often characterized by a strong vasovagal response."
   4. **Situational**: (airplanes, elevators, enclosed places)
   5. **Other type**: (E.g., choking, vomiting, lycanthrophobia, etc.)

II. Epidemiology:

A. DSM-5 estimates annual prevalence of specific phobia at 7%-9% in the U.S. with similar rates in Europe, but lower in Asia, Africa, and Latin America.

B. **Kessler et al, (2005ab):** In U.S., 12-month prevalence of Specific Phobia is 870/10,000 (8.7%); lifetime prevalence is 1250/10,000 (12.5%). Specific Phobia: 12.5%

C. Most likely to develop in childhood, adolescence, and young adulthood. More common in females than in males ratio 2:1.
   1. Animal, natural environment and situational phobias more common in females.
   2. Blood-injections-injury phobia about equal in males and females.

III. Etiology of Phobic disorders

A. Basic problem in etiology is two-fold:
   1. To account for the relatively narrow range of objects and situations that are the subject of phobia.
   2. To relate the specific phobia shown by the individual to some specific triggering factor. Why fear this thing instead of any other?

B. Psychodynamic view: Individual fears some object because it is similar to, related to, or symbolic of some unacceptable unconscious wish. Think of phobia as an adaptation to deal with an inner conflict that is causing anxiety.
   1. Anxiety can arise in three ways:
      a. Ego can fear something in outside world: Reality anxiety.
      b. Ego can fear committing an act that is contrary to moral code: Moral anxiety
      c. Ego can fear punishment for giving in to id impulse: Neurotic anxiety.
   2. Unconscious ego defends against this anxiety by preventing the impulse or wish from reaching consciousness, or by disguising it in some way when it does begin to enter consciousness - defense mechanisms.
      a. Displacement: Wish experienced not against another object.
      b. Reaction formation:
   3. The fear prevents the possibility that a consciously unacceptable urge will be acted out, or may redirect internal anxiety to objects that are less anxiety-producing.
   4. Explains fact that phobias do not occur to a wide variety of stimuli, but only to a restricted list of situations/objects, which have symbolic significance.
   5. Schumer gives examples:
      a. Patient had murderous fantasies toward child; became phobic of kitchen implements such as knives, garbage disposal units and household chemicals.
      b. Suicidal urges produce fear of heights.
      c. Patient thought she might poison her guests; became phobic about entertaining at home.
   6. **Last et al. (1996)**: From 30% to the majority of youths successfully treated for anxiety disorder develop additional anxiety or mood disorders within 3-4 years of their initial evaluation.

C. The Behavioral Model
   1. Based on classical conditioning. Feared object or situation has been paired with an aversive event in the past, and now is a CS for fear. Role of generalization.
   2. How account for the fact that phobias are selective, and do not occur to **any** object in a traumatic or fearful situation?
      a. Prepared classical conditioning: We are more likely to fear objects or situations that are, or once were dangerous to man (heights, animals, etc.)
      b. **Ohman et al. (1976)**: Swedish study. Compared aversive GSR conditioning with shock using pictures as CSs. Pictures were either of 'prepared' (snakes, spiders) or 'unprepared' (houses, faces, flowers) CSs. Found conditioning much more rapid (one pairing) with prepared, but slower (4-5 pairings) with unprepared CSs.
      c. **Hugdahl & Ohman (1977)**: Same as above, then told Ss no more shocks would be delivered. Extinction rapid to nonprepared CSs, but remained to snakes and spiders.
   3. But what about cases in which individual has little or no contact with feared object? How account for phobia? In prepared CSs, little contact is necessary. **Hygge & Ohman (1978)**: Verbal threat of shock produced robust conditioning following prepared signals, but not following unprepared signals.
      a. **Marks (1977)**: Tells of English girl who sees snake in park in England and shows no fear. After going home and injuring hand in car door, shows fear of snakes, not car doors.

General Etiology of Anxiety

I. Introduction

    A. Etiology: A diathesis-stress model is commonly accepted.

    B. As before, we will look at etiology at several different levels of abstraction:
        1. **Behavioral symptoms**: These would be important to those who hold with a behavioral view of the nature of mental disorder, and with behavioral approaches to treatment of anxiety disorders.
            a. Conditioned fear, avoidance and escape behaviors:
                (1) Panic Disorder
                (2) Phobias (Social and Specific)
        2. **Cognitive symptoms**: These are important to those who hold to a cognitive view if the nature and treatment of mental disorders.
            a. Intrusive thoughts
                (1) catastrophizing in GAD, phobias, Panic Disorder
            b. Strong or persistent experience of fear.
        3. **Psychological processes**: These might be important to those with a cognitive view, though they play a smaller role in our analysis of anxiety disorders than they did for ADHD and Autism, and other disorders yet to be discussed.
            a. Emotion regulation: In all Anxiety Disorders
            b. Defense mechanisms (psychodynamic management of anxiety)
        4. Brain function, structure and chemistry
        5. Genetic bases

II. Behavioral mechanisms: Conditioned fear

    A. Introduction: This is one of the most popular and practical levels of analysis, since it forms the basis for important treatment approaches, as we will see.

    B. Panic Disorder:
        1. **Interoceptive conditioning model**: Unconscious internal (interoceptive) stimuli that precede anxiety/panic become conditioned elicitors of anxiety or panic. Panic attacks are unexpected since internal stimuli not conscious. Conditioned anxiety lowers threshold for subsequent panic attacks in self-perpetuating way. (Bouton et al., 2001; Craik &Waters, 2005).
        2. **Ohman & Mineka (2001) and LeDoux (1996)** argue that aversive emotional learning can occur unconsciously, and implicit emotional memories can activate amygdala-based fear systems without conscious awareness of the reasons.

III. Etiology - Cognitive Bases

   A. Panic Disorder: **Catastrophic appraisal model: (Clark, 1986)**: Individuals consciously and/or unconsciously interpret bodily sensations in a catastrophic way.
      1. Hyper vigilance for threat cures and danger-laden judgments
         a. Attentional bias toward threat stimuli reported in PD (e.g., **Maidenberg et al., 1996**), GAD (e.g., **MacLeod et al., 1986**; Social Anxiety Disorder (e.g., **Mogg et al., 2004b**) and Specific Phobias (e.g., **Lavy et al., 1993**)
         b. **Danger-laden judgments**: Individuals high in trait anxiety, and/or with an anxiety disorder, overestimate the personal risk for negative events compared with controls.(**Butler & Matthews, 1987**; **Foa et al., 1996**), and make threatening interpretations of ambiguous stimuli. (e.g., **Taghavi et al., 2000**; **Hirsch & Matthews, 2000**)

IV. Temperament/trait Personality factors in anxiety.

   A. Most trait theories argue for 3-5 core traits that describe personality. Three of these (neuroticism, introversion, negative affectivity) implicated in anxiety disorders.

   B. Eysenck argued that:
      1. Introverts have higher level of cortical arousal, and therefore learn more quickly, and more readily. That includes learning to associate fear with external stimuli.
      2. Individuals high in neuroticism have a strong tendency to experience negative emotions, based on a low threshold for activation of the amygdala and other parts of the brain responsible for negative emotions like fear.
      3. Combination of introversion and neuroticism leads to individuals very ready to experience fear, and to link it with external stimuli.

   C. Link between anxiety disorders generally and introversion. **Rosenbaum et al. (1988)** Found high incidence of introversion (behavioral inhibition) in children of parents with panic disorder and agoraphobia. Suggests genetic basis to introversion, and appropriate link between introversion and anxiety disorder. (learning of anxiety)

   D. Association between neuroticism/negative affectivity and anxiety disorders across the lifespan. (E.g., **Hayward et al., 2000**; **Jorm et al., 2000**). Extreme behavioral inhibition (conceptualized as a behavioral manifestation of neuroticism), is a predictor of anxiety disorders. (E.g., **Biederman et al., 1990, 1993**; **Hirschfeld et al., 1992**)

   E. Argument suggests another trait in addition to neuroticism/negative affectivity; **emotion regulation**: The ability to modulate emotional arousal; thought to be low in anxiety disorders.
      1. **Cardiac vagal tone**: Assessed via heart rate variability (HRV: beat-to-beat changes in heart rate during breathing, also called respiratory sinus arrhythmia). Assesses extent to which heart rate influenced by the vagus nerve of the parasympathetic nervous system.

a. High HRV indicates flexible and adaptive emotional responding to events. Low HRV indicates poorer attention to and discrimination among environmental cues (Thayer et al., 2000; Craik & Waters, 2005).
   b. Notion is that poorer discrimination leads to anxiety being conditioned to a wider variety of stimulus cues, hence general anxiety.
   c. Thayer et al. (2000): GAD Ps had lower tonic HRV, smaller cardiac orienting responses, impaired habituation of cardiac orienting to neutral words compared with non-anxious controls.
   d. Adults with high trait anxiety exhibit low HRV compared with non-anxious controls. (E.g., **Yeragani et al., 1998**)
   e. Low HRV correlated with high behavioral inhibition in children (e.g., **Rubin et al, 1997**; **Fox & Field, 1989**)
   f. But **Friedman & Thayer (1998)** argue for causality in the opposite direction: I.e., that worry and anxiety attenuate cardiac vagal tone. **Crake et al. (2004)**: Cognitive-behavioral treatment for anxiety (nocturnal panic) increases cardiac vagal tone, in support of this reverse causal direction.

V. Brain physiology/chemistry factors in anxiety

   A. Brain structures:
      1. Evidence for the role of the amygdala, and temporal and prefrontal cortices.
      2. **Qin et al (2014)** in fMRI study of 76 children, 7-9 years old, with no psychopathology. Assessed child's anxiety level via parental report.
         a. Found high anxiety levels associated with enlarged basolateral amygdala.
         b. High anxiety also associated with greater connectivity between amygdala and brain areas involved in attention, emotion perception, and regulation.
         c. Machine learning algorithms were able to reliably predict childhood anxiety using measurements of amygdala size and connectivity, with left basolateral amygdala as strongest predictor.
      3. In SAD, interest in **bed nucleus of stria terminalis**. (Between caudate and thalamus) Enervates similar structures as amygdala, but related to diffuse, long-term anxiety not short-term fear.

   B. Hypothalamic-Pituitary-Adrenal (HPA) axis in anxiety:
      1. Attention has been focused on genes related to CRH (corticotropin releasing hormone), which is the primary mediator of HPA activity.
         a. Stress induces release of CRH from hypothalamus.
         b. CRH from hypothalamus causes release of adrenocorticotropin from pituitary
         c. In response to which adrenal cortex releases glucocorticoid stress hormones. (e.g., cortisol)
      2. Altered physiology and function of HPA axis consistently found in anxiety (and depression), e.g. **Strohle & Holsboer (2003)**
      3. Antidepressants of various classes suppress HPA activity.
      4. Early life stress in macaques show adult characteristics reminiscent of anxiety and depression in humans. Changes occur in many areas, including HPA axis. **(Mathew et al., 2002)**

5. Evidence suggests that "early environmental factors establish an HPA axis reactivity that can be set for life and can be transmitted epigenetically to subsequent generations **(Gorman et al., 2002, Weaver et al., 2004)**" (Leonardo & Hen, 2006, page 129)
6. Attention focused on two genes for CRH receptors in the hypothalamus: CRH-R1 and CRH-R2. Mice lacking CRH-R1 gene show reduced anxiety.

C. Evidence also for the role of monoamine neurotransmitters (serotonin, norepinephrine) based on the success of drugs that target those transmitters to alleviate anxiety.

D. Social phobics share the neurochemical profiles of other anxiety disorders: Heightened adrenergic (epinephrine) excitation plus decreased GABA inhibitory regulation **(Argyropoulos et al., 2001)**
 1. But social phobics add evidence of a dysfunction in serotonin and dopamine systems **(Nutt et al., 1998; Potts et al., 1996)**.
 2. Lower dopamine (D2) binding reported in the striatum (caudate, putamen), which correlates in animals with lack of exploration and novelty-seeking and lower social status **(Schneider et al., 2000)**
 3. But are these causes or effects?

E. **Zieman, et al.** (2009). The amygdala detects carbon dioxide and acidosis to elicit fear behavior. *Cell*, 139(5):867-9. Amygdala expresses acid-sensing ion channel-1a (ASIC1a), which is required for normal fear responses. Found that amygdala responded to reduced pH produced by inhaled $CO(2)$ in mice by evoking fear behavior. Inhibiting ASIC1a impaired this activity, and localized ASIC1a expression. Buffering pH reduced fear behavior, while reducing pH with amygdala microinjections reinstated it. May be basis of anxiety and panic disorders

VI. Genetic factors in anxiety

A. Children whose parents have an anxiety disorder about 3-5 times as likely as others to also have an anxiety disorder. (e.g., **Merikangas et al., 1999**)
 1. GAD more common (19.5%) in first-degree relatives than among first-degree relatives of non-anxious controls (3.5%) **(Noyes et al., 1987)**

B. Some evidence from twin studies of constitutional predisposition to high anxiety. In **Slater & Shields (1969)**, 41% of MZ and 4% of DZ twins shared diagnosis of anxiety reaction. Also a high correlation between twins in autonomic measures.

C. Lots of animal work on the genetic bases of endophenotypes of anxiety. Such studies suggest that any single gene accounts for less than 5% of the variance in behavioral measures related to anxiety **(Flint, 2003)**. **Turri et al. (2004)**: Estimate 6 to 14 different loci affect anxiety.

D. 5-HT1A receptor implicated in mediating effects of serotonergic agents in anxiety (and depression). Assume increased serotonin associated with anxiety, and decreased serotonin with depression.

1. Desensitization of 5-HT1A **autoreceptors** on presynaptic neuron (for 5-hydroxytryptamine, or serotonin) postulated as a key change that allows antidepressant action **(Albert & Lemonde, 2004)**
2. Mice lacking the 5-HT1A receptor show increased anxiety on a number of tests. **(Klemenhagen et al., 2005)**
3. Studies with knockout mice show that repression of receptor expression in adult mice has no effect on anxiety, repression of receptor expression until 4 weeks of age produces adult mice with increased anxiety-related behavior.
4. In mice, effect of 5-HT1A knockout on anxiety first appears in 3rd week of life, a period of enhanced synaptic and dendritic growth in the forebrain, and in the hippocampus, which is known to regulate innate anxiety-related behaviors that are abnormal in knockout mice **(Deacon et al, 2002; Kjelstrup et al., 2002)**
5. Human association studies show correlation between "a single functional polymorphism in the promoter of the 5-HT1A receptor and both trait anxiety and depression **(LeMonde et al., 2004; Strobel et al., 2003)**
6. So perhaps altered transcription levels during human development responsible for altered trait anxiety **(Lesch & Gutknecht, 2004)**

E. Serotonin transporter protein (5-HTT; 5-hydroxytryptamine transporter):
1. This protein is the primary target of the SSRIs, which are effective in treating both depression and a wide variety of anxiety disorders.
2. **Holmes et al., (2003)**: Mice lacking 5-HTT genes show anxiety and depression-related behaviors, but this is strange since SSRIs block 5-HTT, so anxiety/depression should be reduced in 5-HTT is absent.
   a. When normal mice treated with fluoxetine at young age (days 4-21), mimicking the 5-HTT knockout, showed anxiety/depression-related activity as adults, like knockout mice, suggesting role of 5-HTT in anxiety has to do with brain development.
3. **Caspi et al. (2003); Kendler et al., 2005)**: Functional polymorphism in human 5-HTT gene moderates effect of early life stress on later development of depression.
   a. People with at least one version of the short (s) allele of 5-HTT-linked polymorphic region (5-HTTLPR) had more depressive symptoms to stressful life events than people with two copies of long allele (l).
4. This vulnerability to depression and anxiety shows up in brain imaging:
   a. Healthy persons with two (s) alleles have higher levels of amygdala activity to stressful stimuli than individuals with two copies of (l). **(Hariri et al., 2002, 2005)**. This is an endophenotype that appears in individuals w/o pathology.
   b. **Pezawas et al. (2005)**: People with (s) allele show uncoupling of cingulate-amygdala feedback circuit found in people carrying the (l) allele.
5. 5-HTT gene located on chromosome 17 (17q11.2). Short allele found in half Caucasians. A single copy of shortened 5-HTT gene makes carriers more susceptible to stress-induced depression, perhaps because lower levels of transporter may lead to less efficient management of stress-related hormone levels.

I. Treatments for anxiety

   A. Pharmacological treatments:
      1. Physiological aspects of anxiety are well handled by drugs, including antidepressants when depression is a concurrent condition, but do not handle the cognitive aspects (i.e, excessive worry) as well.
         a. Anxiolytics are the most prescribed category of drug after birth control pills.
            (1) Benzodiazepines (anxiolytic from 1950's). Increases GABA activity, a major inhibitory transmitter, esp in hippocampus) like Diazepam; Oxazepam; Larazepam; Clorazepate.
         b. Antidepressants:
            (1) venlafaxine (Effexor) - serotonin-norepinephrine reuptake inhibitor
            (2) paroxetine (Paxil) - SSRI
            (3) imipramine (tricyclic) - (Deprenil; Imipramil; Tofranil)
         c. MAO inhibitors (inhibit MAO which catalyses catecholamines (NE, epinephrine, dopamine)

   B. Psychological treatments: Behavioral
      1. Behavior therapy for GAD:
         a. Typically counter conditioning through muscle relaxation training
      2. For phobias
         a. **Systematic desensitization**: Describe for heights
         b. **Flooding**: (implosive therapy): Developed in late 1960's by Stampfl & Levis. Research in 1970's suggests that flooding is equal or superior to systematic desensitization for phobias, especially agoraphobia. Almost no reports of symptom substitution.
         c. **Modeling**: Phobic watches a model perform some behavior that the phobic is not able to do himself.
      3. Evidence comparing clomipramine and behavioral therapy shows clomipramine works best early on (5-10 weeks), but behavior therapy more long lasting. General tenor of literature is that behavioral therapy **alone** is overall more effective than clomipramine alone, and that combination is better than either.
         a. One author suggests that clomipramine helps patient resist temptation to repetition, thus helping behavioral therapy to work.

   C. Psychological treatments: Cognitive
      1. Cognitive therapies not as well-developed or as well established for GAD as for Panic Disorder and Agoraphobia.
      2. General procedure same as for other anxiety disorders
         a. Identification of appraisals of threat and beliefs that are associated with worries
         b. Challenging those beliefs through evidence-seeking and introduction of alternatives
         c. Replacement of dysfunctional appraisals and beliefs with rational alternatives

References

Albert, P.R. & Lemonde, S. (2004). 5-HT1A receptors, gene repression, and depression: Guilt by association. *Neuroscientist*, 10, 575-593.

Argyropoulos, S.V., Bell, C.J & Nutt, D.J. (2001). Brain function in social anxiety disorder. *Psychiatric Clinics of North America*, 24, 707-722.

Biederman, J., Rosenblum, J.F., Hirschfeld, D.R., Faraone, S.V., Bonduc, E.A. et al, (1990). Psychiatric correlated of behavioral inhibition in young children of parents with and without psychiatric disorders. *Archives of General Psychiatry*, 47, 21-26.

Biederman, J., Rosenblum, J.F., Bonduc-Murphy, E.A., Faraone, S.V., Chaloff, J. et al, (1993). A three year follow-up of children with and without behavioral Inhibition. *Journal of the American Academy of Child and Adolescent Psychiatry*, 32, 814-821.

Butler, G. & Matthews, A. (1987). Anticipatory anxiety and risk perception. *Cognitive Therapy Research*, 11(5), 551-565.

Carey, G., & Gottesman, I. I. (1981). Twin and family studies of anxiety, phobic, and obsessive disorders. In D. F. Klein & J. Rabkin (Eds.), *Anxiety: New research and changing concepts* (pp. 117–136). New York: Raven Press.

Caspi, A., Sugden, K., Moffitt, T.E., Taylor, A., Craig, I.W. et al (2003). Influence of life stress on depression: Moderation by a polymorphism in the 5-HTT gene. *Science*, 301, 386-389.

Clark, D.M. (1986). A cognitive approach to panic. *Behaviour Research and Therapy*, 24(4), 461-470.

Crake, M.G. & Waters, A.M. (2005). Panic disorders, phobias, and generalized anxiety disorder. In *Annual Review of Clinical Psychology*, 1, 197-227.

Crake, M.G., Lang, A.J., Atkins, D. & Mystkowski, J. (2005). Cognitive behavioral therapy for nocturnal panic. *Behavior Therapy*, 36(1), 43-54.

Deacon, R.M., Bannerman, D.M. & Rollins, J.N. (2002). Anxiolytic effects of cytotoxic hippocampal lesions in rats. *Behavioral Neuroscience*, 116, 494-497.

Flint, J. (2003). Analysis of quantitative trait loci that influence animal behavior. *Journal of Neurobiology*, 54, 46-77.

Foa, E.B., Franklin, M.E., Perry, K.J. & Herbert, J.D. 91996). Cognitive biases in generalized social anxiety disorder. *Journal of Abnormal Psychology*, 105(3), 433-439.

Fox, N. & Field, T.M. (1989). Individual differences in preschool entry behavior. *Journal of Applied Developmental Psychology*, 10, 527-540.

Friedman, B.H. & Thayer, J.F. (1998). Anxiety and autonomic flexibility: A cardiovascular approach. *Biological Psychology*, 47(3), 243-263.

Gilbertson, M. W., Shenton, M. E., Ciszewski, A., Kasai, K., Lasko, N. B., Orr, S. P. & Pitman, R. K. (2002). Smaller hippocampal volume predicts pathologic vulnerability to psychological trauma. *Nature Neuroscience*, 5, 1111–1113.

Gittelman, M., Klein, R. & Klein, D.F. (1971). Controlled imipramine treatment of school phobia. Archives of General Psychiatry, 25 (1971), 204-207.

Gorman, J.M., Mathew, S. & Coplan, J. (2002). Neurobiology of early life stress: Nonhuman primate models. *Seminars on Clinical Neuropsychiatry*, 7, 96-103.

Gorman, J.M., Kent, J.M., Sullivan, G.M. & Kaplan, J.D. (2000). Neuroanatomical hypothesis of panic disorder, revised. *American Journal of Psychiatry*, 157, 493-505.

Hariri, A.R., Mattay, V.S., Tessitore, A., Kolachana, B., Fera, F. et al. (2002). Serotonin transporter genetic variation and the response of the human amygdala. *Science*, 297, 400-403.

Hariri, A.R., Drabant, E.M., Munoz, K.E., Kolachana, B., Mattsay, V.S. et al, (2005). A susceptibility gene for affective disorders and the response of the human amygdala. *Archives of General Psychiatry*, 62, 146-152.

Hayward, C., Killen, J.D., Kraemer, H.C. & Taylor, C.B. (2000). Predictors of panic attacks in adolescents. *Journal of the American Academy of Child and Adolescent Psychiatry*, 39(2), 207-214.

Hirsch, C.R. & Matthews, A. (2000). Impaired positive inferential bias in social anxiety disorder. *Journal of Abnormal Psychology*, 109(4), 705-712.

Hirschfield, D.R., Rosenbaum, J., Biederman, J., Bolduc, E.A., Faraone, S.V., Snidman, N., Reznick, J.S., & Kagan, J. (1992). Stable behavioral inhibition and its association with anxiety disorder. *Journal of the American Academy of Child and Adolescent Psychiatry*, 31, 103-111.

Holmes, A., Lit, Q., Murphy, D.L., Gold, E. & Crawley, J.N. (2003). Abnormal anxiety-related behavior in serotonin transporter null mutant mice: The influence of genetic background. *Genes, Brain and Behavior*, 2, 365-380.

Hugdahl, K. & Ohman, A. (1977). Effects of instruction on acquisition and extinction of electrodermal responses to fear-relevant stimuli. *Journal of Experimental Psychology: Human Learning and Memory*, 3, 608–618.

Hygge, S. & Ohman, A. (1978). Modeling processes in the acquisition of fears: Vicarious electrodermal conditioning to fear-relevant stimuli. *Journal of Personality and Social Psychology*, 36, 271-279.

Jorm, A.F., Christenson, A., Henderson, A.S., Jacob, P.A., Korten, A.E. & Rodgers, B. (2000). Predicting anxiety and depression from personality: Is there a synergistic effect of neuroticism and extraversion? *Journal of Abnormal Psychology*, 109(1), 145-149.

Kendler, K.S., Kuhn, J.W., Vittum, J., Prescott, C.A. & Riley, B. (2005). The interaction of stressful life events and a serotonin transporter polymorphism in the prediction of episodes of major depression: A replication. *Archives of General Psychiatry*, 62, 529-535.

Kessler, R.C., McGonagle, K., Zhao, S., Nelson, C., Hughes, M. et al (1994). Lifetime and 12-month prevalence of DSM-III-R psychiatric disorders in the United States: Results from the National Comorbidity Survey. *Archives of General Psychiatry*, 51, 8-19.

Kessler, R.C., Berglund, P.A., Demler, O., Jin, R. & Walters, E.E. (2005a). Lifetime prevalence and age-of-onset distributions of DSM-IV disorders in the National Comorbidity Survey Replication (NCS-R). *Archives of General Psychiatry*, 62(6), 593-602.

Kessler, R.C., Chiu, W.T., Demler, O. & Walters, E.E. (2005b). Prevalence, Severity, and Comorbidity of 12-Month DSM-IV Disorders in the National Comorbidity Survey Replication. *Archives of General Psychiatry*, 62, 617-627.

Kjelstrup, K.G., Tuvnes, F.A., Steffenbach, H.A., Murison, R., Moser, E.I. & Moser, M.B. (2002). Reduced fear expression after lesions of the ventral hippocampus. *Proceedings of the National Academy of Science, USA.*, 99, 10825-30.

Klemenhagen, K.C., Gordon, J.A., David, D.J., Hen, R. & Gross, C.T. (2005). Increased fear response to contextual cues in mice lacking the 5-HT1A receptor. Neuropsychopharmacology, 31, 101-111.

Klemenhagen, K.C., Gordon, J.A., David, D.J., Henry, R. & Gross, C.T. (2006). Increased fear response to contextual cues in mice lacking the 5-HT1A receptor. *Neuropsychopharmacology*, 31, 101 - 111.

Last, C.G., Perrin, S., Herten, M. & Kazdin, A.E. (1996). A prospective study of childhood anxiety disorders. *Journal of the American Academy of Child and Adolescent Psychiatry*, 35(11), 1502-1510.

Lavy, E.H., van den Hout, M., & Arntz, A. (1993). Attentional bias and spider phobia: Conceptual and clinical issues. *Behaviour Research and Therapy*, 31, 17-24.

LeDoux, J.E., (1996). *The Emotional Brain*. Simon and Schuster, New York.

LeMonde, S., Du, L., Bakish, D., Hrdina, P. & Albert, P.R. (2004). Association of the (C-1019)G HT1A functional promoter polymorphism with antidepressant response. *International Journal of Psychopharmacology*, 7, 501-506.

Leonardo, E.D. & Hen, Rene (2006). Genetics of Affective and Anxiety Disorders. *Annual Review of Psychology*, 57, 117-138.

Lesch, K.P. & Gutknecht, L. (2004). Focus on the 5-HT1A receptor: Emerging role of a gene regulatory variant in psychopathology and pharmacogenetics. *International Journal of Neuropsychopharmacology*, 7, 381-385.

MacLeod, C., Mathews, A. & Tata, P. (1986). Attentional bias in emotional disorders. *Journal of Abnormal Psychology*, 95, 15-20.

Maidenberg, E., Chen, E., Craske, M., Bohn, P. & Bystristsky, A. (1996). Specificity of attentional bias in panic disorder and social phobia. *Journal of Anxiety Disorders*, 10(6), 529-541.

Marks, I (1977) Phobias and obsessions Clinical phenomena in search of a laboratory model In J Maser & M. Seligman (Eds), *Psychopathology Experimental models* (pp 174-213) San Francisco-Freeman.

Mathew, S.J., Coplan, J.D., Smith, E.L., Scharf, B.A. et al (2002). Cerebrospinal fluid concentration of biogenic amines and corticotropin-releasing factor in adolescent hon-human primates as a function of the timing of adverse early rearing. *Stress*, 5, 185-193.

Merikangas, K.R., Avenoli, S. Dierker, L. & Grillon, C. (1999). Vulnerability factors among children at risk for anxiety disorders. *Journal of Biological Psychiatry*, 99, 172-179.

Mineka, S. & Ohman, A. (2002). Phobias and Preparedness: The Selective, Automatic, and Encapsulated Nature of Fear. *Biological Psychiatry*, 52, 927-937.

Mogg, K., Philippot, P. & Bradley, B. (2004). Selective attention to angry faces in clinical SAD. *Journal of Abnormal Psychology*, 113, 160-165.

Noyes, R., Clarkson, C., Crowe, R.R., Yates, W.R. & McChesney, C.M. (1987). A family study of generalized anxiety disorder. *American Journal of Psychiatry*, 144:1019-1024

Nutt, D.J., Bell, C.J. & Malizia, A.L. (1998). Brain mechanisms of social anxiety disorder. *Journal of Clinical Psychiatry*, 59, 4-11.

Ohman, A., Fredrikson, M., Hugdahl, K., & Rimmö, P. (1976). The premise of equipotentiality in human classical conditioning: Conditioned electrodermal responses to potentially phobic stimuli. *Journal of Experimental Psychology: General*, 105, 313-337.

Öhman, A. & Mineka, S. (2001). Fears, phobias, and preparedness: Toward an evolved module of fear learning. *Psychological Review*, 108, pp. 483-522.

Pezawas, L., Meyer-Lindenberg, A., Drabant, E.M., Verchinski, B.A., Munoz, K.E. et al (2005). 5-HTTLPR polymorphism impacts human cingulate-amygdala interactions: A genetic susceptibility mechanism for depression. *Nature Neuroscience*, 8, 828-834.

Potts, N.L.S., Book, S. & Davidson, J.R.T. (1996). The neurobiology of social phobia. *International Clinical Psychopharmacology*, 11, 43-48.

Qin, S., Young, C.B., Duan, X., Chen, T., Supekar, K. & Menon, V. (2014). Amygdala Subregional Structure and Intrinsic Functional Connectivity Predicts Individual Differences in Anxiety During Early Childhood. *Biological Psychiatry*, 75:892-900.

Rosenbaum, J., Biederman, J., Gersten, M. et al. (1988). Behavioral inhibition in children of parents with panic disorder and agoraphobia. *Archives of General Psychiatry*, 45, 463-470.

Rubin, K.H., Hastings, P.D., Stewart, S.L., Henderson, H.A. & Chen, X. (1997). The consistency and concomitants of inhibitions: Some of the children all of the time. *Child Development*, 68, 467-483.

Schneider, F., Habel, U., Kessler, C., Posse, S. Et al (2000). Functional imaging of conditioning aversive emotional responses in antisocial personality disorder. *Neuropsychobiology*, 42, 192-201.

Slater, E., & J. Shields (1969): Genetical aspects of anxiety. In Lader, M. M. (ed.): *Studies of anxiety*. Royal Medico-Psychological Association, London,

Starcevic, V. (2005). *Anxiety Disorders in Adults: A Clinical Guide*. Oxford, UK: Oxford University Press.

Strobel, A., Guttknecht, L., Rothe, C., Reif, A., Mossner, R. et al (2003). Allelic variation in 5-HT1A receptor expression is associated with anxiety- and depression-related personality traits. *Journal of Neural Transmission*, 110, 1445-1453.

Strohle, A. & Holsboer, F. (2003). Stress responsive neurohormones in depression and anxiety. *Pharmacopsychiatry*, 36(Suppl. 3), 207-214.

Taghavi, M.R., Moradi, A.R., Neeshat-Doost, H.T., Yule, W. & Dalgelish, T. (2000). Interpretation of ambiguous emotional information in clinically anxious children and adolescents. *Cognition and Emotion*, 14(6), 809-822.

Turri, M.G., DeFries, J.C., Henderson, N.D. & Flint, J. (2004). Multivariate analysis of quantitative trait loci influencing variations in anxiety-related behavior in laboratory mice. *Mammalian Genome*, 15, 69-76.

Weaver, I.C., Cervoni, N., Champagne, F.A., D'Alession, A.C., Dharma, S. et al (2004). Epigenetic programming by maternal behavior. *Nature Neuroscience*, 7, 847-854.

Yaffe et al. (2009). Post-traumatic stress disorder and risk of dementia among U.S. veterans. *Alzheimer's and Dementia*, 5 (4): p. 104.

Yeragani, V.K., Sobolewski, E., Igel, G., Johnson, C. Et al (1998). Decreased heart-period variability in patients with PD: A study of Holter ECG records. *Psychiatry Research*, 78(1-2), 89-99.

Zieman, A.E., Allen, J.E., Dahdaleh, N.S., Drebot, I.I. et al (2009). The amygdala is a chemosensor that detects carbon dioxide and acidosis to elicit fear behavior. *Cell*, 139(5):867-9.

Obsessive-Compulsive and Related Disorders

I. Introduction

    A. General list of disorders under this heading (DSM 5): topics in **bold** will be discussed.
        1. **Obsessive-Compulsive Disorder**
        2. Body Dysmorphic Disorder
        3. Hoarding Disorder
        4. Trichotillomanis (Hair-pulling Disorder)
        5. Excoriation (Skin-Picking Disorder)
        6. Substance/Medication Induced Obsessive-Compulsive and Related Disorder
        7. Obsessive-Compulsive and Related Disorder due to another medical condition
        8. Other specified Obsessive-Compulsive and Related Disorder
        9. Other Specified Anxiety Disorder
        10. Unspecified Obsessive-Compulsive and Related Disorder

    B. Characteristic feature are symptoms of anxiety and avoidance behavior. Are the most frequently found in the general population, with specific phobias and social phobia being the most common. Panic disorder most common among people seeking treatment.

    C. 75% of individuals with an anxiety disorder will have their first episode by age 21.5

Obsessive-Compulsive Disorder

I. Description and diagnostic criteria under DSM-5: (all quotations below are from DSM-5, p. 237)

    A. Either obsessions or compulsions, or both:
        1. **Obsessions** as defined by (a) and (b):
            a. "Recurrent and persistent thoughts, urges, or images that are experienced, at some time during the disturbance, as intrusive and unwanted, and that [in most individuals] cause marked anxiety or distress." p. 237 (words in brackets added since DSM-IV)
            b. "The individual attempts to ignore or suppress such thoughts, urges, or images, or to neutralize them with some other thought or action (i.e., by performing a. compulsion.)"
            c. ["The person recognizes that the obsessional thoughts, impulses or images are a product of his or her own mind, (not imposed from without as in thought insertion.)"] dropped in DSM-IV
        2. **Compulsions** defined by (a) and (b):
            a. "Repetitive behaviors (e.g. hand washing, ordering, checking) or mental acts (e.g., praying, counting, repeating words silently) that the individual feels driven to perform in response to an obsession, or according to rules that must be applied rigidly." [Same as DSM-IV]
            b. "The behaviors or mental acts are aimed at preventing or reducing [anxiety or] distress, or preventing some dreaded event or situation; however, these behaviors or mental acts are not connected in a realistic way with what they are designed to neutralize or prevent, or are clearly excessive."([Same as DSM-IV)

B. "The obsessions or compulsions are time-consuming (take more than 1 hour per day) or cause clinically significant distress or impairment in social, occupational, or other important areas of functioning."

C. "The obsessive-compulsive symptoms are not attributable to the physiological effects of a substance (i.e., a drug or abuse, a medication) or another medical condition."

D. "The disturbance is not better explained by the symptoms of another mental disorder...."

E. Specify if:
   1. **With good or fair insight**: The individual realizes that the obsessive-compulsive beliefs are not true or at least that they may or may not be true."
   2. **With poor insight**: The individual thinks the obsessive-compulsive disorder beliefs are probably true.
   3. **With absent insight/delusional beliefs**: The individual is convinced the obsessive-compulsive disorder beliefs are true.

F. Arguably, this definition is broader than that in DSM-IV, because of the elimination of two criteria from DSM-IV:
   1. That the thoughts or impulses are not excessive worries about real-life problems,
   2. That the individual has recognized, at some point, that the obsessive-compulsive symptoms are excessive or unreasonable.

II. Epidemiology

A. **Kessler et al. (2005ab)**: In U.S., 12-month prevalence of OCD is 100/10,000 (1.0%); lifetime prevalence is 160/10,000 (1.6%; Justine said 2.5%).

B. Usually begins in adolescence or early adulthood, but may begin in childhood. Usually chronic, with moderate to severe impairment.

C. In adult OCD, equally prevalent among men and women, but in OCD beginning in childhood, ratio of males to females is 3-1.

III. Etiology: Psychological

A. One thing to note in considering etiology is the relatively limited range of compulsions that appear. Could this be related to the preparedness etiology suggested for simple phobias?

B. The psychodynamic view:

1. Symptom, which has a symbolic link to the underlying problem, is a defense (through displacement & emotional substitution) against consciously unacceptable conflict.
2. Anxiety is displaced onto a less disturbing thought or idea.
3. Conflict is often localized in anal period due to the prevalence of washing, cleaning, contamination obsessions and compulsions.

C. The learning view:
1. Fear is conditioned to some environmental event.
2. Through higher order conditioning, thoughts become associated with feared object.
3. Behavior that alleviates anxiety reinforced by anxiety reduction.

D. The cognitive view: (Rachman & Hodgson)
1. Person gets mildly obsessive thought, but unusually, has difficulty dismissing it.
2. That difficulty causes them some anxiety, which makes it still more difficult to dismiss, causing still more anxiety, etc.
3. Compulsive rituals are strengthened because they cause relief from anxiety.
4. Accounts for maintenance of OCD problems, but not their origin.

IV. Etiology: Biological

A. Genetic evidence: Higher concordance among MZ than among DZ twins for OCD, defined broadly to include any obsessional features. (**Carey & Gottesman, 1981**)

B. Biological bases: Biochemistry: Possible involvement of serotonin (an inhibitory neurotransmitter)
1. Elevated serotonergic activity in OCD.
2. Tricyclic antidepressant clomipramine has higher serotonin-reuptake blocking effects than other tricyclics, and has stronger anti-obsessional properties than other tricyclics.
3. Reduction of OCD symptoms found to coincide with reduction in blood and CSF levels of serotonin and its metabolites (esp 5-hydroxy-indole acetic acid, 5-HIAA). Also, **Thoren et al. (1980)** found that Ss with highest pre-treatment levels of 5-HIAA were most likely to respond to treatment with clomipramine)
4. m-chlorophenyl piperazine (mCPP), a serotonin agonist (mimic), increases obsessions in OCD patients when given acutely.
5. Other drugs that block serotonin uptake (fluoxetin/Prozac, fluvoxamine, zimelidine) also seem to relieve OCD symptoms (at least latter two), but evidence involves small numbers of participants and are therefore inconclusive.
6. So serotonin-using synapses overactive in OCD, and blocking agents reduce that. But why do blood levels go down after successful treatment, since reuptake blockers don't reduce the amount of serotonin, just its location.
    a. Counteracting effects:
    b. High serotonin levels not only activate postsynaptic receptors, but flood presynaptic autoreceptors, that serve as a feedback sensor for the cell. This triggers a throttling of serotonin production. The resulting serotonin deficiency persists for some time, as the transporter inhibition occurs downstream to the cause of the deficiency and therefore, is

not able to counterbalance the serotonin deficiency. The body adapts gradually to this situation by lowering (downregulating) the sensitivity of the autoreceptors.
    c. Downregulation of postsynaptic serotonin 5-HT2A receptors. After use of SSRI, since more serotonin is available, body decreases number of postsynaptic receptors over time and in the long run, this modifies the serotonin/receptor ratio. This downregulation of 5-HT2A occurs when the antidepressant effects of SSRIs become apparent. Deceased suicidal and otherwise depressed patients have had more 5-HT2A receptors than normal, suggesting that 5-HT2A overactivity is involved in pathogenesis of depression.

C. Link with basal ganglia (caudate, putamen, globus pallidus) and caudate nucleus in particular. Basal ganglia a bit mysterious, but seem to be involved in voluntary initiation and cessation of movement.
  1. In both Huntington's chorea and Parkinsonism, synapses degenerate in the basal ganglia, resulting in loss of voluntary control over muscle activity.
  2. Animal research also links basal ganglia with impairment in appropriate initiation and cessation of movement. Damage to one caudate causes animal to circle toward undamaged side.
  3. We saw this link in ADHD with respect to response inhibition.
  4. OCD patients also can't seem to stop, either thoughts or rituals.
  5. Medical literature suggests that obsessive-compulsive symptoms associated with damage to basal ganglia:
     a. **Sydenham's chorea**: A complication of rheumatic fever in children which produces antibodies that attack cells only in the caudate. Physical symptoms involve involuntary jerky movements similar to those in Huntington's. Psychological symptoms involve obsessive thoughts and compulsive rituals. (**Swedo et al., 1989**a)
     b. **Tourette's syndrome**: Grimacing movements of face, jerky movements of hands, and involuntary repetition of sounds or words, esp. profanity. Many patients also meet criteria for OCD. (**Cummings & Frankel, 1985**)
     c. PET scans of OCD patients indicate more metabolic activity in cerebral hemispheres (esp in head of caudate, and orbital cortex just above eyes, and connected to basal ganglia) than in normals or depressives.(**Baxter et al., 1987**; **Baxter et al., 1988**; **Swedo et al., 1989**b)
     d. CAT scans of OCD patients showed caudate about 25% smaller than that in normal subjects (size in 9 of 10 OCD patients was below the mean for normal subjects). No difference in size of other brain structures.

D. **Leonard & Swedo (2001)** suggest that post-streptococcal autoimmunity may be a potential environmental cause of childhood onset OCD. Suggest that in some cases, OCD may develop as a consequence of an autoimmune reaction in which antibodies to streptococcal infections attack and damage the basal ganglia.

E. Sociobiological view: Judith Rapaport at NIMH argues compulsions are hard-wired subroutines: "little computer programs left over from the primitive common ancestors of dogs and humans. 'These behaviors seem phylogenetically old', she says. In her view, the compulsion to wash may be a grooming program gone wild. The compulsion to check that doors are locked. Pictures straightened and ovens turned off may stem from an ancestral need to check the cave for predators and other dangers." (**Scientific American, July 1992.** P. 24)
  1. Dogs exhibit form of compulsion in which they cannot stop washing themselves. Called acral

lick by veterinarians, may be a usable animal model of human OCD.
2. Acral lick responds to treatment with tricyclic antidepressant clomipramine, one of three known antiobsessional drugs, but not to conventional antidepressants. Imaging techniques locate effect in the basal ganglia, which is similar in humans and other animals.

F. In humans, improvement with clomipramine is slow, with maximum occurring 5-12 weeks after start of treatment.
1. When drugs removed, symptoms often reappear. Drugs do not cure disorder, since many patients continue to experience thoughts or impulses, but they are less intrusive, and do not bother them as much.

V. Treatments for OCD:

A. Pharmacological treatments:
1. Clomipramine

B. Psychological treatments: Behavioral
1. Modeling, flooding and response prevention. (**Marks & Rachman, 1978**) (e.g., for washing compulsion spurred by fear of dirt and contamination)
   a. Therapist first models by covering self with dirt.
   b. Patient then does same thing, and tolerates it without washing.
   c. Repeat this process 12 times in one study, and found 65% of patients showed marked improvement after 2 years.
2. Evidence comparing clomipramine and behavioral therapy shows clomipramine works best early on (5-10 weeks), but behavior therapy more long lasting. General tenor of literature is that behavioral therapy **alone** is overall more effective than clomipramine alone, and that combination is better than either.
3. One author suggests that clomipramine helps patient resist temptation to repetition, thus helping behavioral therapy to work.

C. Psychological treatments: Cognitive
1. Cognitive therapies not as well-developed or as well established for GAD as for Panic Disorder and Agoraphobia.
2. General procedure same as for other anxiety disorders.
   a. Identification of appraisals of threat and beliefs that are associated with worries.
   b. Challenging those beliefs through evidence-seeking and introduction of alternatives.
   c. Replacement of dysfunctional appraisals and beliefs with rational alternatives.

References

Baxter, L.R., Phelps, M.E., Mazziota, J.C., Guze, B.H., Schwartz, J.M. & Selin, C.E. (1987). Local cerebral glucose metabolic rates in obsessive-compulsive disorder: A comparison with rates in unipolar depression and in normal controls. *Archives of General Psychiatry*, 44, 211-218.

Baxter, L.R., Schwartz, J.M., Mazziota, J.C., Phelps, M.E., Pahl, J.J., Guze, B.H. & Fairbanks, L. (1988). Cerebral glucose metabolic rates in nondepressed patients with obsessive-compulsive disorder. *American Journal of Psychiatry*, 145, 1560-1563.

Carey, G., & Gottesman, I. I., (1981). Twin and family studies of anxiety, phobic, and obsessive disorders. In D. F. Klein & J. Rabkin (Eds.), *Anxiety: New research and changing concepts* (pp. 117–136). New York: Raven Press.

Kessler, R.C., McGonagle, K., Zhao, S., Nelson, C., Hughes, M. et al (1994). Lifetime and 12-month prevalence of DSM-III-R psychiatric disorders in the United States: Results from the National Comorbidity Survey. *Archives of General Psychiatry*, 51, 8-19.

Kessler, R.C., Berglund, P.A., Demler, O., Jin, R. & Walters, E.E. (2005a). Lifetime prevalence and age-of-onset distributions of DSM-IV disorders in the National Comorbidity Survey Replication (NCS-R). *Archives of General Psychiatry*, 62(6), 593-602.

Kessler, R.C., Chiu, W.T., Demler, O. & Walters, E.E. (2005b). Prevalence, Severity, and Comorbidity of 12-Month DSM-IV Disorders in the National Comorbidity Survey Replication. *Archives of General Psychiatry*, 62, 617-627.

Leonard, H. L., & Swedo, S. E. (2001). Paediatric autoimmune neuropsychiatric disorders associated with treptococcal infection (PANDAS). *International Journal of Neuropsychopharmacology* (4), 191-198.

Leonardo, E.D. & Hen, Rene (2006). Genetics of Affective and Anxiety Disorders. *Annual Review of Psychology*, 57, 117-138.

Marks, I (1977) Phobias and obsessions Clinical phenomena in search of a laboratory model In J Maser & M. Seligman (Eds), *Psychopathology Experimental models* (pp 174-213) San Francisco-Freeman.

Starcevic, V. (2005). *Anxiety Disorders in Adults: A Clinical Guide*. Oxford, UK: Oxford University Press.

Swedo, S.E., Rapoport, J.L., Cheslow, D.L., Leonard, H.L., Ayoub, E.M. Hosier, D.M. & Wald, E.R., (1989a). High prevalence of obsessive-compulsive symptoms in patients with Sydenham's chorea. *American Journal of Psychiatry*, 146, 246-249.

Swedo, S.E., Schapiro, M.B., Grady, C.L., Cheslow, D.L., Leonard, H.L., Kumar, A., Friedland, R., Rapoport, S.I. & Rapoport, J.L. (1989b). Cerebral glucose metabolism in childhood-onset obsessive-compulsive disorder. *Archives of General Psychiatry*, 46, 518-523.

Thoren, P., Asberg, M., Bertillson, L., Mellstrom, B., Sjoqvist, F. & Traskman, L. (1980). Clomipramine treatment of obsessive-compulsive disorder, II. Biochemical aspects. *Archives of General Psychiatry*, 37, 1289-1294.

Weaver, I.C., Cervoni, N., Champagne, F.A., D'Alession, A.C., Dharma, S. et al. (2004). Epigenetic programming by maternal behavior. *Nature Neuroscience*, 7, 847-854.

Yaffe et al. (2009). Post-traumatic stress disorder and risk of dementia among U.S. veterans. *Alzheimer's and Dementia*, 5 (4): p. 104.

Somatic Symptom and Related Disorders

I. Introduction:

    A. What all these disorders share is that they involve the subjective report of physical symptoms that suggest a physical disorder, no obvious signs or organic bases can be found.

    B. Note that these syndromes are different from malingering (a separate category - factitious disorders) since symptom production is not deliberate - they really feel bad, and experience the pain and disability of their symptoms.

    C. There are several good reasons for not spending a lot of time on the somatoform disorders:
        1. The community prevalence appears to be fairly low, and lower today than in the relatively recent past.
        2. There is a relative paucity of research literature on the etiology of the condition.

    D. But we will spend more time here than these considerations suggest for several reasons:
        1. Although the community prevalence is low, the prevalence in clinical settings - especially primary medical care settings - is fairly high.
        2. The disorders have a very long historical record, dating back at least 3,000 years.
        3. Disorders in this category were important in the development of psychological and psychiatric concepts in the late 19th century (by Freud and others) that are still relevant to psychological theorizing and psychiatric practice.
        4. Although the etiology of these disorders is still fairly mysterious, the prevailing view is that the primary etiological factors are psychological/cognitive and (perhaps) behavioral.
        5. The disorders nicely illustrate the **fallacy of mind-body dualism**, showing the power of psychological thought to influence physical functioning.
        6. Many of us have experienced mild forms of these disorders.

II. **DSM-5 Categories and subcategories**:

    A. **Somatic Symptom Disorder** (includes most former cases of hypochondriasis and somatization disorder)

    B. **Illness Anxiety Disorder** (includes some former cases of hypochondriasis]

    C. **Conversion Disorder** (also known as Functional Neurological Symptom Disorder)

    D. **Psychological Factors Affecting Other Medical Conditions**

    E. **Factitious Disorder**

F. Other Specified Somatic Symptoms and Related Disorder
   1. Brief somatic symptoms disorder
   2. Brief illness anxiety disorder
   3. Illness anxiety disorder without excessive health-related behaviors
   4. **Pseudocyesis**

Somatic Symptom Disorder

I. **Diagnostic criteria under DSM-5**: (quotations below from DSM-5 page 311)

   A. One or more somatic symptoms that cause distress, or "significant disruption of daily life."

   B. "Excessive thoughts, feelings, or behaviors related to the somatic symptoms or associated health concerns as manifested by at least one of the following:
      1. Disproportionate and persistent thoughts about the seriousness of one's symptoms.
      2. Persistently high levels of anxiety about one's health or about the symptoms.
      3. Excessive time and energy devoted to these symptoms or health concerns.

   C. Symptoms are persistent, i.e., at least one symptom has been present for more than 6 months.

   D. Additional specifications:
      1. Is the symptom or symptoms **predominantly pain** (DSM-IV Pain Disorder)?
      2. Are the symptoms **persistent** (severe symptoms, marked impairment, and duration more than 6 months)?
      3. What is the level of current severity:
         a. Mild: Only one of the Criterion B symptoms is present
         b. Moderate: Two or more Criterion B symptoms are present
         c. Severe: Two or more Criterion B symptoms are present, and there are multiple somatic complaints (or one very severe somatic symptom.) [matches somatization Disorder in DSM-IV]

II. Epidemiology:

   A. DSM-5 estimate: "The prevalence of somatic symptoms disorder is nor known" (p. 312) but is expected to be somewhere between that of DSM-IV's somatization disorder (less than 1%), and that of DSM-IV's undifferentiated somatoform disorder (about 19%). DSM-5's estimate is 5-5% in the adult population, and "likely" to be higher in females than in males.

B. Comorbidity:
1. **Liskow et al. (1986)** found the following lifetime prevalence rates in outpatients with DSM-III somatization disorder:
   a. Major depression - 87%
   b. Panic disorder - 45%
   c. Mania - 40%
   d. Drug or alcohol dependence - 40%
   e. Phobic disorder - 39%
   f. Obsessive-compulsive disorder - 27%
   g. Schizophrenia - 27%
2. Personality disorders often present as well
   a. Interestingly, Rost et al. (1992) found histrionic and APD less common than avoidant, paranoid, and compulsive PDs.
3. Saxe et al. (1994): Found that 64% of patients with dissociative disorder met the criteria for somatization disorder, with a mean of 12 symptoms per case.

III. Etiology:

A. There is some evidence that it runs in families:
1. **Guze et al., 1986; Woerner & Guze, 1968; Cloninger & Guze, 1970**: An increased prevalence of 10-20% among the first-degree relatives of index cases.
2. **Ford (1983, 1985, 1986)**: Patients often come from chaotic homes marked by evidence of sociopathy and alcoholism. Women appear to marry unstable men, and to have unstable interpersonal relationships.

B. Other predispositions:
1. Male relatives show higher risk for APD and substance-use disorders (**Stoudemire, 1998**, p. 350; citing **Bohman et al., 1984**)
2. **Woodruff et al (1973)**: An increased rate of marital problems, poor work performance, teenage delinquencies, hysteria, in first-degree relatives of patients.

C. Learning probably plays a role because of the **secondary gain**: Symptoms are reinforced by attention, care, concern, etc.

D. **Stoudemire (1984)** says, with commendable understatement that *"the etiologic foundations of somatization disorder are not readily discernible, though familial incidences and association with antisocial and histrionic personality disorder, as well as substance- and alcohol use disorders, suggest a biologic predisposition."* (P. 352)

IV. Treatment:

A. Psychotherapy should be ego-supportive, empathic, and supportive rather than intensive, since ego defenses weak and self-esteem low.

B. Since many patients resistant to psychiatric referral, some recommend that personal physician be advised of diagnosis, and urged to see patient regularly for brief examinations and to avoid unnecessary hospitalizations. **Smith (1986)** found this approach to reduce health care charges for these patients of about 50%.

Illness Anxiety Disorder

I. Diagnostic criteria under DSM-5: (quotations below from DSM-5 page 315)

A. A preoccupation that one has, or that one might get, a serious illness.

B. No somatic complaints, or if there are, they are minor. If there is another medical condition, or a risk for developing one (e.g. because of family history), then the preoccupation is "clearly excessive or disproportionate."

C. The individual is highly anxious about health issues, and is easily alarmed about his or her health.

D. "The individual performs excessive health-related behaviors (e.g., repeatedly checking his or her body for signs of illness) or exhibits maladaptive avoidance (e.g., avoids doctor appointments and hospitals.)"

E. The preoccupation has lasted for at least 6 months, though the specific illness feared may have changed over that time.

F. The preoccupation is not better explained by another mental disorder, such "as somatic symptoms disorder, panic disorder, GAD, body dysmorphic disorder, OCD, or delusional disorder, somatic type.)"

G. Additional specification:
1. **Care-seeking type**: Medical care is frequently used.
2. **Care-avoidant type**: Medical are is rarely used.

H. Note the absence of any mention of impairment, so distress - anxiety - is the primary criterion.

II. Prevalence

    A. Based on DSM-III and IV diagnoses of hypochondriasis, DSM-5 estimates the annual prevalence of this disorder at 1.3% to 10% in the general population, and between 3% and 8% in "ambulatory medical populations". (p. 316)

    B. Prevalence similar in males and females.

Conversion disorder

I. Description: Alteration or loss of physical functioning that is psychologically caused. Onset of symptoms usually associated with some external stress- or anxiety-producing event.

II. History of the categorization of Conversion Disorder.

    A. In **DSM II**, Conversion and Dissociative Disorders were subheadings under Hysterical Neurosis, and conversion disorder was limited to symptoms affecting senses or voluntary nervous systems. Disorders mediated by autonomic nervous system were a separate section.

    B. In **DSM III and III-R, IV**, Dissociative Disorders have their own category; definition of Conversion Disorder broadened to include any medical condition, not neurological symptoms.

    C. **DSM IV** committee considered placing Conversion Disorder in the Dissociative Disorders section, "reflecting the literature that conversion symptoms and dissociative symptoms tend to occur in the same individual and may have related pathogenesis." (ICD-10 also places dissociative disorder and conversion disorder together.)

    D. **DSM-5** adds to name Conversion Disorder the additional name Functional Neurological Symptom Disorder and changes criteria to emphasize the neurological nature of the symptoms, and removed the subtypes.

III. Description and **diagnostic criteria under DSM-5**: (quotations below from DSM-5, pp. 318-319)

   A. Diagnostic criteria:
      1. "One or more symptoms of altered voluntary motor or sensory function."
      2. "Clinical findings provide evidence of incompatibility between the symptom and recognized neurological or medical conditions."
      3. "The symptom or deficit is not better explained by another medical or mental disorder."
      4. "The symptom or deficit causes clinically significant distress or impairment in social, occupational, or other important areas of functioning or warrants medical evaluation."

   B. Specification of symptom type:
      1. Weakness or paralysis
      2. Abnormal movement: Gait disturbances, tics, choreiform movements. Common gait disturbance is "wildly ataxic staggering gait, with gross irregular jerky truncal movements and thrashing and waving arms. Despite this, patients almost never falls
      3. Swallowing symptoms
      4. Speech symptoms
      5. Attacks of seizures
      6. Anesthesia or sensory loss
      7. Special sensory symptoms (e.g., visual, olfactory, or hearing diisturbance)
      8. Mixed symptoms

   C. Specify if **persistent**, or **acute episode** (<6 months)

   D. Specify if **with** or **without psychological stressor**

   E. Associated features:
      1. Ability to function despite symptoms (e.g., avoid obstacles though blind). Relate to **blindsight** situation in which individual with occipital lobe damage is missing visual field, but can still identify objects in it at greater than chance level.)
      2. 'La belle indifference' (though not diagnostically reliable)

IV. Epidemiology

   A. Prevalence estimates are hard to come by, and vary widely. DSM-5 estimates that 5% of patients referred to neurology clinics meet the criteria for the disorder. Though its prevalence in the general population is speculative, the DSM-5 notes that "transient conversion symptoms are common." (p. 320)

   B. Estimates of lifetime prevalence vary widely, including values as high as 33%. Ford (1983) estimates that 20-25% of patients admitted to a general medical setting meet the criteria for Conversion Disorder.

C. Disagreement on sex bias (estimates range from 2 to 5x more frequent in women; (2-3 times according to DSM-5), but most agree that it is diagnosed more frequently in women than in men.

D. Usually appears in adolescence or early adulthood, suddenly after stress; may include 'la belle indifference'.

E. Significant comorbidity with other somatic disorders, anxiety disorders (especially Panic Disorder), depressive disorders, and dissociative disorders
   1. **Sar et al (2004)**: In Turkish study of 38 conversion disorder patients, found
      a. At least one psychiatric diagnosis was found in 89.5% of the patients during follow-up evaluation. Undifferentiated somatoform disorder, generalized anxiety disorder, dysthymic disorder, simple phobia, obsessive-compulsive disorder, major depression, and dissociative disorder not otherwise specified were the most prevalent psychiatric disorders.
      b. A dissociative disorder was seen in 47.4% of the patients. These patients had dysthymic disorder, major depression, somatization disorder, and borderline personality disorder more frequently than the remaining subjects. \
      c. They also reported childhood emotional and sexual abuse, physical neglect, self-mutilative behavior, and suicide attempts more frequently.

V. Etiology: Psychoanalytic view:

A. Freud:
   1. In Freud's time, Conversion Disorder called hysteria, and was considered a nervous disorder.
   2. It was Freud's exploration of the possible psychological roots of hysteria that led him to his theory of the unconscious and its workings.
   3. For Freud, Conversion Disorder was the disguised expression of an unconscious conflict, designed to block direct expression of a forbidden impulse, and/or to allow it to be gratified in a symbolically related way.

B. Modern psychoanalytic view:
   1. Individual is made anxious by some unacceptable unconscious conflict.
   2. Conversion is a defense against this anxiety. The **primary gain**.
   3. Psychic energy is detached from the idea, and transmuted into a somatic loss.
   4. Somatic loss somehow symbolizes the unconscious conflict.
   5. Symptom is a compromise between symbolic expression of impulse and equally unconscious fear of expressing it.
   6. Symptoms develop for several reasons:
      a. To permit the masked expression of forbidden impulse. (e.g., hysterical pregnancy)
      b. To punish oneself for a forbidden impulse via the disabling symptoms.

    c. To remove self from anxiety-producing or threatening situation.
    d. To assume the sick role and allow gratification of dependency needs.
    e. Explains why individual may show indifference to symptom

VI. Etiology: Behavioral

  A. No clear behavioral model of somatoform disorders: Positive or negative reinforcement by parents and other of physical symptoms may lead individual to chose somatic routes to obtain nurturance, attention, love, etc.

  B. Positive reinforcement for affective complaints may lead to increasing use of them: **secondary gain**.

  C. Negative reinforcement of verbal expressions of emotion may leave individual no alternative but somatic complaints to gain attention.
    1. Primary gain: Keeps an internal conflict out of awareness.
    2. Secondary gain: Avoiding activity that is noxious, and gets support from environment.

  D. Communication view - Version 1
    1. Initially, as child, individual expresses some emotions innately, since they are shown by blind babies:
      a. Surprise/startle; Interest/excitement; Enjoyment/joy
      b. Distress; Contempt/disgust; Fear; Shame; Anger/rage
    2. The physical expression of these emotions serve to provide cues for mother to respond to infant's needs.
    3. Later, child learns to verbally label such emotions for communicating with others.
    4. Some people do not learn this as well, and remain in a stage where emotions are primarily experienced and expressed somatically.

  E. Communicative view - Version 2: Argues that patient uses disorder to deal with a variety of negative emotions (eg. anger, guilt, shame, etc.) and to negotiate difficult interpersonal transactions.
    1. Individual expresses underlying distress to himself in the form of a physical complaint, thus distracting himself from that distress.
    2. Physical symptoms also communicate his distress to others; seen as a cry for help with unspoken problems.
    3. Individual chooses illness according to his own conception of a physical illness, perhaps modeled on illnesses of important people in his life.
    4. Symptoms will be crude or sophisticated according to his knowledge about physiology and medicine.
    5. Explains why the types of conversion symptoms seen has changed over the past century, and why they vary with education level.
    6. In urban U.S. dizziness, headache, anesthesias and weakness are more common, while in

more backward rural areas the classic Freudian symptoms - stocking, glove anesthesias, paralysis - still predominate.

VII. Treatment

   A. Prognosis is good for disorders associated with good premorbid condition, recent onset associated with a clearly identifiable external event. Spontaneous remission in such cases 'is the rule rather than the exception'.

   B. Use of supportive and nonconfrontational psychotherapy, together with the suggestion that the symptoms will disappear.

Psychological Factors Affecting Other Medical Conditions

I. Diagnostic criteria under DSM-5: (quotations below from DSM-5 page 322)

   A. "A medical symptom or condition (other than a mental disorder) is present."

   B. "Psychological or behavioral factors adversely affect the medical condition in one of the following ways:"
      1. The are involved in the development, exacerbation, or delayed recovery from, the medical condition (indicated by the temporal association between the psychological factors and the medical condition.)
      2. They interfere with treatment of the medical condition. (e.g., poor adherence)
      3. The factors are themselves well-established health risks for the individual.
      4. They influence the "underlying pathophysiology, precipitating or exacerbating symptoms or necessitating medical attention."

   C. The factors are not better explained by another mental disorder.

   D. Specify current severity:
      1. Mild: Increases medical risk (e.g., inconsistent adherence with antihypertension treatment).
      2. Moderate: Aggravates underlying medical condition (e.g., anxiety aggravating asthma).
      3. Severe: Results in medical hospitalization or emergency room visit.
      4. Extreme: Results in severe, life-threatening risk. (e.g., ignoring heart attack symptoms)

II. Prevalence:

A. DSM-5 notes that it is unclear, though in U.S. insurance billing codes it is more common than somatic symptom disorder.

Factitious Disorder

I. Diagnostic criteria under DSM-5: (quotations below from DSM-5 page 324-325)

    A. **Factitious Disorder Imposed on Self**
        1. Deliberately and deceptively falsifying physical or psychological symptoms, or inducing injury or disease.
        2. "The individual presents himself or herself to others as ill, impaired, or injured."
        3. "The deceptive behavior is evident even in the absence of obvious external rewards."
        4. Behavior not better explained by another mental disorder (e.g., delusional disorder, another psychotic disorder.)

    B. **Factitious Disorder Imposed on Another**
        1. Deliberately and deceptively falsifying physical or psychological symptoms, or inducing injury or disease, in another person.
        2. "The individual presents another individual (victim) to others as ill, impaired, or injured."
        3. "The deceptive behavior is evident even in the absence of obvious external rewards."
        4. Behavior not better explained by another mental disorder (e.g., delusional disorder, another psychotic disorder.)

II. Epidemiology:

    A. Prevalence is unknown, but DSM-5 estimates that about 1% of hospital patients meet the criteria for factitious disorder.

Other Specified Somatic Symptom Disorders

III. Under DSM-5 this includes (among other things):

    A. **Pseudocyesis** (which would no longer be a Conversion Disorder): "False belief of being

pregnant that is associated with objective signs of pregnancy, which may include":
1. Abdominal and/or breast engorgement and secretions
2. Reduced or absent menses
3. Nausea
4. Labor pains at the expected time of delivery
5. Food cravings

B. N.Y. Times,
1. "A few patients with pseudocyesis even test positive on pregnancy tests, said Dr. Paul Paulman, a family practitioner at the University of Nebraska Medical Center. "Every sign and symptom of pregnancy has been recorded in these patients except for three: You don't hear heart tones from the fetus, you don't see the fetus on ultrasound, and you don't get a delivery," Dr. Paulman said. Though the disorder is unusual, cases of false pregnancy have been reported in human societies since ancient times, providing evidence that the phenomenon is not bound by time or culture. In 300 B.C., Hippocrates described 12 women who "believed they were pregnant," and Mary Tudor, the English queen, is widely believed to have suffered from pseudocyesis. (Some commentators say the violent acts that gave her the nickname Bloody Mary were reactions to finding out she was not carrying an heir after all.)" (N.Y. Times, Dec. 5, 2006: http://www.nytimes.com/2006/12/05/health/05pseud.html)

Differential Diagnosis

I. Must distinguish between somatic symptoms and several other problems:

A. **Undiagnosed physical illness**.
B. **Factitious disorder**: Intentionally produced symptoms in order to assume the role of a patient, but with no obvious external incentive.
C. **Malingering** (faking): Same as factitious disorder, except that the malingerer has an obvious external benefit in being sick, e.g. access to drugs, escape from military, improved conditions (e.g., than prison), or legal case based on symptoms.

References

Barsky, A.J. & Klerman, G.L. (1983). Overview: hypochondriasis, bodily complaints, and somatic styles. *American Journal of Psychiatry*, 140, 273-283.

Bohman, M., Cloninger, R., Van Knorring, A-L. Et al (1984). An adoption study of somatoform disorders: III. Cross-fostering analysis and genetic relationship to alcoholism and criminality. *Archives of General Psychiatry*, 41, 872-878.

Brown, F.W., Golding, J.M. & Smith, R. Jr. (1990). Psychiatric Comorbidity in Primary Care Somatization Disorder. *Psychosomatic Medicine*, 52, 445-451.

Brown, R.J., Schrag, A. & Trimble, M.R. (2005). Dissociation, Childhood Interpersonal Trauma, and Family Functioning in Patients With Somatization Disorder. *American Journal of Psychiatry*, 162(5), 899 - 905.

Cloninger, C.R. & Guze, S.B. (1970). Female criminals: Their personal, familial, and social backgrounds. *Archives of General Psychiatry*, 23, 367-372.

Cloninger CR, Guze SB (1970). Psychiatric illness and female criminality: The role of sociopathy and hysteria in ... Their personal, familial, and social backgrounds *Archives of General Psychiatry*, 23:554-558.

Ford, C.V. (1983). *The somatizing disorders. Illness as a way of life*. Elsevier Biomedical, New York.

Ford, C.V. (1986). The somatizing disorders. *Psychosomatics*, 27: 327-337.

Guze, S.B., Cloninger, C.R., Martin, R.L. & Clayton, P.J. (1986). A follow-up and family study of Briquet's Syndrome. *British Journal of Psychiatry*, 149, 17-23.

Hawkley, L. C., Cole, S. W., Capitanio, J. P., Norman, G. J., & Cacioppo, J. T. (2012). Effects of social isolation on glucocorticoid regulation in social mammals. Hormones and Behavior, 62, 314-323.

Liskow B, Othmer E, Penick EC, et al (1986). Is Briquet's syndrome a heterogeneous disorder? *American Journal of Psychiatry*, 143, 626-629.

Rost, K., Akins, R, Brown, F. & Smith, G. (1992). The comorbidity of DSM-III-R personality disorders in somatization disorder. *General Hospital Psychiatry*, 14 (5), 322-326.

Sar, V., Akyüz, G., Kundakç, T., Kizltan, E., & Dogan, O. (2004). Childhood Trauma, Dissociation, and Psychiatric Comorbidity in Patients With Conversion Disorder. *American Journal of Psychiatry*, 161:12, 2271- 1276.

Saxe, G.N., Chinman, G., Berkowitz, R., Hall, K., Lieberg, G., Schwatrz, J. & van der Kolk, B.A. (1994). Somatization in patients with dissociative disorders. *American Journal of Psychiatry*, 151, 1329-1334.

Smith, G.R., Monson, R.A. & Ray, D.C. et al (1986). Psychiatric consultation in somatization disorder. A randomized controlled study. *New England Journal of Medicine*, 314, 1407-1413.

Stoudemire, A. (1998). *Clinical Psychiatry for Medical Students (3rd Edition)*. New York: Lippincott, Williams & Wilkins.

Woerner, P.I. & Guze, S.B. (1968). A family and marital study of hysteria. *British Journal of Psychiatry*, 114, 161-168.

Woodruff, R.A., Robins, L.N., Taibleson, M., Reich, T, Schwin, R, & Frost, N (1973). : A computer-assisted derivation of a screening interview for hysteria. *Archives of General Psychiatry*, 29, 450-454.

Other Sources

Atmaca, M. (2012). Neuroimaging in Somatoform Disorders: A Review. Turkish Journal of Psychiatry 2012.

Browning, M., Fletcher, P. & Sharpe, M. (2011). Can Neuroimaging Help Us to Understand and Classify Somatoform Disorders? A Systematic and Critical Review. *Psychosomatic Medicine*, 73:173–184.

Budinger, M.C., Drazdowski, T.K. & Ginsburg, G.S. (2012). Anxiety-Promoting Parenting Behaviors: A Comparison of Anxious Parents with and without Social Anxiety Disorder. *Child Psychiatry & Human Development*, (online Sept. 2012).

Clauss, J.A. & Blackford, J.U. (2012). Behavioral Inhibition and Risk for Developing Social Anxiety Disorder: A Meta-Analytic Study. *Journal of the American Academy of Child & Adolescent Psychiatry*, Vol. 51(10), pp. 1066-1075.

Creed, F. & Gureje, O. (2012). Emerging themes in the revision of the classification of somatoform disorders. *International Review of Psychiatry*, December 2012; 24(6): 556-567.

Diaz, A. & Bell, M.A. (2012). Frontal EEG Asymmetry and Fear Reactivity in Different Contexts at 10 Months. *Developmental Psychobiology*, 54: 536–545.

Dimsdale, J., & Creed, F. (2009) DSM-V Workgroup on Somatic Symptom Disorders: the proposed diagnosis of somatic symptom disorders in DSM-V to replace somatoform disorders in DSM-IV–a preliminary report. *Journal of Psychosomatic Research*, 66:473–6.

Dimsdale, J., Sharma, N. & Sharpe, M. (2011). What Do Physicians Think of Somatoform Disorders? *Psychosomatics* 2011:52:154–159.

Doehrmann, O. et al (2012). Predicting Treatment Response in Social Anxiety Disorder From Functional Magnetic Resonance Imaging. *Archives of General Psychiatry*. (Published online September 3, 2012).

Fava GA, Fabbri S, Sirri L, et al. (2007). Psychological factors affecting medical condition: a new proposal for DSM-V. *Psychosomatics,* 48:103–11.

Fink P, Schroder A. One single diagnosis, bodily distress syndrome, succeeded to capture 10 diagnostic categories of functional somatic syndromes and somatoform disorders. *Journal of Psychosomatic Research.* 2010;68:415–26.

Fox, A.S. et al (2012). Central amygdala nucleus (Ce) gene expression linked to increased trait-like Ce metabolism and anxious temperament in young primates. *Proceedings of the National Academy of Sciences*, (online, 2012).

Garcia-Campayoa, J., Fayed, N., Serrano-Blancoc, A. & Roca, M. (2009). Brain dysfunction behind functional symptoms: neuroimaging and somatoform, conversive, and dissociative disorders. *Current Opinion in Psychiatry*, 22:224–231.

Gropalis, M., Bleichhardt, G., Witthoft, M. & Hiller, W. (2012). Hypochondriasis, Somatoform Disorders, and Anxiety Disorders Sociodemographic Variables, General Psychopathology, and Naturalistic Treatment Effects. *Journal of Nervous and Mental Disorders,* 200: 406-412.

Gruber, C. Et al (2012). Somatoform Respiratory Disorders in Children and Adolescents-Proposals for a Practical Approach to Definition and Classification. *Pediatric Pulmonology,* 47:199-205.

Hilderink, P.H. et al (2013). Prevalence of somatoform disorders and medically unexplained symptoms in old age populations in comparison with younger age groups: A systematic review. *Ageing Research Reviews* 12, – 156.

Klaus, K. et al (2013). The Distinction Between "Medically Unexplained" and "Medically Explained" in the Context of Somatoform Disorders. *International Journal of Behavioral Medicine*, 20:161-171.

Kleinstäuber M. et al (2013). Pharmacological interventions for somatoform disorders in adults. *The Cochrane Library,* Issue 7.

Knapskaa, E. et al (2012). Functional anatomy of neural circuits regulating fear and extinction. *Proceedings of the National Academy of Sciences,* (online 2012).

Koh, K.B. (Ed.) (2013). *Somatization and Psychosomatic Symptoms.* New York: Springer.

Kroenke, K. (2007). Efficacy of Treatment for Somatoform Disorders: A Review of Randomized Controlled Trials. *Psychosomatic Medicine,* 69:881-888.

Kroenke, K., Sharpe, M. & Sykes, R. (2007) Revising the classification of somatoform disorders: key questions and preliminary recommendations. *Psychosomatics,* 48:277–85.

Kroenke, K. (2007). Somatoform Disorders and Recent Diagnostic Controversies. *Psychiatric Clinics of North America,* 30, 593–619.

Levenson, J.L. (2011). The Somatoform Disorders: 6 Characters in Search of an Author. *Psychiatric Clinics of North America,* 34, 515–524.

Mayou, R., Kirmayer, L.J., Simon, G. et al (2005) Somatoform disorders: time for a new approach in DSM-V. *American Journal of Psychiatry,* 162:847–55.

Morriss, R. & Gask, L. (2009). Assessment and immediate management of patients with medically unexplained symptoms in primary care. *Psychiatry,* 8:5, 179-183.

Morrison, A.S. & Heimberg, R.G. (2013). Social Anxiety and Social Anxiety Disorder. *Annual Review of Clinical Psychology,* 9:249–74.

Newman, M.G. et al (2013). Worry and Generalized Anxiety Disorder: A Review and Theoretical Synthesis of Evidence on Nature, Etiology, Mechanisms, and Treatment. *Annual Review of Clinical Psychology,* 2013. 9:275–97.

Refojo, D. et al. (2011). Glutamatergic and Dopaminergic Neurons Mediate Anxiogenic and Anxiolytic Effects of CRHR1. Science 333, 1903.

Steinbrecher, N., Koerber, S., Frieser, D. & Hiller, W. (2011). The Prevalence of Medically Unexplained Symptoms in Primary Care. *Psychosomatics,* 52:263–271.

Subic-Wrana, C. et al (2010). Theory of Mind and Emotional Awareness Deficits in Patients With Somatoform Disorders. *Psychosomatic Medicine,* 72:404–411.

Tottenham N. (2012). Human Amygdala Development in the Absence of Species-Expected Caregiving. *Developmental Psychobiolpogy.* (Published online, 2011)

Tromp, D.P.M. et al. (2012). Reduced Structural Connectivity of a Major Frontolimbic Pathway in Generalized Anxiety Disorder. *Archives of General Psychiatry,* 2012:69(9) 925-924.

Voigt, K. et al (2012). Predictive validity and clinical utility of DSM-5 Somatic Symptom Disorder—Comparison with DSM-IV somatoform disorders and additional criteria for consideration. *Journal of Psychosomatic Research,* 73, 345–350.

Wollberg, E. et al (2013). Construct validity and descriptive validity of somatoform disorders in light of proposed changes for the DSM-5. *Journal of Psychosomatic Research,* 74, 18–24.

Witthoft, M. & Hiller, W. (2010). Psychological Approaches to Origins and Treatments of Somatoform Disorders. *Annual Review of Clinical Psychology*. 6:257–83.

Dissociative Disorders

I. Introduction:

   A. Basic pattern: Disturbance or alteration in identity, memory or consciousness. Has been defined in various ways, but basically involves the removal of a cluster of associated mental elements from one's conscious awareness and/or conscious willful control. Generally also involves an alteration in sense of identity. Most seem to be traumatically induced. Largest group of cases occur during wartime or in connection with combat or extreme stress.

   B. DSM 5 categories of Dissociative Disorders
      1. **Dissociative Identity Disorder** (former Multiple Personality Disorder)
      2. Dissociative Amnesia (with or without Dissociative Fugue)
      3. Depersonalization/Derealization Disorder
      4. Other Specified Dissociative Disorder
         a. Chronic and recurrent syndromes of mixed dissociative symptoms.
         b. Identity disturbance due to prolonged and intense coercive persuasion: "Individuals who have been subjected to intense coercive persuasion (e.g., brainwashing, thought reform, indoctrination while captive, torture, long-term political imprisonment, recruitment by sects/cults or by terror organizartions) may present with prolonged changes in, or conscious questioning of, their identity." (P. 306)
         c. Acute dissociative reaction to stressful events.
         d. Dissociative trance: "This condition is characterized by an acute narrowing or complete loss of awareness of immediate surroundings that manifests as profound unresponsiveness or insensitivity to environmental stimuli. The unresponsiveness may be accompanied by minor stereotyped behaviors (e.g., finger movements) of which the individual is unaware, and/or that he or she cannot control, as well as transient paralysis or loss of consciousness. The dissociative trance is not a normal part of a broadly accepted collective cultural or religious practice." (P. 307)
      5. Unspecified Dissociative Disorder.

   C. Most experts and clinicians consider dissociation to exist on a continuum that ranges from daydreaming to DID that includes daydreaming, amnesia, hypnosis, OOB experiences, spirit possession, highway hypnosis.

   D. Important to consider that the mind and its functions operates to **adapt** individual to his or her surroundings. To improve our functioning.
      1. Often this involves storing and later providing access to information that we need to make decisions and deal with events. We think of perfect recall as the ideal and best situation.
      2. But consider the possibility that sometimes our best interests in a situation are served by not being able to recall certain experiences or emotions (to dissociate our conscious awareness from them) that might cause disabling anxiety, loss of self-esteem, etc. (During war, disaster, etc.)
      3. Often our memories are distorted, our recall is selective.

    4. If trauma or threat is severe, then the defense mechanism may be equally draconian.

E. May also make us think of (some) disorders a bit differently. What about psychological symptoms arising as the sequelae of attempts to deal cognitively and psychologically with other changes in one's ability to process or interpret information? Perhaps symptoms represent a mixture of 'pure' symptoms resulting from physical malfunction and an adaptive component produced as the individual attempts to make sense of or cope with those changes or deficiencies.
   1. One model is Eysenck's model of extraversion-introversion as strategies for coping with non-optimal levels of cortical arousal.
   2. Perhaps some dissociative and schizophrenic symptoms are similarly caused.

F. Dissociative phenomena, especially DID raise questions about the ways in which the mind works, and pose issues for our models of mental organization and consciousness, particularly the idea of a single organizing self that receives and regulates all other (unconscious) activities.

Dissociative Identity Disorder: (Multiple Personality Disorder)

I. Introduction:

A. DSM-5 diagnostic criteria
   1. "Disruption of identity characterized by two or more distinct personality states, which may be described in some cultures as an experience of possession. This disruption in identity involved marked discontinuity in sense of self and sense of agency, accompanied by related alternations in affect, behavior, consciousness, memory, perception, cognition, and/or sensory-motor functioning. These signs and symptoms may be observed by others or reported by the individual." (P. 292)
   2. "Recurrent gaps in the recall of everyday events, important personal information, and/or traumatic events that are inconsistent with ordinary forgetting."
   3. "The symptoms cause clinically significant distress or impairment in social, occupation, or other important areas of functioning."
   4. The disturbance is not a normal part of a broadly accepted cultural or religious practice." (And in children is not better explained in terms of imaginary playmates or other fantasy play.)
   5. "The symptoms are not attributable to the physiological effects of a substance (e.g., blackouts or chaotic behavior during alcohol intoxication) or to another medical condition (e.g., complex partial seizures.)"

B. Once described as extremely rare: A review of the literature by Sutcliffe & Jones (1962) were able to find only 77 reported cases between 1791 and 1962.

C. The "Three Faces of Eve" case, reported by Corbett Thigpen and Hervey Cleckley was published in 1957. Those authors reported in 1984 that despite hundreds of referrals over the following 25 years they never saw another valid case of MPD. (Kihlstrom, 2005, page 228)

D. "Sybil" case published in 1973, based on case of Shirley Mason. Made into TV movie in 1976. 16 alters
  1. In 1998, Robert Schreiber presented a paper at APA meeting based on tape recordings he had received from the book author.
  2. Argued that Mason did not suffer from MPD, but was very suggestible manipulated by Dr. Cornelia Wilbur to secure a book deal with publishers who weren't interested in a book on a case of hysteria.
  3. Position supported by Dr. Herbert Spiegel, who briefly treated Mason while Wilbur on vacation. Spiegel said Wilbur responded to assertion that Mason wasn't MPD by saying publisher wouldn't publish the book unless they said she was.
  4. Case remains controversial; Wilbur's files sealed, and she and Mason dead.

E. But between late 1970s and late 1980s there was what a number of psychologists described as an epidemic of MPD, with hundreds or reported cases, dozens of books, journal articles, and conferences devoted to MPD.
  1. While there were only eight reports of MPD published between 1944 and 1970, 36 published between 1970 and 1979 (**Greaves 1980**).
  2. In 1982, Frank Putnam et al. (1986) had developed a case registry of 100 cases "currently or recently in treatment"
  3. Richard Kluft (1984) analyzed outcomes for 171 patients who had been diagnosed with MPD.
  4. International Society for the Study of Multiple Personality and Dissociation (renamed the International Society for the Study of Dissociation, then renamed International Society for the Study of Trauma and Dissociation) held its first annual conference in 1984.
  5. First scholarly monographs devoted to MPD also appeared at this time (Bliss 1986, Ross 1986)" (**Kihlstrom, 2005**, page 228-229)

F. Recent cases in the DID "epidemic" involve many more alters per case. In classic literature, vast majority were dual personalities (**Sutcliffe & Jones 1962, Taylor & Martin 1944**). Most new cases compiled by Greaves (1980) presented at least three alters; in two other series, the average number of alter egos was more than 13 (Kluft 1984, Putnam et al., 1986).

G. Eve appeared to have three personalities (Osgood & Luria 1954, Thigpen & Cleckley 1954). But when popular and professional interest in MPD stimulated by case of Sibyl - reported to possess 16 different personalities (Schreiber 1973), Eve replied with her own account of her illness, eventually claiming 22 (Sizemore & Huber 1988). The proliferation of alter egos within cases, as well as the proliferation of cases, has been one of the factors leading to skepticism about the disorder itself." (Kihlstrom, 2004, page 231)

II. Description:
  A. The Host and alters:

1. Host generally presents to therapist with complaints about depression, fears, persistent headache. Are often rigid, frigid, compulsively good, conscience-stricken and masochistic.
2. Alters often encapsulate affects as well as memories, and their appearance my be triggered by specific external cues, perhaps those that are associated with a particular affect.
3. Some alters have very specific roles, and appear only in very specific situations - sexual, social, work, etc.
4. Many alters do not believe themselves to be in need of therapy, and report that they come only because the host needs help.
5. Alter types:
    a. Majority of multiples have **prosecutor personality** (or two) who insults and berates the host, who threatens (and sometimes engages in) self-damaging behavior. These tend to be child or adolescent personalities.
    b. The ISH: Many reports in the literature than some (though not all, perhaps 50-80%) of multiples have an **internal self helper** personality.
        (1) Typically physically passive, relatively emotionless.
        (2) Provide information and insights into the workings of the personality matrix.
        (3) May discuss patient's strengths and weaknesses, tell therapist what needs to be done to help patient.

B. Sometimes many personality states (half cases have 10 or more). Recent estimates of median number of personalities is 7, with a mode under 5, and a modal range of 8-13.

C. Generally, at least two personalities take full control of the individual at one time or another, with sudden transition between the two.
1. Transition often triggered by stress or individually meaningful social or environmental cues.
2. Functional personalities may alternate with others that are dysfunctional, or who appear to have a specific mental disorder, including mood disorders, personality disorders.

D. Relationship between personalities varies:
1. May be aware of some or all of the others to some degree.
2. May be experienced as adversaries or friends or as hallucinatory voices.
3. Personality that comes for treatment often has little knowledge or understanding of the others.

E. Most personalities are aware of amnesic periods in their recall.

F. Personalities may different in a number of interesting ways:
1. Psychological differences:
    a. Self-perceived ages, ethnic background, ancestry
    b. Accents, vocabularies
    c. Several animal alters
2. Physiological differences:
    a. Headaches specific to one personality (**Coons et al., 1988; Packard & Brown, 1986**)
    b. Hives specific to one personality (**Coons, 1984**)
    c. Visual acuity (**Coons, 1988a**)
    d. Handedness (**Putnam et al., 1986**; Smith & Sager, 1971)

    e. Changes in handwriting (Coons, 1980; Thigpen & Cleckley, 1954)
    f. Different reactions to the same drugs (Barkin et al, 1986; **Coons, 1988a**; Putnam, 1989a; **Putnam et al, 1986**)
    g. Different allergies (Braun, 1983)
    h. Heart rate; blood pressure, respiration (Bahnson & Smith, 1975; Larmore et al, 1977)
    i. Different IQs
    j. Different menstrual cycles.

G. Signs of multiplicity (**Cummings, 1985**) (% as reported by **Ross et al, 1990**) in 102 MPD patients from four centers):
    1. Sense of another person existing inside: 90%
    2. Hearing voices talking: 87%
    3. Voices coming from inside: 82%
    4. Another person taking control: 81%
    5. Amnesia for childhood: 81%
    6. Using the word 'we' during the course of an interview: 74%
    7. Person inside has a different name: 71%
    8. Reports of time distortions, lapses and discontinuities, blank spells: 68%
    9. Being told of behavioral episodes by others that are not remembered by patient. (63%)
    10. Feelings of unreality: 57%
    11. Being recognized by others or called by another name by people the patient does not recognize. (44%)
    12. Other personalities elicited under hypnosis or during amobarbital interviews.
    13. Patient finds articles (drawings, writings, clothing, etc.) among belongings that cannot be accounted for or are not recognized.

H. Before DSM-III in 1980, dissociative disorders classified as psychoneuroses, or forms of hysteria.

I. It can be difficult to discriminate between the dissociative disorders and bipolar disorder, borderline personality disorder, and even schizophrenia. When enthusiastic clinicians are determined to find it, DID can be diagnosed merely from the normal situational variability of behavior, or instances where otherwise "normal" people just "don't feel like themselves" (Piper 1995).

J. Especially true if clinician sees DID as "superordinate" diagnosis, "such that presenting symptoms such as phobias, obsessions, and compulsions, which might normally call for a primary diagnosis of anxiety disorder, can be attributed to one of a patient's alter egos instead (Putnam et al. 1984), or if it is believed that alter egos can appear only once in the patient's life, in order to perform some specific task, never to be manifest again (Bliss 1980, Kluft 1991)." (Kihlstrom, 2005, pp. 229-230)

III. Epidemiology:

A. Prevalence
1. "At the height of clinical interest in the dissociative disorders, the Clinton administration's Task Force on Health Care Financing Reform received a report claiming a prevalence of dissociative disorder of "about ten percent in the general population" (**Loewenstein 1994**, p. 3)
2. Study of large acute psychiatric hospital, using SCID-D (Structured Clinical Interview for DSM-IV Dissociative Disorders) to diagnose DID, yielded estimate of 1% among recent admissions (Rifkin et al. 1998). Suggests that prevalence of DID in population likely much lower. (Kihlstrom, 2005, p. 230-231)
3. Using DES [Dissociative Experiences Scale] and DDIS [Dissociative Disorders Interview Schedule], Ross (Ross, 1991; Ross, Joshi, & Currie, 1990) examined 1005 randomly selected people from population of Winnipeg. Study estimated lifetime prevalence of dissociative disorders at 11.2%. List below shows prevalence of dissociative disorders in ca 500 respondents in original study. (Lowenstein, 1994, p. 5). Prevalence in sample:
   a. Psychogenic amnesia: 7%
   b. Depersonalization Disorder: 2.4%
   c. Multiple Personality Disorder: 1.3%
   d. DDNOS: 0.2%
   e. All Dissociative Disorders: 11.2%
4. DSM-5 estimates prevalences as follows:
   a. DID: Annual prevalence in "small U.S. community sample" was 1.5% (1.6% for males; 1.4% for females)
   b. Dissociative Amnesia: Annual prevalence in "small U.S. community sample" was 1.8% (1.0% for males; 2.6% for females)
   c. Depersonalization/Derealization Disorder: Lifetime prevalence in U.S. and non-U.S. countries estimated at 2% (ranging from .8% to 2.8%) with no gender bias)

B. Onset almost always in childhood, usually before the age of nine, and is chronic. Much more common (3-9 times) in females. To date, 75-90% of cases female.
1. May reflect the fact that women are generally over represented in the patient population.
2. Perhaps MPD males end up being dealt with by the criminal justice system, where Bliss (1986) has reported a number of male MPD patients.

C. Impairment varies from mild to severe, depending primarily on relationship between personalities.

D. Problems of differential diagnosis:
1. False negatives are common because patient may resist sharing information, or present in a personality that has no access to essential information.
2. Putnam et al. (1986) reported that 100 MPD patients averaged 6.8 years between first appearance of symptoms of MPD and the accurate diagnosis. In meantime, received an average of 3.6 inaccurate diagnoses.
3. One problem with diagnosis occurs when individual who shows all the signs required when seen at one time do not show them as clearly at another time. Kluft (1985) reports that

80% of 200 cases followed longitudinally show waxing and waning of the clinical phenomenology. Only 20% show had classic features over prolonged period of time. Argues for a 'window of diagnosability' for most patients.

E. Kluft suggests several signs that may indicate MPD:
1. Prior treatment failure
2. Three or more prior diagnoses
3. Concurrent somatic and psychiatric symptoms
4. Fluctuating symptoms and level of functioning
5. Severe headaches
6. Others noting observable changes
7. Patients may exhibit first-rank symptoms indicative of schizophrenia:
    a. Feelings of imposed ideas or behaviors
    b. Voices arguing in the head, of commenting on one's behavior
8. Others may show symptoms of a variety of disorders
    a. Depression, anxiety, PTSD
    b. May have hallucinations, delusion-like features
9. Malingering a big problem, but often present more polarized, less complex and consistent than real cases.

IV. Etiology:

A. **Psychodynamic view.** Dissociative states are a form of repression in which an active process of removing threatening or unacceptable contents from conscious awareness.

B. Dissociation as a defense against trauma
1. Kluft (1987) suggests that almost all cases follow abuse (often sexual) or other emotional trauma in childhood. In two large series, 97 and 98% had experienced child abuse, usually physical, sexual and psychological maltreatment: "**...MPD is a posttraumatic pathology with no specific psychodynamic underpinning and without an origin in a specific developmental phase. It emerges in the context of efforts of an overwhelmed child, unable to either fight or take flight, to flee inwardly by abandoning sense of ownership of what is intolerable and unacceptable.**"

C. Two factors here:
1. First, there must be a predilection for dissociation
2. Then the traumatizing event that is dealt with using dissociation
    a. Dissociation seen as a different process from repression, which blocks anxiety-producing material in the unconscious
    b. Dissociation said to block it into another pocket of consciousness from that occupied by the ego
3. Two controversies:
    a. Is there evidence for dissociation (or repression)?

  b. Is there evidence that trauma is followed by forgetting (whether dissociation or repression)?

D. The debate over the validity of the trauma-memory argument:
1. "A plausible traumatic origin can be identified in most cases of amnesia and fugue, e.g., sexual assault (Eisen 1989, Kaszniak et al., 1988), physical assault (Glisky et al. 2004), or death of family member (Schacter et al., 1982).
2. But trauma history sometimes absent (Dalla Barba et al., 1997). Trauma not difficult to find with a broad definition. Even when trauma unequivocal, must show that trauma caused amnesia, and explain psychological mechanisms responsible. (Kihlstrom, 2004; p. 232)
3. Proponents cite the literature on disaster victims, combat, prisoners and torture victims, and victims and perpetrators of violent crime (e.g., Arrigo & Pezdek 1997, Brown et al., 1998, Gleaves et al., 2004, Scheflin & Brown 1996)
4. But Pope and his colleagues (**Pope et al., 1998, 2000**) reviewed 63 studies of trauma victims including more than 10,000 subjects, and found that all cases of amnesia for the trauma could not be explained by organic factors, infantile and childhood amnesia, ordinary forgetting, or other normal memory processes.
5. In response to the critiques of trauma-memory literature by Pope et al.(1998,2000), Brown et al.(1999) reviewed literature on "naturally occurring dissociative or traumatic amnesia for childhood sexual abuse," and concluded, "Not a single one of the 68 data-based studies failed to find it" (Brown et al., 1999, p. 126).
6. Prospective study by Williams (1994a,b), frequently cited: Found that 38% of a group of women who had suffered documented sexual abuse as children failed to report it to interviewer some 17 years later."
  a. Williams had independent corroboration of trauma, but she did not distinguish between traumatic repression and ordinary time-dependent forgetting, infantile and childhood amnesia, or even reluctance to report embarrassing memories to a stranger.
  b. Genuine memory failures not common in careful inquiries of individuals abused as children, as long as they were old enough to encode memory in the first place (Goodman et al., 2003, Widom & Morris 1997, Widom & Shepard 1996)." (Kihlstrom, 2004)
7. But Brown and colleagues (1999) argued that some studies cited by Pope et al. (1998,2000) offer evidence for traumatic amnesia (see also Brown et al., 1998). However, Piper et al.'s (2000) re-examination of the evidence supported Pope's initial conclusions.
  a. E.g., two individuals amnesic for lightning strike were "side-flash" victims who received the equivalent of electroconvulsive shock.
  b. Some children amnesic for flood disaster were two years old at the time of the flood, and though ca one third of older children who were earthquake survivors were reported as having psychogenic amnesia for event, more than two thirds of control group not exposed to trauma met the same criterion.
8. Cardena & Spiegel (1993) did report high rate of dissociative symptoms on DES among those who experienced Loma Prieta earthquake of 1989, but there was no evidence that any subject forgot earthquake. (Kihlstrom, 2004; p. 234)

E. Trauma-memory argument sometime revised to distinguish between has suggested that memory is enhanced for **Type I traumas** involving single, surprising, well-defined events, while **Type II traumas**, such as incest, that are repeated for extended time, lead to denial, psychic numbing, dissociation, and amnesia. (Terr, 1991, 1994)

F. Jennifer Freyd (1994, 1996) argues that memory enhanced for "terror" traumas, such as combat, but impaired by dissociation for "betrayal" traumas, such as incest. (Kihlstrom, 2004)

G. Dissociation: Continuum versus taxon:
1. One view, as we have seen, has it that dissociation, and dissociative phenomena exist on a continuum from daydreaming, amnesia, hypnosis, OOB experiences, to DID.
2. Another view is that there is a distinct subgroup- or taxon - of pathological dissociatiors:
   a. Putnam, co-author of DES (continuum-based measure of dissociation), aware that frequency and type of dissociative experiences reported by certain diagnostic groups suggested existence at least two discrete dissociative types. (Putnam, 1997, p. 66).
   b. Irwin (1999): Frequency and severity of dissociative taxon experiences not normally distributed, suggesting that dissociation taxon represents category not a dimension. (Collins, 2004)
   c. Waller (1995) confirmed this in his psychometric review of the DES, leading to description of the dissociation taxon (Waller, Putnam & Carlson, 1996)." (Collins, 2004)
      (1) Waller et al. (1996): Identified both pathological and non-pathological dissociative phenomena, and two corresponding groups of dissociators.
      (2) pathological type (or taxon) of dissociative phenomena includes amnesia and identity alteration, depersonalisation and derealisation.
      (3) Waller et al's (1996) analysis suggests that ca 3% of general population belongs to pathological dissociative taxon, with frequent and profound experiences of amnesia and/or depersonalization.
   d. But Watson (2003) found that assessments of dissociative taxon have extremely low test-retest reliability, casting existence of taxon into doubt.

H. More common in first-degree relatives of sufferers. Often occurs in several generations of the same family, and in siblings.
1. Perhaps due to transgenerational abuse.
2. Inability of dissociating parent to protect child from abuse.
3. Identification of child with dissociating parent.

V. Treatment and prognosis:

A. Most current therapeutic approaches to DID based on assumption that DID caused by childhood trauma. Typically, therapy is psychodynamic and insight-oriented, focusing on uncovering, abreacting, and working through trauma and other conflictual issues, and getting the patient to abandon dissociative defenses. Therapist seeks to integrate patient's alters into single cohesive identity, such that therapeutic alliances must be established between each alter and therapist, but also among alters themselves. (Kihlstrom, 2004)

B. Kluft believes that treatment can be highly successful for motivated patients who are treated specifically with respect to MPD. Suggests several generally sequential steps:
1. Share diagnosis with patient.
2. Make contact with as many alters as possible, taking no sides (perhaps through hypnosis)
3. Therapy may involve hypnosis, and asking other alters to come forward and speak while patient listens, and is told to remember later. Then patient is told that she can, and should defeat the other personalities.
4. Each alter receives treatment for its concerns, encouraging emotional abreaction.
5. Encourage communication between alters.

C. Literature evaluating success of such therapies typically do not involve standard treatment protocols and no-treatment controls, so are hard to evaluate (Merskey & Piper 1998, Powell & Howell 1998; for a reply, see Ross & Ellason 1998).

D. Studies also lack comparison with alternative treatments: If no causal link between sexual abuse and DID, then no reason to focus therapy on working through recovered memories of trauma. Indeed, process of identifying, negotiating with, and integrating patient's alters may reinforce dissociative symptoms (Bowers 1991; Piper 1995, 1997), which may help explain the increase in number of alters per DID case. (Kihlstrom, 2004)

E. No evidence that hypnosis facilitates recovery of repressed or dissociated memories, and much evidence that it can distort memory (Kihlstrom & Eich 1994). Memories recovered through hypnosis must have corroboration. (Kihlstrom, 2004)

VI. Controversy remains

A. "More than 200 years after the first published case study of multiple personality, more than a century after the syndromes were formally recognized by mental health professionals, and fully 20 years since the current revival of interest in them began, the dissociative disorders continue to invite controversy... The case of Sybil, which arguably marks the onset of the MPD "epidemic" of the 1980s and 1990s, has now been thoroughly discredited" (Borch-Jacobsen 1997, 2002; Rieber 1999).

B. Other "sociocognitive" theorists propose that DID is "a syndrome that consists of rule-governed and goal-directed experiences and displays of multiple role enactments that have been created, legitimized, and maintained by social reinforcement" (Lilienfeld et al., 1999, p. 507; Lilienfeld & Lynn 2003). ... Recent surveys suggest that more than half of American and Canadian psychiatrists harbor reservations about the validity of the diagnosis and its inclusion in the DSM (Lalonde et al., 2001, Pope et al., 1999)" (Kihlstrom, 2004, p. 243-244)

C. "the possibility that some – probably many, perhaps most – recent cases of DID and other dissociative disorders are iatrogenic or misdiagnosed mean that the occasional genuine case should not be taken seriously. As rare as they may be, the dissociative disorders provide a unique perspective on fundamental questions concerning consciousness, identity, the self, and the unity of personality. As complex as they surely are, they deserve to be studied in a spirit of open inquiry that avoids both the excessive credulity of the enthusiast and the dismissal of the determined skeptic." (Kihlstrom, 2004, p. 244)

Derealization/Depersonalization Disorder:

I. DSM-5 diagnostic criteria:

   A. "The presence of persistent or recurrent experiences of depersonalization, derealization, or both."
      1. Depersonalization: "Experiences of unreality, detachment, or being an outside observer with respect to one's thoughts, sensations, body, or actions..."
      2. Derealization: "Experiences of unreality or detachment with respect to surroundings (e.g., individuals or objects are experienced as unreal, dreamlike, foggy, lifeless, or visually distorted.)"

   B. "During the depersonalization or derealization experience, reality testing remains intact."

   C. "The symptoms cause clinically significant distress or impairment in social, occupational, or other important areas of functioning."

   D. "The disturbance is not better explained by another mental disorder, such as schizophrenia, panic disorder, major depressive disorder, acute stress disorder, posttraumatic stress disorder, or another dissociative disorder."

   E. "The symptoms are not attributable to the physiological effects of a substance (e.g., a drug of abuse, medication) or to another medical condition (e.g., seizures.)"

References

Arrigo, J.M. & Pezdek, K. (1997). Lessons from the study of psychogenic amnesia. *Current Directions in Psychological Science*, 6, 148–52.

Bahnson, C.B. & Smith, K. (1975). Autonomic changes in a multiple personality. *Psychosomatic Medicine*, 37, 85-86.

Barkin R, Braun B, Kluft R. (1986). The dilemma of drug therapy for multiple personality disorder. In Braun, B.G., (Ed.). *Treatment of multiple personality disorder*. Washington, DC: American Psychiatric Press, 107-132.

Bliss, E.L. (1986). *Multiple Personality, Allied Disorders, and Hypnosis*. New York: Oxford University Press.

Borch-Jacobsen M. (1997). Sybil—the making of a disease: An interview with Dr. Herbert Spiegel. *New York Review of Books*, 44, 60–64.

Borch-Jacobsen M. (2002). *Folie `a Plusieurs: De l'Hysterie `a la Depression*. Paris: Le Seuil.

Bowers, K.S.. (1991). Dissociation in hypnosis and multiple personality disorder. *International Journal of Clinical and Experimental Hypnosis*, 39, 155-76.

Brown, D, Scheflin. A.W. & Hammond, D.C. (1998). *Memory, Trauma Treatment, and the Law*. New York: Norton.

Brown, D, Scheflin, A.W. & Whitfield, C.L. (1999). Recovered memories: the current weight of the evidence in science and in the courts. *Journal of Psychiatry and Law*, 27, 5–156.

Cardena, E. & Spiegel, D. (1993). Dissociative reactions to the San Francisco Bay area earthquake of 1989. *American Journal of Psychiatry*, 150, 474–78.

Collins, C., Burazeri, G., Gofin, J., & Kark, J. D. (2004). Health status and mortality in holocaust survivors living in Jerusalem 40–50 years later. *Journal of Traumatic* Stress, 17, 403–411.

Coons, P.M. (1980). Multiple personality: Diagnostic considerations. *Journal of Clinical Psychiatry*, 41, 330336.

Coons, P.M. (1984). The differential diagnosis of multiple personality: A comprehensive review. *Psychiatric Clinics of North America*, 7, 51-67.

Coons, P.M. (1988a). Psychophysiological aspects of multiple personality disorder: A review. *Dissociation*, 1, 47-53.

Coons, P.M., Bowman, E.S., & Milstein, V. (1988). Multiple personality disorder: A clinical investigation of 50 cases. *Journal of Nervous and Mental Disease*, 176, 519-527.

Cummings, J.L. (1985). Dissociative states, depersonalization, multiple personality, episodic memory lapses. In *Clinical Neuropsychiatry*. Orlando Fla.: Grune & Stratton, p. 122.

Dalla Barba, G., Mantovan, M.C., Ferruzza, E. & Denes, G. (1997). Remembering and knowing the past: a case study of isolated retrograde amnesia. *Cortex* 33:143–54.

Eisen, M.R. (1989). Return of the repressed: Hypnoanalysis of a case of total amnesia. *International. Journal of Clinical and Experimental Hypnosis*, 37, 107–19.

Freyd, J. (1996). *Betrayal Trauma: The Logic of Forgetting Childhood Abuse*. Cambridge, MA: Harvard Univ. Press.

Freyd, J.J. (1994). Betrayal trauma: traumatic amnesia as an adaptive response to childhood abuse. *Ethics & Behavior*, 4, 307–29.

Gleaves, D.H., Smith, S.M., Butler, L.D. & Spiegel, D. (2004). False and recovered memories in the laboratory and clinic: a review of experimental and clinical evidence. *Clinical Psychology: Science and Practice*, 11:3–28.

Glisky, E.L., Ryan, L, Reminger, S., Hardt, O., Hayes, S.M. & Hupbach, A. (2004). A case of psychogenic fugue: I understand, aber ich verstehe nichts. *Neuropsychologia* 42:1132–47.

Goodman, G.S., Ghetti, S., Quas, J.A., Edelstein, R.S. & Alexander, K.W.(2003). A prospective study of memory for child sexual abuse: new findings relevant to the repressed-memory controversy. *Psychological Science*, 14, 113–18.

Greaves, G.B. (1980). Multiple personality: 165 years after Mary Reynolds. *Journal of Nervous and Mental Disease*, 168, 577-596.

Irwin, H. J. (1999). Pathological and nonpathological dissociation: The relevance of childhood trauma. *Journal of Psychology: Interdisciplinary and Applied*, 133, 157–164.

Kaszniak, A.W., Nussbaum, P.D., Berren, M.R., & Santiago, J. (1988). Amnesia as a consequence of male rape: a case report. *Journal of Abnormal Psychology*, 97, 100-4.

Kihlstrom, J.F. (2005). Dissociative Disorders. *Annual Review of Clinical Psychology*, 1, 227-253.

Kihlstrom, J.F, & Eich, E. (1994). Altering states of consciousness. In *Learning, Remembering, and Believing: Enhancing Performance*, ed. D Druckman, RA Bjork, pp. 207–48. Washington, DC: Natl. Acad. Press.

Kluft, R.P. (1984). Treatment of Multiple Personality Disorder: A study of 33 cases. *Psychiatric Clinics of North America*, 7, 9-29.

Kluft, R.P. (1985). The natural history of multiple personality disorder. In R.P. Kluft (Ed.), *Childhood antecedents of multiple personality* (pp. 197-238). Washington, DC: American Psychiatric Press.

Kluft, R.P. (1987). First rank symptoms as diagnostic indicators of multiple personality disorder. *American Journal of Psychiatry*, 144, 293-298.

Lalonde, J.K., Hudson, J.I., Gigante, R.A. & Pope, H.G. (2001). Canadian and American psychiatrists' attitudes toward dissociative disorders diagnoses. *Canadian Journal of Psychiatry*, 46, 407–12.

Larmore, K., Ludwig, A.M., Cain, R.L. (1977). Multiple personality: An objective case study. *British Journal of Psychiatry*, 131, 35-40.

Lilienfeld, S.O., Kirsch, I., Sarbin, T.R., Lynn, S.J. & Chaves, J.F. (1999). Dissociative identity disorder and the sociocognitive model: Recalling the lessons of the past. *Psychological Bulletin*, 125:507–23.

Lilienfeld, S.O. & Lynn, S.J. (2003). Dissociative identity disorder: multiple personalities, multiple controversies. In *Science and Pseudoscience in Clinical Psychology*, ed. SO Lilienfeld, SJ Lynn, pp. 109–42. New York: Guilford.

Loftus, E.F., Garry, M. & Feldman, J. (1994). Forgetting sexual trauma: What does it mean when 38% forget? *Journal of Consulting and Clinical. Psychology*, 62, 1177–81.

Lowenstein, R.J. (1994). Diagnosis, epidemiology, clinical course, treatment, and cost effectiveness of treatment for dissociative disorders and MPD: report submitted to the Clinton Administration Task Force on Health Care Financing Reform. *Dissociation*, 7, 3–12.

Merskey H, & Piper A. (1998). Treatment of dissociative identity disorder. *American Journal of Psychiatry*, 155, 1462–63.

Osgood, C.E. & Luria, Z. (1954). A blind analysis of a case of multiple personality using the semantic differential. *Journal of Abnormal and Social Psychology*, 49, 579–91.

Packard, R.C. & Brown, F. (1986). Multiple headaches in a case of multiple personality disorder. *Headache*, 26, 99-102.

Piper, A. (1995). A skeptical look at multiple personality disorder. In *Dissociative Identity Disorder: Theoretical and Treatment Controversies*, ed. LM Cohen, JN Berzoff, MR Elin, pp. 135–73. New York: Jason Aronson.

Piper A. (1997). *Hoax and Reality: The Bizarre World of Multiple Personality Disorder*. New York: Jason Aronson.

Piper, A., Pope, H.H., & Borowiecki, B.S. (2000). Custer's last stand: Browm, Schefllin, and Whitfield's latest attempt to salvage "dissociative amnesia". *Journal of Psychiatry and Law*, 28, 149-213.

Pope, H.G., Hudson, J.L., Bodkin, J.A. & Oliva, P. (1998). Questionable validity of "dissociative amnesia" in trauma victims: Evidence from prospective studies. *British Journal of Psychiatry*, 172, 210-215.

Pope, H.G. Jr, Oliva, P.S., Hudson, J.I., Bodkin, J.A. & Gruber, A.J. (1999). Attitudes toward DSMIV dissociative disorders diagnoses among board-certified American psychiatrists. *American Journal of Psychiatry*, 156, 321–23.

Powell, R.A., & Howell, A.J. (1998). Treatment outcome for dissociative identity disorder. *American Journal of Psychiatry*, 155, 1304–5.

Putnam, F.W., Guroff, J.J., Silverman, E.K. et al. (1986). The clinical phenomenology of multiple personality disorder: Review of 100 recent cases. *Journal of Clinical Psychiatry*, 47, 285-293.

Rieber RW. (1999). Hypnosis, false memory, and multiple personality: a trinity of affinity. *History of Psychiatry*, 10, 3–11.

Rifkin, A, Ghisalbert, D, Dimatou, S, Jin, C. & Sethi, M. (1998). Dissociative identity disorder in psychiatric inpatients. *American Journal of Psychiatry*, 155, 844–45.

Ross, C.A. (1986). *Multiple Personality Disorder: Diagnosis, Clinical Features, and Treatment*. New York: Wiley.

Ross, C. (1991). The epidemiology of multiple personality disorder and dissociation. *Psychiatric Clinics of North America*, 14, 503-517.

Ross, C.A. & Ellason, J.W. (1998). "Treatment of dissociative identity disorder": Dr. Ross and Ms. Ellason reply. *American journal of Psychiatry*, 155:1462-1463.

Ross, C. A., Joshi, S., & Currie, R. (1990). Dissociative experiences in the general population. *American journal of Psychiatry*, 147, 1547-1552.

Ross, C.A., Miller, S.D., Reagor, P., Bjornson, L., Fraser, G.A. & Anderson, G. (1990). Structured interview data from 102 cases of multiple personality disorder from four centers. *American Journal of Psychiatry*, 147, 596.

Schacter, D.L., Wang, P.L., Tulving, E. & Freedman, M. (1982). Functional retrograde amnesia: a quantitative case study. *Neuropsychologia*, 20:523–32

Scheflin, A.W. & Brown, D. (1996). Repressed memory or dissociative amnesia: what the science says. *Journal of Psychiatry and Law*, 24, 143–88.

Sutcliffe, J.P. & Jones, J. (1962). Personal identity, multiple personality, and hypnosis. *International Journal of Clinical Experimental Hypnosis*, 10, 231–69.

Terr, L. (1991). Childhood traumas: an outline and overview. *American Journal of Psychiatry*, 48, 10–20.

Terr, L. (1994). *Unchained Memories: True Stories of Traumatic Memories, Lost and Found*. New York: Basic Books.

Thigpen, C.H., Cleckley H. (1954). A case of multiple personality. *Journal of Abnormal and Social Psychology*, 135–51

Thigpen, C.H., Cleckley, H. (1984). On the incidence of multiple personality disorder. International *Journal of Clinical and Experimental Hypnosis*, 32, 63–66.

Waller, N.G., Putnam, F.W., & Carlson, E.B. (1996). Types of dissociation and dissociative types: A taxometric analysis of dissociative experiences. *Psychological Methods*, 1, 300–321.

Watson D. (2003). Investigating the construct validity of the dissociative taxon: stability analyses of normal and pathological dissociation. *Journal of Abnormal Psychology*, 112, 298-305.

Widom, C.S. & Morris, S. (1997). Accuracy of adult recollections of childhood victimization. Part 2: childhood sexual abuse. *Psychological Assessment*, 9, 34–46.

Widom, C.S. & Shepard, R.L. (1996). Accuracy of adult recollections of childhood victimization. Part 1: childhood physical abuse. *Psychological Assessment*, 8, 412–21.

Williams, L.M. (1994a). Recall of childhood trauma: a prospective study of women's memories of child sexual abuse. *Journal of Consulting and Clinical. Psychology*, 62, 1167–78.

Williams, L.M. (1994b). What does it mean to forget child sexual abuse? A reply to Loftus, Garry, and Feldman 1994. *Journal of Consulting and Clinical. Psychology*, 62, 1182–86.

Other Sources

Auerbach, Carl F., Mirvis, Shoshana, Stern, Susan andSchwartz, Jonathan(2009) 'Structural Dissociation and Its Resolution Among Holocaust Survivors: A Qualitative Research Study', *Journal of Trauma & Dissociation*, 10: 4, 385 - 404.

Bliss, E. L. (1984). Spontaneous self-hypnosis in multiple personality disorder. *Psychiatric Clinics of North America*, 7, 135–148.

Brand, B.L., Lanius, R., Vermetten, E., Loewenstein, R.J. & Spiegel, D. (2012) Where Are We Going? An Update on Assessment, Treatment, and Neurobiological Research in Dissociative Disorders as We Move Toward the DSM-5 , *Journal of Trauma & Dissociation*, 13:1, 9-3.

Brand, B. et al (2009). A Naturalistic Study of Dissociative Identity Disorder and Dissociative Disorder Not Otherwise Specified Patients Treated by Community Clinicians. *Psychological Trauma: Theory, Research, Practice, and Policy*, Vol. 1, No. 2, 153-171.

Carlson, E. B., Putnam, F. W., Ross, C. A., Torem, M., Coons, P., Bowman, E. S., et al. (1993). Predictive validity of the Dissociative Experiences Scale. *American Journal of Psychiatry*, 150, 1030–1036.

Coons et al, (1988). Multiple Personality Disorder: A Clinical Investigation of 50 cases. *Journal of Nervous and Mental Disease*, 176(9), 519-527.

Coons, P. M. (1994). Confirmation of childhood abuse in child and adolescent cases of multiple personality disorder and dissociative disorder not otherwise specified. *Journal of Nervous and Mental Disease*, 182, 461–464.

Coons, P. M., Bowman, E. S., & Milstein, V. (1988). Multiple personality disorder: A clinical investigation of 50 cases. *Journal of Nervous and Mental Disease*, 176, 519–527.

Coons, P. M., & Milstein, V. (1986). Psychosexual disturbances in multiple personality: Characteristics, etiology, and treatment. *Journal of Clinical Psychiatry*, 47, 106-111.

Ellason, J. W., & Ross, C. A. (1997). Two-year follow-up of inpatients with dissociative identity disorder. *American Journal of Psychiatry*, 154, 832–839.

Ellason, J. W., & Ross, C. A. (1996). Millon Clinical Multiaxial Inventory-II followup of patients with dissociative identity disorder. *Psychological Reports*, 78, 707–716.

Ellason, J. W., & Ross, C. A. (2004). SCL-90-R norms for dissociative identity disorder. *Journal of Trauma and Dissociation*, 4(5), 85–91.

Friedl MC, Draijer N, de Jonge P. (2000). Prevalence of dissociative disorders in psychiatric in-patients: the impact of study characteristics. *Acta Psychiatrica Scandinavica*, 102, 423–428.

Gleaves, D. H., May, M. C., & Cardena, E. (2001). An examination of the diagnostic validity of dissociative identity disorder. *Clinical Psychology Review*, 21, 577–608.

Gleaves, D.H., May, M.C., & Cardeña, E. (2001). An examination of the diagnostic validity of dissociative identity disorder. *Clinical Psychology Review*, 21, 577–608.

Goldsmith, Rachel E., Cheit, Ross E. and Wood, Mary E.(2009) 'Evidence of Dissociative Amnesia in Science and Literature: Culture-Bound Approaches to Trauma in Pope, Poliakoff, Parker, Boynes, and Hudson (2007)', *Journal of Trauma & Dissociation*, 10: 3, 237- 253.

Goldsmith, Rachel E., Cheit, Ross E. and Wood, Mary E.(2009) 'Ignoring Nina: Avoidance and Denial in Pope, Poliakoff, Parker, Boynes, and Hudson (2009)', *Journal of Trauma & Dissociation*, 10: 3, 258-260.

Hornstein, N. L., & Putnam, F. W. (1992). Clinical phenomology of child and adolescent multiple personality disorder. *Journal of the American Academy of Child and Adolescent Psychiatry*, 31, 1055–1077.

Huntjens, R.J.C., Peters, M.L., Woertman, L., Bovenschen, L.M., Martin, R.C. & Postma, A. (2006). Inter-identity amnesia in dissociative identity disorder: a simulated memory impairment? *Psychological Medicine*, 36, pp 857-863.

Kluft, R. P. (1995). The confirmation and disconfirmation of memories of abuse in DID patients: A naturalistic clinical study. *Dissociation*, 8, 253–258.

Kong, Lauren L.; Allen, John J. B.; Glisky, Elizabeth L. (2008). Interidentity memory transfer in dissociative identity disorder. *Journal of Abnormal Psychology*, 117(3), 686-692.

Lambert, K., & Lilienfeld, S. O. (2007, October/November). Brain stains. *Scientific American Mind*, 46–53.

Lilienfeld S.O., Kirsch, I., Sarbin. TR, Lynn, S.J., Chaves, J.F., et al. (1999). Dissociative identity disorder and the sociocognitive model: recalling the lessons of the past. *Psychological Bulletin*, 125, 507–23.

Loewenstein RJ. (1994). Diagnosis, epidemiology, clinical course, treatment, and cost effectiveness of treatment for dissociative disorders and MPD: *report submitted to the Clinton Administration Task Force on Health Care Financing Reform. Dissociation* 7:3–12.

Lynn, S.J., Lilienfeld, S.O., Merckelbach, H., Giesbrecht, T. & van der Kloet, D. (2012). Dissociation and Dissociative Disorders : Challenging Conventional Wisdom. *Current Directions in Psychological Science*, 21: 48.

MacDonald, Kai and MacDonald, Tina (2009). 'Peas, Please: A Case Report and Neuroscientific Review of Dissociative Amnesia and Fugue', *Journal of Trauma & Dissociation*, 10: 4, 420-435.

McNally, R. J., & Geraerts, E. (2009). A new solution to the recovered memory debate. *Perspectives on Psychological Science*, 4(2), 126–134.

McNally, R. J. (2007). Betrayal trauma theory: A critical appraisal. *Memory*, 15(3), 280–294; discussion 295–311.

McNally, R. J. (2004). Is traumatic amnesia nothing but psychiatric folklore? *Cognitive and Behavioral Therapy*, 33(2), 97–101; discussion 102–104, 109–111.

McNally, R. J. (2005). Debunking myths about trauma and memory. *Canadian Journal of Psychiatry*, 50, 817–822.

Merskey, H. (1992). The manufacture of personalities: The production of multiple personality disorder. *British Journal of Psychiatry*, 160, 327–340.

Piper, A., & Merskey, H. (2004a). The persistence of folly: A critical examination of dissociative identity disorder. Part I. The excesses of an improbable concept. *Canadian Journal of Psychiatry*, 49, 592–600.

Piper, A., & Merskey, H. (2004b). The persistence of folly: A critical examination of dissociative identity disorder. Part II. The defence and decline of multiple personality or dissociative identity disorder. *Canadian Journal of Psychiatry*, 49, 678–83.

Pope, H. G., Hudson, J., Bodkin, J. A., & Oliva, P. (1998). Questionable validity of 'dissociative amnesia' in trauma victims. Evidence from prospective studies. *British Journal of Psychiatry*, 172, 210–215.

Pope, H. G., Poliakoff, M. B., Parker, M. P., Boynes, M., & Hudson, J. I. (2007). Is dissociative amnesia a culture-bound syndrome? Findings from a survey of historical literature. *Psychological Medicine*, 37, 225–233.

Pope Jr., Harrison G., Poliakoff, Michael B., Parker, Michael P., Boynes, Matthew and Hudson,IJames (2010) 'Letter to the Editor', *Journal of Trauma & Dissociation*, 11: 1, 19 - 20.

Pope Jr., Harrison G., Poliakoff, Michael B., Parker, Michael P., Boynes, Matthew andHudson, James I.(2009) 'Response to R. E. Goldsmith, R. E. Cheit, & M. E. Wood, "Evidence of Dissociative Amnesia in Science and Literature: Culture-Bound Approaches to Trauma in Pope et al. (2007)"', *Journal of Trauma & Dissociation*, 10: 3, 254-257.

Putnam, F. W., Guroff, J. J., Silberman, E. K., Barban, L., & Post, R. M. (1986). The clinical phenomenology of multiple personality disorder: Review of 100 recent cases. *Journal of Clinical Psychiatry*, 47, 285-293.

Rofé, Y. (2008). Does repression exist? Memory, pathogenic, unconscious and clinical evidence. *Review of General Psychology*, 12(1), 63–85.

Ross, C. A. (1991). Epidemiology of multiple personality disorder and dissociation. *Psychiatric Clinics of North America*, 14, 503-517.

Ross, C. A. (1997). *Dissociative identity disorder: Diagnosis, clinical features, and treatment of multiple personality* (2nd ed.). New York: Wiley.

Ross, C. A. (2000). *The trauma model: A solution to the problem of comorbidity in psychiatry*. Richardson, TX: Manitou Communications.

Ross, C. A., & Burns, S. (2007). Acute stabilization in a trauma program: A pilot study. *Journal of Psychological Trauma*, 6, 21-28.

Ross, C. A., Duffy, C. M. M., & Ellason, J. W. (2002). Prevalence, reliability and validity of dissociative disorders in an inpatient setting. *Journal of Trauma and Dissociation*, 3, 7-17.

Ross, C. A., & Ellason, J. W. (2001). Acute stabilization in an inpatient trauma program. *Journal of Trauma and Dissociation*, 2, 83-87.

Ross, C. A., & Ellason, J. W. (2005). Discriminating among diagnostic categories using the Dissociative Disorders Interview Schedule. *Psychological Reports*, 96, 445-453.

Ross, C.A. et al (2008). 'A Cross-Cultural Test of the Trauma Model of Dissociation, *Journal of Trauma & Dissociation*, 9(1), 35-49.

Ross, C. A., Heber, S., Anderson, G., Norton, G. R., Anderson, B., del Campo, M., et al. (1989). Differentiating multiple personality disorder and complex partial seizures. *General Hospital Psychiatry*, 11, 54-58.

Ross, C. A., Heber, S., Norton, G. R., & Anderson, G. (1989). Differences between multiple personality disorder and other diagnostic groups on structured interview. *Journal of Nervous and Mental Disease*, 179, 487-491.

Ross, C. A., Heber, S., Norton, G. R., Anderson, G., Anderson, D., & Barchet, P. (1989). The Dissociative Disorders Interview Schedule: A structured interview. *Dissociation*, 2, 169-189.

Ross, C. A., Miller, S. D., Bjornson, L., Reagor, P., Fraser, G. A., & Anderson, G. (1991). Abuse histories in 102 cases of multiple personality disorder. *Canadian Journal of Psychiatry*, 36, 97-101.

Ross, C. A., Miller, S. D., Reagor, P., Bjornson, L., Fraser, G. A., & Anderson, G. (1990). Structured interview data on 102 cases of multiple personality disorder from four centers. *American Journal of Psychiatry*, 147, 596-601.

Ross, C. A., Norton, G. R., & Wozney, K. (1989). Multiple personality disorder: An analysis of 236 cases. *Canadian Journal of Psychiatry*, 34, 413-418.

Ross, C.A. & Ness, L. (2010). Symptom Patterns in Dissociative Identity Disorder Patients and the General Population. *Journal of Trauma & Dissociation*, 11:4, 458-468.

Ross, C. A., & Haley, C. (2004). Acute stabilization and three-month follow-up in a trauma program. *Journal of Trauma and Dissociation*, 5, 103-112.

Ross, C.A. (2006). Dissociative identity disorder. *Current Psychosis and Therapeutics Reports*, 4(3), 112-116.

Ross, Colin A.(2009) 'Errors of Logic and Scholarship Concerning Dissociative Identity Disorder', *Journal of Child Sexual Abuse*, 18: 2, 221- 231.

Sar, V., Middleton, W. & Dorahy, M.J. (2012). The Scientific Status of Childhood Dissociative Identity Disorder: A Review of Published Research. *Psychotherapy and Psychosomatics*, 81:183-184.

Sar, V. & Ozturk, E. (2007). Functional Dissociation of the Self: A Sociocognitive Approach to Trauma and Dissociation. *Journal of Trauma & Dissociation*, 8(4), 69-89.

Schultz, R. K., Braun, B. G., & Kluft, R. P. (1989). Multiple personality disorder: Phenomenology of selected variables in comparison to major depression. *Dissociation*, 2, 45-51.

Spanos, N. P. (1996). *Multiple identities & false memories: A sociocognitive perspective*. Washington, DC: American Psychological Association.

Stein, D.J., Craske, M.G., Friedman, M.J. & Phillips, K.A. (2011). Meta-structure Issues for the DSM-5: How Do Anxiety Disorders, Obsessive-Compulsive and Related Disorders, Post-Traumatic Disorders, and Dissociative Disorders Fit Together? *Current Psychiatry Report*, 13:248-250.

Steinberg, M., Rounsaville, B., & Cicchetti, D. V. (1990). The Structured Clinical Interview for DSM-III-R Dissociative Disorders: Preliminary report on a new instrument. *American Journal of Psychiatry*, 147, 76-82.

Spiegel, D. Et al (2013). Dissociative Disorders in DSM-5. *Annual Review of Clinical Psychology*. 9:299-326.

Steinberg, M. (1995). *Handbook for the assessment of dissociation*. Washington, DC: American Psychiatric Press.

Depressive Disorders & Bipolar and Related Disorders

I. Introduction:

   A. In DSM-IV, this was a single category called Mood Disorders. Now separated into two categories, partly because of increasing evidence suggesting separate etiological pathways for mood disorders with and without manic episodes.

   B. This is a disorder category that many of us are familiar with from personal or family experience. It is also the case that quite a number of well-known individuals have experienced depression:
      1. Kurt Cobain, Jim Carrey, Drew Carey, Drew Barrymore
      2. Gwyneth Paltrow, Brooke Shields, Britney Spears, Hugh Laurie
      3. Charles Dickens, Charles Darwin, J.K. Rowling, Ernest Hemingway
      4. Princess Diana, Harrison Ford, Mike Wallace.

   C. Depression, though often having severe and debilitating effects on an individual's life, is now among the most treatable of mental disorders.

Depressive and Related Disorders

I. DSM-5 categories of Depressive Disorders:

   A. Disruptive Mood Regulation Disorder [New to DSM-5; all quotations from DSM-5, p. 156]
      1. "In order to address concerns about the potential for the over diagnosis and treatment for bipolar disorder in children, a new diagnosis, disruptive mood regulation disorder, referring to the presentation of children with persistent irritability and frequent episodes of extreme behavioral dyscontrol is added to the depressive disorders for children up to 12 years of age. Its placement in this chapter reflects the finding that children with the symptom pattern typically develop unipolar depressive disorders or anxiety disorders, rather than bipolar disorders, and the mater into adolescence and adulthood." (P. 155)
      2. Summary of diagnostic criteria:
         a. "Severe recurrent temper outbursts manifested verbally ... and/or behaviorally (e.g., physical aggression towards people or property) that are grossly out of proportion in intensity or duration to the situation or provocation."
         b. "The temper outbursts are inconsistent with developmental level."
         c. "The temper outbursts occur, on average, three or more times per week."
         d. "The mood between temper outbursts is persistently irritable or angry most of the day, nearly every day, and is observable by others."

- e. "Criteria A-D have been present for 12 or more months. Throughout that time, the individual has not had a period lasting 3 or more consecutive months without all of the symptoms in Criteria A-D."
- f. "Criteria A through D are present in at least two of three settings (i.e., at home, at school, with peers) and are severe in at least one of these."
- g. "The diagnosis should not be made for the first time before the age of 6 years or after the age of 18 years."
- h. "By history or observation the age of onset of Criteria A-E is before 10 years."
- i. "There has never been a distinct period lasting more than 1 day during which the full symptom criteria, except duration, for a manic or hypomanic episode have been met."
- j. "The behaviors do not occur exclusively during an episode of major depressive disorder and are mnot better explained by another mental disorder (e.g., ASD, PTSD, separation anxiety...)."
  - (1) Note: This diagnosis cannot coexist with ODD, bipolar disorder, or intermittent explosive disorder...
- k. The symptoms are not due to the physiological effects of a substance, or to another medical or neurological condition.

B. **Major Depressive Disorder**

C. Persistent Depressive Disorder (Dysthymia) [New in DSM-5]

D. Premenstrual Dysphoric Disorder

E. Substance/Medication-Induced Depressive Disorder

F. Depressive Disorder Due to Another Medical Condition

G. Other Specified Depressive Disorder
   1. Recurrent brief depression
   2. Short-duration depressive episode
   3. Depressive episode with insufficient symptoms

H. Unspecified Depressive Disorder

II. **Major Depressive Disorder** diagnostic criteria in DSM-5

A. "Five (or more) of the following symptoms have been present during the same 2-week period and represent a change from previous functioning. At least one of the symptoms is either (1) depressed mood, or (2) loss of interest or pleasure."
   1. **Depressed mood** most of the day, nearly every day, as indicated by either subjective report (e.g., feels sad, empty, hopeless) or observation made by others (e.g., appears tearful.) (Note: In children or adolescents can be irritable mood)."

2. Markedly **diminished interest or pleasure** in all, or almost all, activities most of the day, nearly every day (as indicated by either subjective account or observation).
3. **Significant weight loss when not dieting or weight gain** (e.g., a change of more than 5% in body weight in a month), or decrease or increase in appetite nearly every day. (Note: In children consider failure to make expected weigh gains.)
4. **Insomnia or hypersomnia** nearly every day.
5. **Psychomotor agitation or retardation** nearly every day (observable by others, not merely subjective feelings of restlessness or being slowed down).
6. **Fatigue or loss of energy** nearly every day.
7. **Feelings of worthlessness or excessive/ or inappropriate guilt** (which may be delusional) nearly every day (not merely self-reproach or guilt for being sick).
8. **Diminished ability to think or concentrate, or indecisiveness**, nearly every day (either by subjective account opr as observed by others.)
9. **Recurrent thoughts of death** (not just fear of dying), recurrent suicidal ideation without a specific plan, or a suicide attempt or a specific plan for committing suicide.".
    a. About 15% of the seriously depressed eventually commit suicide (30 times the rate for the general population) - risk is greatest in first 5 years after onset. Risk factors include:
       (1) Chronic depression, or depression severe enough to require hospitalization.
       (2) History of previous suicide attempts.
       (3) Family history of suicide.
       (4) Change from inpatient to outpatient status.

B. "The symptoms cause clinically significant distress or impairment in social, occupational, or other important areas of functioning."

C. "The episode is not attributable to the physiological effects of a substance or to another medical condition." [Note: Criteria A through C represent a major depressive episode.]

D. "The occurrence of the major depressive episode is mnot better explained by schizoaffective disorder, schizophrenia, schizophreniform disorder, delusional disorder, or other specified and unspecified schizophrenia spectrum and other psychotic disorders."

E. "There has never been a manic episode or a hypomanic episode." (Unless all the manic or hypomanic-like episodes are substance induced, or are attributable to the physiological effects of another medical condition.)

F. Additional coding with this diagnosis includes:
   1. Whether it is a single or recurrent episode
   2. Its severity and course
      a. Mild
      b. Moderate
      c. Severe
      d. With psychotic features [only if full criteria for major depressive episode are met]
      e. In partial or full remission [only if full criteria for major depressive episode not met]
      f. Unspecified

3. Additional specifiers:
   a. With anxious distress
   b. With mixed features
   c. With melancholic features
   d. With atypical features
   e. With mood-congruent psychotic features
   f. With catatonia
   g. With peripartum onset [postpartum depression]
   h. With seasonal pattern [SAD, for recurrent episode only]

III. **Persistent Depressive Disorder (Dysthymia):** DSM-5 criteria: "This disorder represents a consolidation of DSM-IV-defined chronic major depressive disorder and dysthymic disorder." (P. 168)

   A. "Depressed mood for most of the day, for more days than not, as indicated by either subjective account or observation by others, for at least 2 years. Note: In children and adolescents, mood can be irritable and duration must be at least 1 year."

   B. Presence, when depressed, of two (or more) of the following:"
      1. Poor appetite or overeating
      2. Insomnia or hypersomnia
      3. Low energy or fatigue
      4. Low self-esteem
      5. Poor concentration or difficulty making decisions
      6. Feelings of hopelessness

   C. "During the 2-year period ... of the disturbance, the individual has never been without the symptoms in Criteria A and B for more than 2 months at a time."

   D. "Criteria for a major depressive disorder may be continuously present for 2 years." [In this case, both diagnoses - Major Depression and Persistent Depressive Disorder should be given.]

   E. "There has never been a manic episode or a hypomanic episode, and criteria have never been meet for cyclothymic disorder."

   F. "The disturbance is not better explained by a persistent schizoaffective disorder, schizophrenia, delusional disorder, or other specified or unspecified schizophrenia spectrum and other psychotic disorder."

   G. The symptoms are not due to the effects of a drug or to another medical condition.

   H. "The symptoms cause clinically significant distress or impairment in social, occupational or other important areas of functioning."

Bipolar and Related Disorders

I. In DSM-5, the introduction to this category indicates that it is separated from, and placed between Depressive Disorders and Schizophrenia and Related Disorders because Bipolar and Related Disorders are seen "as a bridge between the two diagnostic classes in terms of symptomatology, family history, and genetics." (P. 123)

II. DSM-5 categories for Bipolar and Related Disorders

    A. **Bipolar I Disorder**
        1. DSM-5 (p. 123) notes that this category "represents the modern understanding of the classic manic-depressive disorder or affective psychosis described in the nineteenth century, differing from that classic description only to the extent that neither psychosis nor the lifetime experience of a major depressive episode is a requirement.."

    B. **Bipolar II Disorder**
        1. DSM-5 (p. 123) notes that this category "requiring the lifetime experience of at least one episode of major depression and at least one hypomanic episode, is no longer thought to be a 'milder' condition than bipolar I disorder, largely because of the amount of time individuals with this condition spend in depression and because the instability of mood experienced by individuals with bipolar II disorder is typically accompanied by serious impairment in work and social functioning."

    C. **Cyclothymic Disorder**
        1. DSM-5 (p. 123) says of this diagnosis that it "is given to adults who experience at least 2 years (for children, a full year) of both hypomanic and depressive periods without ever fulfilling the criteria for an episode of mania, hypomania, or major depression."

    D. Substance/Medication-Induced Bipolar and Related Disorder

    E. Bipolar and Related Disorder Due to Another Medical Condition

    F. Other Specified Bipolar and Related Disorder

    G. Unspecified Bipolar and Related Disorder

III. Description and DSM-5 criteria for Bipolar Disorders:

A. This diagnosis is made for disorder involving mania (unipolar mania was always rare, is now almost unknown, and seems to resemble bipolar mania in terms of clinical course, family history of affective disorder, and treatment response) and depression when there is a previous history of mania or hypomania.

B. For a diagnosis of Bipolar I disorder, DSM-5 requires that the individual have met the following criteria for a manic episode: (p. 124)
    1. "A distinct period of abnormally and persistently elevated, expansive, or irritable mood and abnormally and persistently increased goal-directed activity or energy, lasting at least 1 week and present most of the day, nearly every day (or any duration of hospitalization is necessary.)
    2. "During this period of mood disturbance an increased energy and activity, three (or more) of the following symptoms (four if the mood is only irritable) have persisted, represent a noticeable change from usual behavior, and have been present to a significant degree:"
        a. "Inflated self-esteem or grandiosity."
        b. "Decreased need for sleep (e.g., feels rested after only 3 hours of sleep)."
        c. "More talkative than usual, or pressure to keep talking."
        d. "Flight of ideas, or subjective experience that thoughts are racing."
        e. "Distractibility (i.e., attention too easily drawn to unimportant or irrelevant external stimuli) as reported or observed."
        f. "Increase in goal-directed activity (either socially, at work or school, or sexually) or psychomotor agitation."
        g. "Excessive involvement in activities that have a high potential for painful consequences (e.g., engaging in unrestrained buying spree, sexual indiscretions, or foolish business investments)."
    3. "The mood disturbance is sufficiently severe to cause marked impairment in social or occupational functioning or to necessitate hospitalization to prevent hard to self or others, or there are psychotic features."
    4. "The episode is not attributable to the physiological effects of a substance (e.g., a drug of abuse, a medication, other treatment) or to another medical condition."
    5. "Note: Criteria A-D [1 through 4] constitute a monic episode. At least one lifetime manic episode is required for the diagnosis of bipolar I disorder."
    6. **NOTE**: Although it is **NOT** necessary for this diagnosis that the individual now meets, or has ever met, criteria for a major depressive episode, though cases in which major depressive episodes are present are the norm for this diagnostic category.

C. For a Bipolar II diagnosis, the individual must have met the following criteria for a hypomanic episode. **AND** the criteria for a past or current major depressive episode:

D. DSM-5 described the criteria for a hypomanic episode as follows: (p. 124-125)
    1. "A distinct period of abnormally and persistently elevated, expansive, or irritable mood and abnormally and persistently increased activity or energy, lasting at least 4 consecutive days and present most of the day, nearly every day."
    2. "During the period of mood disturbance and increased energy and activity, three (or more) of the following symptoms (four if the mood is only irritable) have persisted, represent a noticeable change from usual behavior, and have been present to a significant degree."
        a. "Inflated self-esteem or grandiosity"

    b. "Decreased need for sleep (e.g., feels rested after only 3 hours of sleep)."
    c. "More talkative than usual, or pressure to keep talking."
    d. "Flight of ideas, or subjective experience that thoughts are racing."
    e. "Distractibility (i.e., attention too easily drawn to unimportant or irrelevant external stimuli) as reported or observed."
    f. "Increase in goal-directed activity (either socially, at work or school, or sexually) or psychomotor agitation."
    g. "Excessive involvement in activities that have a high potential for painful consequences (e.g., engaging in unrestrained buying spree, sexual indiscretions, or foolish business investments)."
3. "The episode is associated with an unequivocal change in functioning that is uncharacteristic of the individual when not symptomatic."
4. "The disturbance in mood and the change in functioning are observable by others."
5. "The episode is not severe enough to cause marked impairment in social or occupational functioning, or to necessitate hospitalization. If there are psychotic features, the episode is, by definition, manic."
6. "The episode is not attributable to the physiological effects of a substance (e.g., a drug of abuse, a medication, other treatment)."
7. "Note: Criteria A-F [1 through 6] constitute a hypomanic episode. Hypomanic episodes are common in bipolar I disorder but are not required for the diagnosis of bipolar I disorder."

E. DSM-5 describes the criteria for a major depressive episode as follows: (quotations from pp 133-134.

  1. At least five of the following symptoms "have been present during the same 2-week period, and represent a change from previous functioning; at least one of the symptoms is either (1) depressed mood or (2) loss of interest or pleasure."
     a. Depressed mood, most of the day, nearly every day, as indicated by either subjective report (e.g., feels sad, empty or hopeless) of observation made by others (e.g., appears fearful). (Note: In children or adolescents it can be irritable mood.)"
     b. "Markedly diminished interest or pleasure in all, or almost all, activities most of the day, nearly every say (as indicated by ether subjective account or observation.)"
     c. "Significant weight loss when not dieting or weight gain (e.g., a change of more than 5% of body weight in a month), or decrease or increase in appetite nearly every day (Note: In children, consider failure to make expected weight gain.)"
     d. "Insomnia or hypersomnia nearly every day."
     e. "Psychomotor agitation or retardation nearly every day (observable by others; not merely subjective feelings of restlessness or being slowed down.)"
     f. "Fatigue or loss of energy nearly every day."
     g. "Feelings of worthlessness or excessive or inappropriate guilt (which may be delusional) nearly every day (not merely self-reproach or guilt about being sick.)"
     h. "Diminished ability to think or concentrate, or indecisiveness, nearly every day (either by subjective account or as observed by others.)"
     i. "Recurrent thoughts of death (not just fear of dying), recurrent suicidal ideation without a specific plan, a suicide attempt, or a specific plan for committing suicide."

2. "The symptoms cause clinically significant distress or impairment in social, occupational, or other important areas of functioning."
3. "The episode is not attributable to the physiological effects of a substance or another medical condition."

F. In addition to meeting the criteria for a major depressive episode and a hypomanic episode, the diagnosis of bipolar II disorder requires meeting the following additional criteria:
1. No history of a manic episode
2. The symptoms are not better explained by any disorder from the category Schizophrenia and Other Psychotic Disorders.
3. "The symptoms of depression, or the unpredictability caused by frequent alternation between periods of depression and hypomania causes clinically significant distress or impairment in social, occupational, or other important areas of functioning."
4. Additional specifications:
   a. Whether current or most recent episode is hypomanic or depressed
   b. Whether with anxious distress (fearful, tense, restless) or mixed features (manic or hypomanic criteria met, but also depressive features present)
   c. Whether in partial or full remission, if all criteria for depressive or manic/hypomanic episode not met.
   d. Whether mild, moderate or severe in severity.

IV. Cyclothymic Disorder

A. DSM-5 Diagnostic Criteria: (p. 139-140) - very much the same as in DSM-IV TR
1. "For at least two years (at least 1 in children and adolescents) there have been numerous periods with hypomanic symptoms that do not meet criteria for a hypomanic episode and numerous periods with depressive symptoms that do not meet criteria for a major depressive episode."
2. "During the above 2-year period (1 year in children and adolescents), the hypomanic and depressive periods have been present for at last half the time and the individual has not been without the symptoms for more than 2 months art a time."
3. "Criteria for a major depressive, manic, or hypomanic episode have never been met."
4. The symptoms in criterion A [criterion 1] are not better explained by schizoaffective disorder, schizophrenia, schizophreniform disorder, delusional disorder, or other specified and unspecified schizophrenia spectrum and other psychotic disorders."
5. "The symptoms are not attributable to the physiological effects of a substance...or another medical condition."
6. "The symptoms cause clinically significant distress or impairment in social, occupational, or other important areas of functioning."

V. Epidemiology

   A. Major Depressive Disorder:
   1. DSM-5 estimates annual prevalence in U.S. as 7%, with prevalence 3x higher in 18-29-year olds than in individuals over 59 years of age.
   2. DSM-5 estimates female:male ratio in prevalence to be 1.5-3:1 - call it 2:1
   3. Other estimates put point prevalence at 5-9% for females, 2-4% for males; l Lifetime prevalence estimated at 10-25% for women, 5-12% for men.
   4. Age at onset: Ranges from 20's to 50's averaging mid to late-30's.
   5. No bias as a function of social class or race.
   6. Comorbidity: Mostly anxiety disorders, ADHD, ODD, conduct disorder, substance abuse.

   B. **Bromet et al (2011)**: Examined prevalence of major depressive episodes in 18 countries based on face-to-face interviews with 89,000 adults using the WHO's Composite International Diagnostic Interview (CIDI).
   1. Mean annual and lifetime prevalence estimates of DSM-IV MDE were 5.5% and 14.6% in 10 high income countries: (Belgium, France, Germany, Israel, Italy, Japan, Netherlands, New Zealand, Spain, U.S.A.)
   2. Mean annual and lifetime prevalence estimates of DSM-IV MDE were and 5.9% and 11.1% in 8 low-middle income countries: (Brazil, Colombia, India, Lebnanon, Mexico, China, Ukraine)
   3. Mean age of onset 25.7 in high and 24.0 in low-middle income countries.
   4. Female:male ratio was ~ 2:1.
   5. In high income countries, younger age associated with higher 12-month prevalence
   6. In several low-middle income countries, older age was associated with greater likelihood of MDE.
   7. Strongest demographic correlate in high income countries = being separated; in low-middle income countries = being divorced or widowed.

   C. Bipolar Disorder
   1. DSM-5 estimates U.S. annual prevalence of 0.6% for bipolar I, with roughly equal prevalence among makes and females (very slight edge to males).
   2. DSM-5 estimates U.S. annual prevalence of bipolar II disorder to be 0.8%; somewhat lower (ca .3% internationally). No clear indication of gender bias in community samples, but some evidence of preponderance of females in clinical samples.
   3. Lifetime prevalence of bipolar disorder estimated at just under 1%, though this may be an underestimate. 6-month prevalence of manic episode is .7%
   4. Onset about late adolescence or early adulthood. Patients first hospitalized in late 20s or early 30s.
   5. No sex bias, no race bias, somewhat more frequent in higher socioeconomic classes.
   6. Comorbidity: Mostly anxiety disorders, ADHD, ODD, conduct disorder, substance abuse. DSM-5 notes that:
      a. 60% of individuals with bipolar II disorder meet the criteria for 3 other mental disorder:
         (1) 75% have an anxiety disorder (for both Bipolar I and II)
         (2) 37% have substance use disorder

VI. Psychological Etiology in Affective Disorders

   A. **Psychoanalytic Theory**: Freud argued (after Abraham's initial 1911 formulation) saw depression as a reaction to the real, imagined or threatened loss of a love object.
      1. When maternal love withdrawn, individual fixates at the oral stage, and is dependent on oral sources of gratification, and on others to supply emotional gratification.
      2. Individual feels angry toward person who has been lost, and instead of working through the mourning, loosening bond to lost person, depressive turns anger inward to the self, where lost person set up as an introjection. Resulting in dysphoria, guilt, and loss of self-esteem.
      3. So individual reacts to real, potential or perceived loss with depression.
      4. Some evidence that parental loss for reasons other than death leads to depression more than other disorders, but relationship weak.

   B. Learned helplessness, learned hopelessness (**Seligman, 1975; Abramson, Seligman & Teasdale, 1978; Abramson, Metalsky & Alloy, 1989**): We will focus on the 1978 version of the model, though there is a newer (1989) version that your text discusses:
      1. Basic idea is that the individual's interpretation of negative events determines whether individual will experience depression as a result of those events; a particular causal explanations produce depression following negative events:
         a. That the cause of the events is internal to the person rather than something external about the situation. Produces a loss of self-esteem.
         b. That the cause is a stable factor that will persist over time, rather than something that is transitory. Produces chronic depressive symptoms, rather than transitory (if transitory cause assumed).
         c. That the cause is global, and affects a wide range of areas of living rather than specific, and limited to this particular event. (produces pervasive depressive symptoms (compared with circumscribed symptoms if specific causes assumed).

   C. Beck's Cognitive-Behavioral Theory (**Kovacs & Beck, 1978**): Depression results from the activation of specific cognitive distortions (**depressogenic schemata**) that are present in depression-prone people.
      1. Depressogenic schemata relate to experiences concerning self-evaluation and interpersonal relationships.
      2. Once activated by stressor, schemata lead depression-prone people to unrealistically negative and demeaning view of selves, world, and future (the 'cognitive triad').
      3. Depressogenic schemata associated with four systematic errors in logic:
         a. **Arbitrary inference**: Drawing conclusions in the absence of or contrary to evidence.
         b. **Selective abstraction**: Focusing on elements of situation that are most consistent with person's negative views, ignoring other elements.
         c. **Magnification** of negative events or faults and minimization of positive events, attributes and accomplishments.
         d. **Overgeneralization**: Basing far-reaching conclusions on single, minor experiences or incidents.

4. These errors lead to erroneous and exaggerated negative views of self and experiences, and subsequently to depression.

D. General reaction to life events. Depressives report more significant life events before onset of illness than normal controls. **Paykel et al. (1969)** found depressives in New Haven reported 3 times as many events in 6 months before onset as matched controls from local population.

VII. Etiology - the amine hypothesis has dominated thinking for the past 30 years.

A. Original hypothesis argued that depression resulted from functional deficit, and mania from functional excess, of amine neurotransmitter. Three candidates for the monoamine involved:
1. dopamine (catecholamine)
2. norepinephrine (catecholamine)
3. serotonin (5-HT) (indoleamine)

B. How do neurotransmitters work?
1. Synaptic release
2. Activation of receptors
3. Breakdown of transmitter in the synapse:
   a. Degrading enzymes for monoamines = **monoamine oxidase** (MAO) in the presynaptic terminal and in the synaptic cleft, and **catechol-O-methyl transferase** (COMT) are in the synaptic cleft.
4. Reuptake into presynaptic neuron: There is reuptake of transmitters at presynaptic terminals by transporters.

C. Why would we think these amines are involved? Evidence from drug action:
1. Two kinds of antidepressant, tricyclics and monoamine oxidase inhibitors (MAOI) facilitate transmission in aminergic neuron systems.
   a. Tricyclics inhibits the reuptake from synaptic cleft by presynaptic neuron.
   b. MAOI inhibit the oxidation of the amine in the presynaptic storage vesicles.(outer membrane of mitochondria)
   c. Tricyclics, MAO inhibitors, and ECT all reduce the number of post-synaptic beta-adrenergic receptors, and increase response to serotonergic and alpha-adrenergic stimulation.
   d. Chronic lithium (for bipolar disorder):
   (1) Chronic lithium stabilizes midbrain serotonin systems, preventing over activity in serotonergic systems.
      (a) Decreases norepinephrine beta-receptor density, while reducing serotonin receptors in some areas; prevents dopamine receptor supersensitivity.
      (b) Decreases uptake of serotonin precursor tryptophan into nerve endings.
      (c) Increases synthesis of tyrosine hydroxylase, enzyme involved in serotonin synthesis.

- e. Drugs that deplete storage of amines (eg reserpine) may result in severe depression, though recent evidence suggests otherwise.).
- f. Four types of adrenoceptor: Alpha1, Alpha2, Beta1, Beta2. Evidence focuses on A2. Several studies suggesting fewer A2 receptors in depression. But data confusing..

D. Evidence re neurotransmitter metabolites in cerebrospinal fluid (CSF), blood, urine (low levels = low levels of activity in brain).
  1. Evidence for **dopamine** involvement: Metabolite is homovanillic acid (HVA):
     a. L-DOPA, a dopamine precursor, enhances the antidepressant action of phenelzine (an MAO inhibitor), and may precipitate hypomania in bipolar patients.
     b. But HVA no lower in CSF of depressed patients than in controls.
     c. Suggest CSF HVA related to psychomotor state: motorically retarded patients have lower levels.
  2. Evidence for involvement of **serotonin** pathways: Metabolite is 5-hydroxyindoleacetic acid (5-HIAA).
     a. Serotonin precursor tryptophan has antidepressant effects in relatively mild depression.
     b. Bare majority of studies find lower CSF levels of 5HIAA in depressed patients:
     c. Levels of 5-HIAA levels more closely related to:
        (1) suicidal tendencies and suicide (Ashberg et al, 1976). Serotonin levels lower in the brain stems of suicide victims than in control brains.
        (2) impulsivity
        (3) aggression linked to levels.
  3. Evidence for involvement of **norepinephrine** pathways: Metabolite is 3-methoxy-4-hydroxyphenylglycol (MHPG).
     a. Overall, evidence suggests that MHPG levels lower in depressed patients than in controls.
     b. MHPG levels reported as significantly lower in bipolar than in monopolar depression in majority of studies.

E. Since single-transmitter data confusing, perhaps several transmitter systems involved: The **permissive serotonin hypothesis**:
  1. Reduced serotonergic damping of other neurotransmitter systems (esp. norepinephrine or dopamine) allows wider excursions between mania and depression in bipolar illness.
  2. Based partly on reports of low CSF levels of 5-HIAA in both mania and depression, and persistence of low levels after recovery.
  3. Also based on finding that chronic lithium use enhances or stabilizes central serotonin systems.
  4. Based also on some clinical reports of successful prevention of depression with serotonin precursors alone, or combined with lithium.
  5. Hypothesis is improvement over single-transmitter model, since it could account for fact that mania and depression are not always opposites in clinical presentation.

F. Problems with metabolite and other data:
  1. Several drugs (mianserin & iprindole) relieve depression despite having little or no affect on amine reuptake.

2. Neurotransmitters adapt to change in transmitter concentration.
   a. Antidepressants that increase intrasynaptic norepinephrine subsequently cause a decrease (down regulation) in number or functional activity of beta adrenoceptors, some to alpha receptors.

VIII. New view on biochemistry of depression

   A. Several researchers, including Dr. Paul Andrews of McMaster's PNB Department, have argued that in depression, as in anxiety, serotonin levels are too high, not too low Andrews et al, in press). The evidence for this is growing, and includes the observations that:
   1. Serotonin cannot be directly measured in the human brain without invasive techniques
      a. Serotonin cannot cross blood-brain barrier, so peripheral measures of serotonin may not accurately reflect brain levels.
      b. 5-HIAA, the main serotonin metabolite, can cross blood brain barrier, but peripheral measures of 5-HIAA are often contaminated by peripheral sources of 5-HIAA.
   2. Some drugs that inhibit serotonin reuptake (e.g., cocaine, amphetamine) do not relieve depression.
   3. Reserpine, which decreases serotonin, may actually have antidepressant properties (Healy, 2002; Davies and Shepherd, 1955; Price et al., 1987).
   4. SSRIS and other antidepressant medications increase serotonin within hours, (Bymaster et al., 2002; Rutter and Auerbach, 1993), but do not reduce symptoms for several weeks (Charney et al., 1981; Oswald et al., 1972).
   5. Reducing serotonin by reducing tryptophan does not reliably trigger depression in non-depressed individuals (Ruhe et al., 2007).
   6. In rats, neonatal exposure to SSRIs causes depressive symptoms in adulthood. (Ansorge et al., 2004; Hansen et al., 1997).
   7. Genetic downregulation of serotonin transporter (SERT, or 5-HTT) increases synaptic serotonin, and increases depressive symptoms (Holmes et al., 2003).
   8. Meta-analyses suggest that antideressants only slightly more effective than placebos in treating depression (**Fournier et al., 2010; Khan et al., 2011; Khan et al., 2005; Khan et al., 2002; Kirsch et al., 2008**).

IX. Etiology - Neuroendocrine system involvement.

   A. Depressed patients, both mono- and bipolar, often high in cortisol, secreted by adrenal cortex. Cortisol level usually falls to normal upon recovery. In 1970's, this reaction thought to be non-specific reaction to stress, since normals show this increase prior to stressful events.

   B. But recent developments that allow 24-hour monitoring of urinary cortisol level by sampling at 20-30 minute intervals from catheter show that this is not normal stress.

1. In normals, cortisol secretion generally in morning, between 4 am and noon, with low levels otherwise.
2. In depressives, morning peak starts earlier, is more pronounced, and last longer. Seems to be secondary to increased secretion of ACTH by pituitary.

C. Rapid manic-depressive cycling related to reduced thyroid function, which is controlled by HPA axis.

D. Biochemical mechanism of cortisol production:
1. Neurotransmitter (could be acetylcholine, NA, SA, and GABA) stimulates hypothalamus to release corticotropin-releasing-factor (CRF). Transmitter involved depends on particular condition leading to release, such as stress, circadian rhythms, etc.
2. CRF stimulates pituitary to produce adrenocorticotropin (ACTH).
3. ACTH stimulates adrenal glands to produce cortisol.

E. Flurry over dexamethasone (DM) suppression test (DST) for cortisol hypersecretion. DM is synthetic steroid that inhibits ACTH secretion by pituitary, and therefore inhibits cortisol output.
1. In normals DM suppresses cortisol secretion for up to 24 hours.
2. **Carroll et al (1981)**: Reported that 60% of patients with melancholic (endogenous) depression had both high cortisol levels, and failed to show suppression from DST. Claimed that their test had 96% specificity for melancholia, and 67% sensitivity.
3. But **Kocsis et al (1985)**, working with 132 depressives from 6 centers in NIMH Psychobiology of Depression program found no endocrine differences between endogenous and non-endogenous depressions, or between psychotic and non-psychotic depressions.
4. **Berger et al. (1984)**: Studied 231 inpatients at Max Planck Institute in Munich, and reported same results as Kocsis et al. (1985). Reported high incidence of non-suppression from manics, schizophrenics, dementia, and non-endogenous depressions.

F. New test combining DST and corticotropin-releasing hormone (CRH) into the dex/CRH test seems to have better results.
1. Developed in late 1980s (von Bardeleben and Holsboer, 1989) to overcome deficiencies. In DST. "dex/CRH test seems to be more sensitive (i.e. abnormal more often in mood disorder patients) than DST (Heuser et al., 1994) and may reveal HPA axis disturbances not detected by DST.
2. Inject dex at 11 pm, then sample cortisol at 1 pm following day (DST).
3. Same as above for dex/CRH, but inject CRH at 3 pm following day and measure cortisol at 15-min intervals for several hours.
4. "In control subjects, pretreatment with DEX suppresses pituitary–adrenal responses to CRH but in hospitalized depressed patients, the same procedure has been reported to enhance ACTH and cortisol responses (Holsboer et al., 1987; von Bardeleben and Holsboer, 1989). Compared to the standard DST test, the combined DEX/CRH test has a higher sensitivity, of up to 80% (Heuser et al., 1994) and it has been shown that among various parameters such as weight, age and nicotine consumption, only female gender is weakly correlated with the neuroendocrine test response (Kunzel et al.,

2003). It has also been reported that the kind of antidepressant treatment or intake of benzodiazepines do not affect the outcome of the test (Kunzel et al., 2003; Zobel et al., 2001). On the contrary, lithium and carbamazepine interfere with plasma CTH and cortisol concentrations at baseline and under CRH stimulation (review in Kunzel et al., 2003)."

5. **Watson et al (2006)** comparing DST with dex/CRH test found that:
   a. In 82 mood disorder patients and 28 controls, similar cortisol responses on the two tests but ROC analysis showed dex/CRH test had better diagnostic performance.
   b. Sensitivity of delta cortisol (from dex/CRH) was 62% and specificity 71%. Sensitivity of 1500 h cortisol (DST) was 67% and specificity was 48%.
      (1) Sensitivity is % of patients who show suppression of cortisol release on the test.
      (2) Specificity is % of non-patients who do NOT show cortisol suppression on test.
   c. Concluded that both tests measure same pathology but dex/CRH test better for diagnosis.
6. Since 1990, dex/CRH test widely used in studies of depression and bipolar disorder as a dependent variable and predictor. Mixed results relating dex/CRH values to treatment outcomes.
7. **Ising et al (2005)** reported no differences between premorbid dex/CRH results for high-risk relatives of probands who later had depressive episodes and controls - so HPA reactivity not a predictor of subsequent depression.

X. Etiology of Affective Disorders - Genetic/Twin Studies

A. **McGuffin & Katz (1986)** reviewed data from 15 studies over the previous 20 years, finding concordance rates in first-degree relatives of probands ranging from 6-40%, varying with clinical features of the proband's illness, and with age of onset (early onset = 19%, late onset = 10%). [Note: A 'proband' in epidemiological terms is the individual who has the disorder being studied.]

B. Data are complicated by the fact that it appears that bipolar and unipolar disorders are genetically separate. In bipolar (BP) probands, the concordance is higher for BP than for unipolar (UP) probands.
   1. % Risk in 1st-Degree (**McGuffin & Katz, 1986**)
      a. BP probands: concordance for UP = 11.4%; for BP = 7.8% (< 1% BP in population)
      b. UP probands: concordance rate for UP = 9.1%; for BP = 0.6% (3% UP in population)
   2. **McGuffin et al. (2003)**: Concluded that heritability of BP about 85%-90%, with no shared environmental effects. "Fitting a correlated liability model revealed a genetic correlation of 0.65 ... between mania and depression and a correlation of 0.59 ... for nonfamilial environment. Approximately 71% of the genetic variance for mania was not shared with depression. ... As defined by the DSM-IV, BP highly heritable. There are substantial genetic and nonshared environmental correlations between mania and

depression, but most of the genetic variance in liability to mania is specific to the manic syndrome."

C. These studies do not concern neurotic depression (dysthymia or cyclothymia), only major or psychotic forms of depression.

D. Twin studies indicate that MZ concordance rate is 65-75%, and DZ concordance rate is 15-20%.

E. Again, must consider UP-BP distinction.
1. **Allen (1976):** Found MZ concordance rate for UP was 40%, DZ=11%. MZ concordance rate for BP=72%, DZ=14%
2. **Bertelsen et al. (1977)** used Danish twin register to do same sort of study. Zygosity based on blood testing.: with 110 twin pairs: Found MZ concordance rate for UP was 54%, DZ=24%. MZ concordance rate for BP=79%, DZ=19%.
3. Currently believed that transmission is poly- rather than monogenic. Considered that both UP and BP lie on same continuum, with BP the narrower, more severe end.

F. **Betancur C. (2011)** reviewed literature to find genes and genomic imbalances linked to etiology of ASD.
1. Found 103 genes and 44 genomic loci reported in subjects with ASD or autistic behavior.
2. All genes and loci causally implicated in intellectual disability.
3. "these findings clearly show that autism is not a single clinical entity but a behavioral manifestation of tens or perhaps hundreds of genetic and genomic disorders. Increased recognition of the etiological heterogeneity of ASD will greatly expand the number of target genes for neurobiological investigations and thereby provide additional avenues for the development of pathway-based pharmacotherapy.

XI. Treatment of Depression

A. Physical and pharmacological therapies:
1. Tricyclic or heterocyclic antidepressants are treatment of choice for unipolar depression.
   a. Controlled studies clearly demonstrate effectiveness over placebos. Improvement rates over studies range from 50-85%, averaging 65%. [though see recent work by Irving Kirsch at Harvard University suggesting no effect - post YouTube video of 60 Minutes segment]
   b. But tricyclics have cardiovascular side effects: about 5% of patients develop postural hypertension and tachycardia.
   c. About 40% of patients do not respond to medication.
2. Recent research (**Lesperance et al, 2010**) suggests that omega-3 acids nearly as, or as effective as traditional antidepressants for depressed patients without comorbid anxiety disorders, at least over the short term.
3. Rapid-acting, glutamate-based antidepressants.

a. **Diazgranados et al (2010)**. Rapid (within 40 minutes) and through day 3, positive response to intravenous ketamine vs placebo in bipolar depression. 71% of subjects responded to ketamine, 6% to placebo at some point during the trial.
b. (**Berman et al, 2000**; Typically used as general anesthetic for children, in lower doses rapidly relieves depression. Initial clinical studies suggest, ~70% of treatment-resistant patients improved within hours of receiving ketamine. Must be administered intravenously with medical supervision, may cause acute psychotic symptoms. (Also used as a recreational drug: "Special K" or just "K.")
   (1) In rats, ketamine acts on synaptogenic pathway in prefrontal cortex that quickly forms new connections between neurons.
   (2) Found critical point in pathway where enzyme mTOR controls protein synthesis required for new synaptic connections.
c. Scopolamine: Also works on glutamate using synapses, and - like ketamine - produces rapid antipressant effects.
4. **Weeks et al (2013)**: Reported that isoflurane anesthetic might be effective alternative to ECT. therapy (ECT), though early replications of its antidepressant effect failed.
   (1) Studied patients whose depression did not respond to medication, comparing 10 treatments of ECT with same of isoflurane over 3 weeks.
   (2) Depression severity (Hamilton Rating Scale for Depression-24) and neurocognitive responses (anterograde and retrograde memory, processing speed and verbal fluency) assessed Pretreatment, Post all treatments, and at 4-week Follow-up.
   (3) Both treatments produced reductions in depression at Post-treatment and 4-week Follow-up; however, ECT had modestly better antidepressant effect at follow-up in severity-matched patients.
   (4) Immediately Post-treatment, ECT (but not isoflurane) patients showed declines in memory, fluency, and processing speed. At Follow-up, only autobiographical memory remained below Pretreatment level for ECT patients, but isoflurane patients had greater test-retest neurocognitive score improvement.
5. SSRIs
6. MAO inhibitors
7. ECT (EST): Was the first really effective therapy for severe depression. Several studies show higher response rate among endogeneous depression than to tricyclics, especially among more severe cases. Works more rapidly than antidepressants, and has side effects of retrograde amnesia (esp when administered bilaterally) and sometimes anterograde amnesia.
8. Transcranial magnetic stimulation: An experimental approach so far.
   a. **Loo & Mitchell (2005)**: Mostly to left (predominantly) or right prefrontal lobes. Lots of variability in parameters, generally positive results.
9. Deep brain stimulation: VERY new; published in vol. 64,(4) of Biological Psychiatry, 2009.(**Mayberg, 2008**) Stimulation through electrodes implanted in the **nucleus accumbens**.
   a. Located at the underside of the prefrontal lobes, with connections to hypothalamus and amygdala, in addition to prefrontal areas.
   b. Important part of our reward system; involved in reactions to recreational drugs, among other things.

c. "Dopaminergic input thought to modulate activity of neurons in nucleus accumbens. These terminals also site of action of addictive drugs such as cocaine and amphetamine, which cause a increase in dopamine levels in nucleus accumbens. Indeed, almost every recreational drug increases dopamine levels in nucleus accumbens.

B. Psychological therapies
1. Cognitive therapy: Beck

XII. Treatment of Mania

A. Three different drugs used in the treatment of manic episodes:
1. Chlorpromazine
a. Haloperidol
2. Lithium: Not sure how lithium works.
a. May reduce brain inflammation by adjusting metabolism of health-protective omega-3-fatty acid called DHA.
b. Believed that lithium reduces brain inflammation during manic phase, Mireille Basselin and colleagues at the National Institute of Aging and University of Colorado, Denver used mass spectrometry to analyze chemical composition of brain samples of control and lithium-treated rats stressed by brain inflammation.
(1) Found that rats given six-week lithium treatment had reduced levels of arachidonic acid and its products, which can contribute to inflammation.
(2) Also showed lithium increased metabolite 17-OH-DHA in response to inflammation. 17-OH-DHA is formed from the omega-3 fatty acid DHA (docosahexaenoic acid) and is precursor to wide range of anti-inflammatory compounds known as docosanoids.
(3) Other anti-inflammatory drugs, like aspirin, are known to also enhance docosanoids in their mode of action.
(4) Basselin and colleagues noted that concentration of DHA did not increase, which suggests that lithium may increase 17-OH-DHA levels by affecting the enzyme that converts DHA to 17-OH-DHA.
(5) By reducing pro-inflammatory arachnidoic acid products, and increasing anti-inflammatory DHA profaducts, lithium exerts a double-protective effect which may explain why it works well in bipolar treatment.
3. Several studies equivocal on whether any of these is any better than any of the others.

B. Psychological therapies
1. Cognitive therapy: Aaron Beck
a. Depressed patient suffers from unbidden, 'automatic' negative thoughts about themselves, their present lives, and the future.
b. Therapy helps patients recognize those thoughts, and re-evaluate them in light of realistic evidence.

References

Abramson, L.Y., Seligman, M.E.P. & Teasdale, J.D. (1978). Learned helplessness in humans: Critique and reformulation. *Journal of Abnormal Psychology*, 87, 49-74.

Abramson, L.Y., Metalsky, G.I. & Alloy, L.B. (1989). Hopelessness depression: A theory-based subtype of depression. *Psychological Review*, 96, 358-372.

Allen, M.G. (1976). Twin studies of affective illness. *Archives of General Psychiatry*, 33(12), 1476-1478.

Andrews, P., Bharwani, A., Fox, M., & Lee, K. R. (In press). Is serotonin an upper or a downer? An integrated account of the evolution of the serotonergic system and its role in depression and the antidepressant response. In press.

Ansorge, M.S., Zhou, M., Lira, A., Hen, R., Gingrich, J.A (2004). Early-life blockade of the 5-HT transporter alters emotional behavior in adult mice. *Science*, 306, 879-881.

Asberg, M., Traskman, L. & Thoren, P. (1976). 5-HIAA in the cerebrospinal fluid: a biochemical suicide predictor. *Archives of General Psychiatry*, 33, 93-97.

Berger, M., Pirke, K.M., Doerr, P. et al., (1984). The limited utility of the dexamethasone suppression test for the diagnostic process in psychiatry. *British Journal of Psychiatry* 145, 372-382.

Bertelsen, A., Harvald, B. & Hauge, M. (1977). A Danish twin study of manic-depressive disorders. *British Journal of Psychiatry*, 130, 330-351.

Betancur C. (2011) Etiological heterogeneity in autism spectrum disorders: more than 100 genetic and genomic disorders and still counting. *Brain Research*, 2011; 1380: 42–77..

Bymaster, F.P., Zhang, W., Carter, P.A., Shaw, J., Chernet, E., Phebus, L., Wong, D.T., Perry, K.W., (2002). Fluoxetine, but not other selective serotonin uptake inhibitors, increases norepinephrine and dopamine extracellular levels in prefrontal cortex. *Psychopharmacology* 160, 353-361.

Carroll, B.J., Feinberg, M., Greden, J.F., Tarika, J., Albala, A.A., Haskett, R.F., James, N.M., et al (1981). A specific laboratory test for the diagnosis of melancholia. *Archives of General Psychiatry*, 38, 15-22.

Charney, D.S., Menkes, D.B., Heninger, G.R. (1981). Receptor sensitivity and the mechanism of action of antidepressant treatment: Implications for the etiology and therapy of depression. *Archives of General Psychiatry*, 38, 1160-1180.

Davies, D.L., Shepherd, M., (1955). Reserpine in the treatment of anxious and depressed patients. The Lancet 266, 117-120.

Ferster, C.B. (1973). A functional analysis of depression. *American Psychologist,* 28, 857-870.

Fournier, J.C., DeRubeis, R.J., Hollon, S.D., Dimidjian, S., Amsterdam, J.D., Shelton, R.C., Fawcett, J. (2010). Antidepressant drug effects and depression severity: A patient-level meta-analysis. *Jama-Journal of the American Medical Association,* 303, 47-53.

Goldapple, K., Segal, Z., Garson, C., Beiling, P., Lau, M., Kennedy, S. & Mayberg, H. (2004). Modulation of cortical-limbic pathways in major depression: Treatment specific effects of cognitive behavior therapy compared to Paroxetine. *Archives of General Psychiatry.* 61, 34-41.

Hansen, H., Sanchez, C., Meier, E. (1997). Neonatal administration of the selective serotonin reuptake inhibitor Lu 10–134-C increases forced swimming-induced immobility in adult rats: A putative animal model of depression? *Journal of Pharmacology and Experimental Therapeutics,* 283, 1333-1341.

Healy, D., 2002. The creation of psychopharmacology. Harvard University Press, Cambridge, MA.

Holmes, A., Murphy, D.L., Crawley, J.N. (2003). Abnormal behavioral phenotypes of serotonin transporter knockout mice: Parallels with human anxiety and depression. *Biological Psychiatry,* 54, 953-959.

Lewinsohn, P.M. A behavioral approach to depression. In *The Psychology of Depression: Contemporary Theory and Research.* R. Friedman & M. Katz (Eds.), New York: John Wiley, 1974.

Khan, A., Bhat, A., Faucett, J., Kolts, R., Brown, W.A. (2011). Antidepressant-placebo differences in 16 clinical trials over 10 years at a single site: Role of baseline severity. *Psychopharmacology,* 214, 961-965.

Khan, A., Brodhead, A.E., Kolts, R.L., Brown, W.A. (2005). Severity of depressive symptoms and response to antidepressants and placebo in antidepressant trials. *Journal of Psychiatric Research,* 39, 145-150.

Khan, A., Leventhal, R.M., Khan, S.R., Brown, W.A. (2002). Severity of depression and response to antidepressants and placebo: An analysis of the Food and Drug Administration database. *Journal of Clinical Psychopharmacology,* 22, 40-45.

Kirsch, I., Deacon, B.J., Huedo-Medina, T.B., Scoboria, A., Moore, T.J., Johnson, B.T. (2008). Initial severity and antidepressant benefits: A meta-analysis of data submitted to the Food and Drug Administration. *Plos Medicine,* 5, 260-268.

Kocsis, J.H., Davis, J.M., Katz, M.M., Koslow, S.H., Stokes, P.E., Casper, R. & Redmond, D.E. (1985). Depressive behavior and hyperactive adrenocortical function. *American Journal of Psychiatry,* 142, 1291-1298.

Loo, C.K. & Mitchell, P.B. 2005. A review of the efficacy of transcranial magnetic stimulation (TMS) treatment for depression, and current and future strategies to optimize efficacy. Journal of Affective Disorders, 88, 255–267.

Kovacs, M. & Beck, A.T. (1978) Maladaptive cognitive structures in depression. *American Journal of Psychiatry*, 1978, 135, 525-533.

Mahmoud, T. (2001). Serotonin and bipolar disorder. *Journal of Affective Disorders*, 66(1), 1 - 11.

Malone Jr., D.A., Dougherty, D.D., Rezai, A.R., Carpenter, L.L. et al (2009). Deep Brain Stimulation of the Ventral Capsule/Ventral Striatum for Treatment-Resistant Depression. *Biological Psychiatry*, 65 (4), 267-275.

Mayberg, H. (2008). Deep brain stimulation for treatment-resistant depression. *Journal of Affective Disorders*, 107, Supplement 1, S23.

McGuffin, P. & Katz, R. (1986). Nature, nurture and affective disorder. In The Biology of Depression (ed. J. F. W. Deakin). London: Royal College of Psychiatrists, Gaskell Press.

Mendlewicz, J, & Rainer J.D. (1977) Adoption study supporting genetic transmission in manic-depressive illness. *Nature* 268:327–329.

Oswald, I., Brezinova, V., Dunleavy, D.L.F., (1972). On the slowness of action of tricyclic antidepressant drugs. *The British Journal of Psychiatry*, 120, 673-677.

Paykel E.S., Myers, J.K., Dienelt, M.N., Klerman, G.L., Lindenthal, J.J., & Pepper, M.P. (1969). Life events and depression: A controlled study. *Archives of General Psychiatry*, 21, 753-760.

Price, L.H., Charney, D.S., Heninger, G.R., (1987). Reserpine augmentation of desipramine in refractory depression: Clinical and neurobiological effects. *Psychopharmacology* 92, 431-437.

Ruhe, H.G., Mason, N.S., Schene, A.S. (2007). Mood is indirectly related to serotonin, norepinephrine and dopamine levels: A meta-analysis of monoamine depletion studies. *Molecular Psychiatry*, 12, 331-359.

Rutter, J.J., Auerbach, S.B., (1993). Acute uptake inhibition increases extracellular serotonin in the rat forebrain. *Journal of Pharmacology and Experimental Therapeutics* 265, 1319-1324.

Seligman, M.E.P. (1975) *Helplessness: On Depression, Development and Death*. San Francisco: Freeman.

von Bardeleben, U. & Holsboer, F. (1989) Cortisol response to a combined dexamethasone-human corticotropin-releasing hormone (CRH) challenge in patients with depression. *Journal of Neuroendocrinology*. 1, 485–488.

Watson, S., Gallagher, P., Smith, M.S., Ferrier, I.N. & Young, A.H. (2006). The dex/CRH test—Is it better than the DST? *Psychoneuroendocrinology*, 31, 889–894.

Weeks, H.R., Tadler, S.C., Smith, K.W. et al. (2013). Antidepressant and Neurocognitive Effects of Isoflurane Anesthesia versus Electroconvulsive Therapy in Refractory Depression. *PLoS ONE*, 2013; 8 (7): e69809

Zarate Jr., C.A., Singh, J.B., Carlson, P.J., et al. (2006). A Randomized Trial of an N-methyl-D-aspartate Antagonist in Treatment-Resistant Major Depression. *Archives of General Psychiatry*, 63, 856

Other Sources

Abramson, L.Y., Seligman, M.E.P. & Teasdale, J.D. (1978). Learned helplessness in humans: Critique and reformulation. *Journal of Abnormal Psychology*, 87, 49-74.

Schizophrenia Spectrum and Other Psychotic Disorders

I. Introduction: The History of Schizophrenia

   A. The history of understanding mental disorder is first a history of classification and discrimination.

   B. Until 19th century, mental disorders were recognized as being of only two general sorts: Nervous disorders (neuroses) and true madness or insanity. The latter included all cases in which the individual seemed to lose contact with objective reality.

   C. In late 19th century, Emil Kraepelin (1896) distinguished two categories within insanity or madness:
      1. **Manic-depressive psychoses**, which were seen as having a sudden onset and a fluctuating course, but with complete recovery between relapses.
      2. **Dementia praecox** (schizophrenia)
         a. Believed it was a biological disorder that began in adolescence and had no cure.
         b. Perhaps due to chemical imbalance produced by malfunctioning sex glands, which affected nervous system.
         c. Distinguished by the tendency toward a deteriorating course.

   D. In 1911, Eugen Bleuler at Burghölzi clinic of University of Zurich, coined the term **schizophrenia**.
      1. Thought that it was caused by brain disease.
      2. His description emphasized not the course of the disorder, but underlying disturbances in certain psychological processes or functions, and the separation of psychological function and affect.

   E. **Schneider, 1958**: Distinguished so-called first-rank symptoms that distinguished schizophrenia from other psychotic conditions:
      1. Delusions of being controlled by an external force
      2. Delusions of thought insertion, withdrawal, or broadcast to other people
      3. Hallucinatory voices that comment on one's thoughts or actions or that have a conversation with other hallucinated voices

II. Description of symptoms: Characteristic symptoms involving disturbances in several areas:

 A. **Disorders in the Form and Content of thought**:
   1. Form of thought (formal thought disorder):
      a. Loosening of associations
      b. poverty of content in speech
      c. vague abstract speech.
      d. Less common are neologisms, perseveration, clanging.
   2. Thought content:
      a. Multiple, fragmented or bizarre delusions (involving a phenomenon that would be regarded as implausible in the person's culture).
      b. May be persecutory, delusions of reference (objects and people have special negative significance for the individual).
      c. Some delusions more common in schizophrenia than in other disorders:
         (1) Thought broadcast, insertion, withdrawal
         (2) Delusions of external control

 B. **Perception**: Hallucinations most common.
   1. Schneider considered certain kinds of hallucinations as first-rank symptoms of schizophrenia:
   2. Auditory hallucinations: External voices most common.
      a. Audible voices commenting about the patient's behavior, usually negatively
      b. Repeating aloud the patient's thoughts
      c. Commanding behaviors of the individual
      d. Often in treatment, voices move from outside the head to inside, then are experienced as part of the patient's own thoughts.
   3. Other hallucinations
      a. Tactile: tingling or burning sensations
      b. Somatic: Snakes crawling inside the abdomen
      c. Synesthesias
   4. These are found in 28-70% of schizophrenics, also found in 10% of affective disorders, and are not effective in predicting outcome.

 C. **Affect**: Flat or inappropriate affect.

 D. **Sense of self**: 'Loss of ego boundaries' - individual shows perplexity about own identity and/or the meaning of existence, or feels controlled by some outside force.

 E. **Avolition**: Disturbance in self-initiated goal-directed activity. Inadequate interest, inability to follow a course of action to its conclusion. Ambivalence about what course of action to take can lead to paralysis of action. [similar to depression]

 F. **Impaired interpersonal functioning and relationship to the external world**: Social withdrawal, emotional detachment. May be preoccupied with egocentric and illogical ideas and fantasies.

G. **Psychomotor behavior**: Most common in the chronically severe and florid forms of disorder.
   1. May be reduction in spontaneous movement, in extreme, a complete isolation form the environment with rigid posture and resistance to being moved (catatonic stupor)
   2. May make purposeless and stereotyped motor movements unrelated to external stimuli (catatonic excitement). Not very common today.
   3. Waxy flexibility, strange grimaces or odd mannerisms may occur.

H. Associated features: Can include almost any symptom.
   1. Poverty of speech, ritualistic or stereotyped behaviors.
   2. Dysphoric mood, depression, anger
   3. Depersonalization, derealization, delusions of reference

I. Frequent symptoms of schizophrenia:
   1. Lack of insight   - 94%
   2. Blunted affect   - 82%
   3. Asociality   - 79%
   4. Delusions   - 73%
   5. Autism   - 72%
   6. Lack of interest   - 65%
   7. Apathy   - 60%
   8. Thought derailment - 58%
   9. Suspiciousness   - 51%

J. **Andreason & Olsen (1982)** (and most clinicians distinguish between positive and negative symptoms in schizophrenia:
   1. **Positive symptoms**: involve normal functions that have been distorted, or are operating in an excessive manner. Positive symptoms typically include:
      a. Hallucinations
      b. Delusions
      c. Formal thought disorder as indicated by the individual's speech (incoherence, derailment, tangentiality or illogicality)
      d. Bizarre, disorganized, or catatonic behavior
   2. **Negative symptoms**: involve normal functions that have been lost, or reduced in activity. Negative symptoms typically include:
      a. Reduced speech, or reduced speech content (alogia)
      b. Reduced emotional expressiveness (mask-like facial expressions, no emotion in tone of voice, or in body language). (flattened affect)
      c. Anhedonia-asociality (inability to experience pleasure, few social contacts)
      d. Avolition (loss of will)-apathy
   3. This is an important distinction, theoretically, since several attempts to understand the etiology of SZ are based on possible etiological distinctions between these two categories.

III. DSM-5 Treatment of schizophrenia spectrum and other psychotic disorders

   A. Categories for schizophrenia spectrum disorder and other psychotic disorders
      1. Schizotypal (Personality) Disorder
      2. Delusional Disorder
      3. Brief Psychotic Disorder
      4. Schizophreniform Disorder (same criteria as for schizophrenia, but lasting less than 6 months, and without the necessity for diminished functioning)
      5. **Schizophrenia**
      6. Schizoaffective Disorder
      7. Substance/Medication-Induced Psychotic Disorder
      8. Psychotic Disorder Due to Another Medical Condition
      9. Catatonia
         a. Catatonia Associated with Another Medical Condition (Catatonia Specifier)
         b. Catatonia Disorder Due to Another Medical Condition
         c. Unspecified Catatonia
         d. Other Specified Schizophrenia Spectrum and Other Psychotic Disorder
         e. Unspecified Schizophrenia Spectrum and Other Psychotic Disorder

   B. Key features that define the psychotic disorders (described in more detail below)
      1. **Delusions**: Fixed beliefs that don't easily change despite contrary or conflicting evidence.
      2. **Hallucinations**: Perceptions without the presence of corresponding external stimuli. Can occur in any sense, but are most prominent and noticeable in the visual and auditory senses.
      3. Disorganized thinking (and consequent speech):
         a. See [http://www.youtube.com/watch?v=2yUKBnJn4G8]
      4. Grossly disorganized or abnormal motor behavior (including catatonia):
      5. Negative symptoms:
         a. Diminished emotional expression
         b. Avolition
         c. Alogia
         d. Anhedonia
         e. Asociality

IV. DSM-5 Criteria for schizophrenia (p. 99-100)

   A. "Two (or more) of the following, each present fr a significant potion of the time during 1-month period (or less if successfully treated). At least one of these most be (1), (2), or (3)."
      1. Delusions
      2. Hallucinations
      3. Disorganized speech (e.g., frequent derailment or incoherence)
      4. Grossly disorganized or catatonic behavior
      5. Negative symptoms (i.e., diminished emotional expression or avolition)

B. "For a significant portion of the time since of the onset of the disturbance, level of functioning in one or more major areas, such as work, interpersonal relations, or self-care., is markedly below the level achieved prior to the onset (or when the onset is in childhood or adolescence, there is failure to achieve expected level of interpersonal, academic, or occupational functioning)."

C. "Continuous signs of the disturbance persist for at least 6 months. This 6-month period must include at least 1 month of symptoms (or less if successfully treated) that meet Criterion A (i.e., active-phase symptoms) and may include periods of prodromal or residual symptoms. During these prodromal or residual periods, te signs of the disturbance may be manifested by only negative symptoms or by to or more symptoms listed in Criterion A present in an attenuated form (e.g., odd beliefs, unusual perceptual experiences)."
   1. "Prodromal" refers to early symptoms and signs of an illness before the full and characteristic manifestations of the illness appear, and a diagnosis is possible.
   2. In schizophrenia and psychotic disorders, these prodromal signs are varied, but involve disturbances in behavior and thought that precede the full development of symptoms.

D. "Schizoaffective disorder and depressive or bipolar disorder with psychotic features have been ruled out because either 1) no major depression or manic episodes have occurred concurrently with the active-phase symptoms, or 2) if mood episodes have occurred during active-phase symptoms, they have been present for a minority of the total duration of the active and residual periods of the illness."

E. "The disturbance is not attributable to the physiological effects of a substance)e.g., a drug of abuse, a medication) or another medical condition."

F. "If there is a history of autism spectrum disorder or a communication disorder of childhood onset, the additional diagnosis of schizophrenia is made only if prominent delusions or hallucinations, in addition to the other required symptoms of schizophrenia, are also present for at least 1 month (or less if successfully treated)."

V. Course of Schizophrenia

A. **Watt et al. (1983), WHO (1979),** five typical patterns of the disorder:
   1. Pattern 1: One episode, with full recovery. (25% of cases)
   2. Pattern 2: Episodic course, full remission (20% of cases)
   3. Pattern 3: Episodic course, partial remission (25% of cases)
   4. Pattern 4: Episodic course, merging into chronicity (15% of cases)
   5. Pattern 5: Chronic deterioration (15% of cases)

B. Symptom pattern may change with time, with tendency to change from positive to negative symptoms

VI. Incidence and Prevalence of Schizophrenia

   A. Studies on prevalence are problematic:
      1. Lack of common definition of the disorder
      2. Inconsistent use of diagnostic instruments
      3. Different methods of locating cases

   B. Point prevalence:
      1. ECA study in U.S. (Regie et al., 1984) estimated point prevalence at 70/10,000
      2. Point prevalence estimates: about 50-60 per 10,000 in Canada and US

   C. Lifetime prevalence:
      1. DSM-5 estimates lifetime prevalence of .3% to .7%
      2. ECA study in U.S. (Regie et al, 1984) estimated lifetime prevalence at 150/10,000
      3. Recent ECA study (1984), sponsored by NIMH found lifetime prevalence rates of 100-190 per 10,000. No good explanation for the difference between these and earlier estimates.
      4. Lifetime prevalence estimates: 40-80 per 10,000 (Scotland, Iceland, India, Ireland).

   D. Usually appears during adolescence or early adulthood, but may begin in middle or later adult life. Suggestions of earlier onset in males.:
      1. Estimates of male-female ratios run from 1:1 to 2:1 (call it 1.5 male-female ratio).

VII. General Diathesis-Stress Model of the Etiology of SZ: Individual inherits some abnormality that leads to a predisposition to schizophrenia in the presence of some environmental factor or stressor.

   A. What about the diathesis? What is inherited? What is the mode of inheritance?

   B. What about the stress? What is it in the environment (prenatally, postnatally, family relationships, etc.) that causes predisposition to become activated?

VIII. Etiology - Psychological

   A. **Freud's psychoanalytic model**:
      1. Schizophrenia is defect in interpersonal relationships. Withdrawal of libido into self causes individual to be unable to relate to others. Regression of libido into narcissistic focus promotes primitive, primary process thought. Hallucinations, delusions compensate for lack of interpersonal relationships. Unable to make contact with outside world because of libidinal regression. Since patient cannot develop transference, cannot be helped using

psychoanalysis.

IX. Etiology - Sociocultural hypotheses

   A. **Faris & Dunham (1939)**: Indirectly link between low social class and schizophrenia. Found higher rates for mental hospital admissions, including for SZ, in slum areas than in suburban areas. Replicated in other US and European cities. Led to Hare's (1956) 'breeder hypothesis': Stress from social disorganization, poverty, general adverse influences of poor housing breed schizophrenia.

X. Etiology - Neurological disorder or dysfunctions

   A. CAT studies show ventricular enlargement, which is also observed in other disorders, such as Alzheimer's and alcoholism.
      1. Proportion of patients in which ventricular enlargement reported varies widely, from 6% to 60% of patients. One study (**Jernigan et al., 1982**) reported no differences between a population of young SZ and controls.
      2. **Gross et al. (1982)**: Found overall prevalence of 28% ventricular enlargement in SZ patients, but difference between SZ and normals only above age 50.
         a. In general, these symptoms seem to be associated with:
            (1) Poor premorbid functioning
            (2) Age and/or chronicity
            (3) Negative symptoms
            (4) Presence of cognitive impairment
            (5) Poor response to treatment.
         b. Data also suggest that enlarged ventricles associated with history of birth complications and a negative history of psychiatric disorders in other family members.
      3. **Meduri et al. (2010)**: Total lateral ventricle volume, right ventricle volume and left ventricle volume higher in schizophrenia patients than in controls.

   B. Some suggestion schizophrenics more likely to show abnormalities in the asymmetry of brain lateralization, with higher proportion of ambidexterity and sinistrality than normals.

   C. MRI studies show schizophrenics have decrease in cerebral size almost totally due to decrease in size of frontal lobes. Also have smaller craniums. Since this determined during first 2 years, suggests early causality. (prenatal insults, birth injuries, etc.)

   D. Other studies show additional neuroanatomical irregularities in schizophrenia, particularly cell atrophy or loss in hippocampus, limbic and periventricular areas.

E. Higher hippocampal metabolism, and smaller hippocampal size in schizophrenia. **(Schobel et al, 2013)**. Hippocampal hypermetabolism at baseline predicted hippocampal atrophy, which occurred during progression to psychosis.

F. **Kochunov et al (2013)** found cerebral white matter showed accelerated aging in schizophrenia, but not in Major Depressive Disorder. White matter tracts that matured later in life appeared more sensitive to the pathophysiology of schizophrenia

G. Some suggestion that schizophrenics more likely than normals to show abnormalities in the asymmetry of brain lateralization, with higher proportion of ambidexterity and sinistrality than normals.

H. Magnetic Resonance Imaging (MRI) studies show that schizophrenics have decrease in cerebral size that is almost totally due to decrease in size of frontal lobes. Also have smaller craniums. Since this determined during first 2 years, suggests early causality. (prenatal insults, birth injuries, etc.)

I. Some researchers (one at least) argue that schizophrenia may be produced by genetic transmission or by perinatal damage resulting (among other things) in ventricular enlargement.

XI. Etiology - Differences in Brain Activity Patterns

A. Studies of cerebral blood flow in normals indicates a pattern of higher activity in frontal lobes, with a gradient of decrease to posterior parts of brain.

B. Similar studies with schizophrenics suggest a **hypofrontality syndrome**, in which activity is significantly lower in the frontal lobes, and higher in posterior areas, than in normals.

C. EEG studies of brain wave patterns:
 1. Several studies support the conclusion that SZ associated with left hemisphere abnormalities, while affective disorders associated with right hemisphere abnormalities. **Coger et al (1979)**, among others, reports increased beta activity in left temporal and frontal areas in SZ.
 2. **Walker & McGuire (1982)** report increased EEG variability from temporal lobes, more power in higher frequencies in left hemisphere, less left hemisphere alpha. Also report SZ activation of non-dominant hemisphere regardless of nature of task.
 3. Report of increased frontal system delta activity in schizophrenics.

D. Evoked potentials (EPs) - brain waves elicited in response to presented stimuli. Special attention paid to P300 component, a large amplitude positive wave peaking between 275-450 msec after stimulus presentation, maximal in parietal regions. Argued to be relatively stimulus independent, and to be related to attention on task, or to significance of stimulus.
 1. Found to be lower in SZ than in normals (**Roth & Cannon, 1972**)

2. Increases in normals when prediction of nature of next stimulus required, but not so in SZ (**Levit et al., 1973**)
3. Increases in normals when incentives given for speed or accuracy of detection. Not so in SZ (**Brecher & Begleiter, 1983**), despite no normal-SZ differences in speed or accuracy. Suggests it is not a deficit on conscious attention or relevance.
4. **Morihasa et al. (1983)**: Used BEAM (Brain Electrical Activity Mapping) to examine both EP and EEG data. Argue that data consistent with the view that the SZ cortex is 'irritable' if not epileptogenic.

E. **Fuster (1980)**: Injury to prefrontal cortex leads to symptoms like negative symptoms of SZ:
1. Disorders of cognitive function:
   a. concreteness
   b. impaired attention
   c. trouble with categorization and abstraction
2. Diminished spontaneity in speech
3. Decrease in voluntary motor behavior
4. Decreased will and energy
5. Abnormalities of affect and emotion.

F. Other schizophrenia symptoms like those in temperolimbic disease:
1. Auditory hallucinations.
2. Disorganized speech.
3. Note that dopaminergic system drives substantial part of the limbic system.

XII. Etiology: Viral Agents

A. Suggested primarily by the tendency of SZ patients to be born during the winter months. This seasonal effect has been known for some time. (See, e.g., **Watson, 1990; Torrey & Bowler, 1990; Pulver et al., 1990**, and on the other side **Lewis, 1990**)
1. Excess of winter (December to April) births in SZ compared with normal controls averages about 15%.
2. Overage in Australia occurs during June through August (**Jones & Frei, 1979**)
3. Not due to pattern of parental procreation, since siblings of SZ offspring show no such effect.

B. Differences within the winter season effect:
1. **Machon et al. (1983)**: Reasoned that if viral infection responsible, then incidence of SZ should be higher in high-risk individuals (those with familial SZ) born in the city - where viral exposure higher - as opposed to the country. Using Danish sample of **Mednick & Schulsinger (1968)**, found following: (% high risk Ss diagnosed SZ as function of time and place of birth)

(1)	Urban	Non-Urban	
(2) Winter	23%	0%	(15.2%)
(3) Non-winter	8.4%	6.3%	(7.8%)

C. Several viruses peak in winter and spring, including influenza, rubella and measles.

D. In general population, maternal viral infections are associated with a number of congenital abnormalities, including those of CNS (**Coffey & Jessop, 1959**)

E. **Tyrell et al (1979)** and **Albrecht et al. (1980)** reported elevated levels of antibodies to common viruses in the CSF of SZ compared with non-psychiatric patients and normals

F. **Soderlund et al. (2009):** Found that patients with recent-onset schizophrenia have higher levels of interleukin-1beta, which is released in response to inflammation. Barely measurable in healthy control patients. Suggests brain's immune defense system activated in schizophrenia. Perhaps due to infection?
   1. Major hypothesis relates schizophrenia to overactive dopamine system, and studies show interleukin-1beta can upset dopamine system in rats in similar way to schizophrenia in humans.
   2. Question now under investigation is whether the inflammatory process only activated in schizophrenia, or in other chronic disorders.

G. **Ellman et al. (2010)**: In schizophrenia, fetal exposure to increased IL-8 (mother's response to infections) in trimesters 2 and 3 associated with:
   1. increases in ventricular cerebrospinal fluid
   2. decreases in left entorhinal cortex volumes
   3. decreases in right posterior cingulate volumes.
   4. Decreases approaching significance found in volume of:
      a. right caudate
      b. the putamen (bilaterally)
      c. the right superior temporal gyrus.
   5. No significant associations observed among controls.
   6. Concluded fetal exposure to high maternal IL-8 = structural neuroanatomic alterations in brain regions implicated in schizophrenia. In utero exposure to high IL-8 may partially account for brain disturbances common in schizophrenia.

H. **Canetta et al (2014)** found maternal C-reactive protein levels (a reliable biomarker for inflammation) associated with schizophrenia in offspring (adjusted odds ratio=1.31. Relationship was significant even after adjusting for parental history of psychiatric disorders, urbanicity, and maternal socioeconomic status."

XIII. Etiology - Perinatal Complications: The argument is that individuals with a genetic predisposition to SZ may be triggered or moved toward the threshold by stresses associated with birth complications.

XIV. Etiology - Biochemical: The dopamine hypothesis

   A. Some believe that most promising avenue lies in neurochemistry, particularly in parts of the brain that use dopamine as a transmitter. The argument is that these pathways are **overactive** in schizophrenia.

   B. Dopamine is a monoamine neurotransmitter, like dopamine, serotonin (5-HT) and norepinephrine, and is a catecholamine

   C. Evidence from the action of neuroleptic drugs:
      1. Drugs (phenothiazines such as chlorpromazine) that are most effective in reducing symptoms of SZ produce greatest blockade of dopamine receptors in animals.
         a. But action of phenothiazines also seen in manics and other acute psychotics.
         b. Not all schizophrenics respond to phenothiazine.
         c. Effect may be indirect
      2. Dopamine antagonists, like reserpine, reduce symptoms of SZ, though with strong side effects, so rarely used clinically.
      3. Dopamine agonists increase symptoms of schizophrenia; amphetamine overdose leads to amphetamine psychosis similar to paranoid SZ.

   D. Problems with the hypothesis and drug effects:
      1. **Van Kammen et al. (1981)** Lit review through 1981 suggests picture not quite clear.
         a. In 12 studies, only 72/285 (25%) patients showed worsened symptoms after amphetamine administration; 81 (28%) improved; 132 (46%) no change.
         b. **Haracz (1982)** agrees, noting the wide variability in response to administration of dopamine agonists across 24 studies.
      2. Administration of MAO inhibitors, which should indirectly increase dopamine by inhibiting MAO, does not reliably exacerbate SZ symptoms. **Brenner & Shopsin (1980)** reviewed 14 studies involving large numbers of SZ patients and found 71% unchanged, 26% improved, only 3% worsened with MAO-I administration.

   E. But recent evidence:
      1. **Hart et al (2014)** found that SNPs associated with decreased susceptibility to schizophrenia (and to ADHD) overlap with set of SNPs that create the euphoric response to d-amphetamine.
      2. "These results reinforce idea that dopamine plays role in schizophrenia and ADHD. ... we found that alleles associated with increased euphoric response to d-amphetamine were associated with decreased risk for schizophrenia and ADHD."

XV. Dopamine receptors?

   A. Overall, data suggest hyperactivity of dopaminergic pathways in SZ. Is it too much dopamine,

or something to do with the receptors?
1. Failure to find excess of dopamine metabolites (esp homovanillic acid - HVA) in cerebrospinal fluid of schizophrenia suggests problem with receptor rather than transmitter neurons.

B. Two types of dopamine receptors on post-synaptic neurons, D1 and D2. Most clinically effective drugs produce more D2 than D1 blockade.

C. Data from dopamine studies also suggest distinction between different types of SZ:
1. **Crow et al. (1982)**: Compared the action of alpha- and beta-flupenthixol and a placebo on SZ symptoms. Alpha- selectively blocks D2 receptors, while beta is much less specific.
   a. Found that beta- and a placebo both had little effect on either positive or negative symptoms.
   b. Alpha- D2 blockade selectively reduced positive symptoms such as hallucinations, delusions and disorganized speech, but had little effect on negative symptoms such as blunted affect or poverty of speech.
2. Likewise, clinical studies suggest that antipsychotics (phenothiazines neuroleptics) are particularly effective in reducing positive symptoms such as delusions and hallucinations.
   a. **Crow (1980)** suggests distinction between Type 1 and Type 2 and two mechanisms:
   b. Type1: Positive symptoms, usually acute, no structural brain damage, good prognosis. Seen to be primarily due to hyperdopaminergic activity.
   c. Type 2: Negative symptoms, intellectual impairment, poor prognosis. Seen as due to some other mechanism such as neuron loss.

XVI. Etiology of Schizophrenia - Genetic

A. Twin studies consistently demonstrate high concordance rates for schizophrenia among MZ twins compared to DZ twins. Range of MZ-DZ rates is moderately large from different studies: (all using systematic registers)
1. **Kringlen (1967)**: MZ=45%; DZ=15%
2. **Pollin et al (1969)**: MZ=43%; DZ=9%
3. **Gottesman & Shields (1972)**: MZ=58%; DZ=12%
4. **Fischer (1973)**: MZ=56%; DZ=26%
5. **Gottesman & Shields (1982)**. MZ = 46%; DZ = 14%

B. Family study methods
1. Rates of schizophrenia much higher in families of probands than in population at large. Lifetime risk for various relatives of schizophrenics (**Gottesman & Shields, 1982**)
   a. Child (both parents affected): 46%
   b. Child (one parent affected): 12%
   c. Child (one parent, one sib): 17%
   d. Siblings: 10%
   e. Parent of schizophrenic: 6% **

        f. Grandchild: 4%
        g. Uncle/aunt/niece/nephew: 3%
        h. Unrelated: ca 1%
    2. Why is rate in parents of a schizophrenic so low?
        a. One argument is that SZ reduces individual's ability to marry, so parents of SZ are likely to be unaffected carriers, or have children before disorder develops.
        b. When one parent of proband affected, is likely to be mother.

C. Genes involved?
    1. Several strong linkages have emerged.
        a. Best-supported regions: 6p24-22, 1q21-22 and 13q32-34
        b. Other promising regions include 8p21-22, 6q21-25, 22q11-12, 5q21-q33, 10p15-p11 and 1q42.
        c. Specific genes: [**DO NOT** try to learn these!]
            (1) NRG1 (neuregulin-1 on chromosome 8p21)
            (2) DTNBP1
            (3) COMT (catechol-O-methy transferase) at 22q11: Inactivates catecholamine transmitters
            (4) RGS4
            (5) G72/G30 (13q33):
            (6) PRODH, proline dehydrogenase (22q11):
            (7) DISC1 (Disrupted in Schizophrenia 1): Located in 1q42. Not known whether its expression is altered in schizophrenia.
            (8) MUTED : ZDHHC8 (zinc finger DHHC domain-containing protein 8)
            (9) OLIG2 (oligodendrocyte lineage transcription factor 2)
            (10) GLUR7, CACNG2, AKAP5 - involved in glutamate signaling.
            (11) DAOA/G30: DAO: AKT1: CNP: GRM3 (glutamate receptor 3 gene)
            (12) SEMA6A (Semaphorin6A): PLXNA2: PPP3CC
            (13) CHRNA7, DRD3; ERBB4, GABRB2, GRID1, GRIK3, GRIK4, GRIN2B, HTR2A, NCAM1, NEUROG1, NOTCH4, SLC1A2, SLC6A3,
    2. "the genetic signature of schizophrenia, much like autism, is more complicated than that, involving dozens or even hundreds of genes, whose function has been disrupted by duplications or deletions of DNA." (**Walsh et al., 2008**) (http://www.abc.net.au/science/articles/2008/03/28/2201595.htm)
    3. **Girard et al. (2011a):** Montreal researchers and many colleagues identify de novo SNP mutations in a number of genes found in patients with schizophrenia, but not in either of their parents. Genes implicated include:
        a. ZNF565; NRIP1; LRP1; CCDC137
        b. KPNA1; ZNF480; EIF5; ALS2CL
        c. CHD4; KDM2B; LAMA1; CASP4
        d. SDF4; PIK3CB; SBNO1
    4. **Stefansson et al. (International Schizophrenia Consortium) (2009):** Genome-wide association study (GWAS) of 3,322 European individuals with schizophrenia and 3,587 controls. Show that common genetic variation underlies schizophrenia risk.
        a. Implicate the major histocompatibility complex.
        b. Evidence for substantial polygenic component to schizophrenia risk involving

thousands of common alleles of very small effect.
c. Also show that this component contributes to risk of bipolar disorder.
5. **Girard et al (2011a)** estimated that GWAS implicated more than 1,000 genes in the etiology of schizophrenia, but that additional genetic effects existed but remained unidentified.
6. **Aberg et al (2013)** integrated results from meta-analysis of 18 genome-wide association studies (GWAS) involving over 1,000,000 SNPs. 8,107 most promising SNPs genotyped in independent family-based replication study. Replication results showed a highly significant enrichment of SNPs with small effects.
   a. Replicated SNPs in TCF4, NOTCH4 that are among the most robust SCZ findings.
   b. More novel findings included POM121L2, AS3MT, CNNM2, NT5C2.
   c. The most significant pathways involved neuronal function (axonal guidance, neuronal systems, and L1 cell adhesion molecule interaction) and the immune system (antigen processing, cell adhesion molecules relevant to T cells, and translocation to immunological synapse).
7. **Timms et al (2013).** performed genome-wide array comparative genomic hybridization, linkage analysis, and exome sequencing in multiplex families with schizophrenia.
   a. Analysis of select variants was performed in cultured cells to assess their functional consequences.
   b. In all families, exome sequencing detected rare protein-altering variants in 1 of 3 genes associated with the N-methyl-D-aspartate (NMDA) receptor. Genes involved included GRM5, PPEF2, LRP1B, all involved with glutamate signalling.
8. **Lett et al (2013)** examined influence of genome-wide schizophrenia risk variant rs1625579 near MIR137 gene on age-at-onset of psychosis and brain structure.
   a. MIR137 risk genotype strongly predicts earlier age-at-onset of psychosis across four different samples of schizophrenia patients.
   b. In subsample including matched controls, patients with schizophrenia who had MIR137 risk variant had reduced white matter integrity throughout the brain, smaller hippocampi and larger lateral ventricles
   c. Brain structure of patients who carried protective allele was same as healthy controls.

XVII. Mode of Transmission if Schizophrenia is Genetic

A. Debate about monogenic vs polygenic etiology still goes on, and is apparent in recent reviews:
   1. **Mullan & Nurray (1989), Pardes et al. (1989)** focus on single-gene models.
   2. **Reiss et al (1991)**, and **Risch (1990)** argue that these reviews are one-sided, ignore environmental contributions, and are incompatible with a large body of data.

B. Data most consistent with polygenic mode of inheritance, with inheritance of susceptibility in the presence of certain environmental conditions. Explains several features of SZ:
   1. Dimension of severity (number of genes possessed).
   2. Concordance higher for probands with severe chronic schizophrenia rather than milder forms.

3. Higher risk for individuals with more than one relative affected.
4. Persistence of schizophrenia in the population despite low reproductive rate of schizophrenics (each gene itself is normal, only the combination is pathogenic).

XVIII. New look: Schizophrenia and Copy Number Variations (CNV)

A. Two kinds of genetic differences:
1. **Single Nucleotide Polymorphism (SNPs)**: Difference in one base pair (e.g., C-G rather than A-T) in a gene sequence, or non-gene sequence, inter-gene sequence.
2. **Copy Number Variations (CNVs)**: Chunks of DNA missing (deletions), or duplicated (insertions).

B. Recent interest in **rare copy number variations** as a substrate for schizophrenia:
1. Especially 1q21.1; 15q11.2; 15q13.1, 15q13.3, 3q29, 16p11.2, 22q11.2
2. Maybe it's the number rather than the location of CNVs; more in schizophrenia.

XIX. Treatment Approaches:

A. Pharmacological agents: Antipsychotics (neuroleptics). No dose-response curve for these drugs, even 30 years after their introduction.
1. Tardive dyskinesia: "neurological syndrome caused by long-term use of neuroleptic drugs. ... characterized by repetitive, involuntary, purposeless movements. Features of the disorder may include grimacing, tongue protrusion, lip smacking, puckering and pursing, and rapid eye blinking. Rapid movements of the arms, legs, and trunk may also occur. Involuntary movements of the fingers may appear as though the patient is playing an invisible guitar or piano." (http://www.ninds.nih.gov/disorders/tardive/tardive.htm)

B. Electroconvulsive therapy: Introduced in 1938, after found that patients with affective disorders were improved after spontaneous seizures.
1. Only about 17% of those given ECT have schizophrenia.
2. **May et al (1976)** found that ECT better than psychoanalytic or milieu therapy, but worse than antipsychotics in institutionalized chronic schizophrenics.
3. Primarily used in catatonia, secondary depression superimposed on schizophrenia, and for those not responding to antipsychotics.
4. Several studies suggest that ECT has only short-lived benefits to acute schizophrenics, and is not of practical importance in such cases. (**Brandon et al., 1985**)

C. **Individual psychotherapy**: Long-term studies suggest it to be of little value in treating chronic schizophrenia compared with ECT, antipsychotics or milieu therapy. But therapeutic relationship important in helping patient develop new coping strategies.

D. **Group psychotherapy**: Generally oriented toward providing support, and environment in which patient can develop social skills, and format to allow friendships to begin. Seeking of insights may be counterproductive.

E. **Family therapy**: Has focused on families that show high expressed emotion. Studies suggest that, combined with antipsychotics, can be valuable in preventing relapse.

XX. Etiology Summary:

A. In 2008, Tandon, Keshavan & Nasrullah summarized our understanding of the etiology of schizophrenia this way:
   1. "its causes and pathogenesis remain obscure." (P. 1)
   2. It runs in families, and incidence varies, with "urbanicity, male gender, and a history of migration being associated with a higher risk for developing the illness." (P. 1)
   3. "Genes and gene-environment interactions contribute over 80% of the liability for developing schizophrenia", but "no single gene variation has been consistently associated with a greater likelihood of developing the illness and the precise nature of the genetic contribution remains obscure ..."
   4. There are a number of environmental factors associate with increased risk of developing schizophrenia, and these include:
      a. Marijuana use
      b. prenatal infection or malnutrition
      c. perinatal complications
      d. a history of winter birth
   5. "the exact relevance or nature of these contributions is, however, unclear", and "how various genetic and environmental factors interact to cause schizophrenia and via which precise neurobiological mechanisms they mediate this effect is not understood."
   6. "The ability to question some of our basic assumptions about the etiology and nature of schizophrenia and greater rigor in its study appear critical to improving our understanding about its causation." (**Tandon, Keshavan & Nasrallah, 2008**), p. 1.

References

Aberg, K.A. et al (2013) A Comprehensive Family-Based Replication Study of Schizophrenia Genes. *JAMA Psychiatry*, 70(6), 573-581.

Albrecht, P., Torrey, E.F., Boone, E., Hicks, J.T. & Daniel, N. (1980). Raised cytomegalovirus-antibody level in cerebrospnal fluid of schizophrenic patients. *Lancet*, ii, 767-772.

Andreassen, N.C. & Olsen, S. (1982). Negative and positive schizophrenia. *Archives of General Psychiatry*, 39, 89-794.

Andreason, N.C., Smith, M.R., Jacoby, C.G., Dennert, J.W. & Olsen, S.A. (1982). Ventricular enlargement in schizophrenia: Definition and prevalence. *American Journal of Psychiatry*, 139, 292-296.

Barch, Deanna M. (2005). The Cognitive Neuroscience of Schizophrenia. *Annual Review of Clinical Psychology*, 1:321-354

Bateson, G., Jackson, D.D., Haley, J. & Weaklund, J.H. Toward a theory of schizophrenia. (1956). *Behavioural Science*, 1, 251-264.7

Birchwood, M., Hallett, S. & Preston, M. (1988). *Schizophrenia: An Integrated Approach to Research and Treatment*. London: Longmans.

Boklage, C.E. (1977). Schizophrenia, brain asymmetry development and twinning: Cellular relationship with etiological and possibly prognostic implications. *Biological Psychiatry*, 12, 19-35.

Brandon, S., Gonley, P., McDonald, C., Neville, P., Palmer, R. & Wellstood-Eason, S. (1985). Leicester ECT trials: Results in schizophrenia. *British Journal of Psychiatry*, 146, 177-183.

Brecher, M. & Begleiter, H. (1983). Event-related brain potentials to high incentive stimuli in unmedicated schizophrenic patients. *Biological Psychiatry*, 18, 661-674.

Brenner, R. & Shopsin, B. (1980). The use of monoamine oxidase inhibitors in schizophrenia. *Biological Psychiatry*, 15, 633-647.

Brown, G.W., Monck, E.M., Carstairs, G.M. & Wing, J.K. (1962). Influence of family life on the course of schizophrenic illness. *British Journal of Preventive and Social Medicine*, 16, 55-68.

Canetta, S., Sourander, A., Surcel, H-M., Hinkka-Yli-Salomäki, S., Leiviskä, J., Kellendonk, C., McKeague, I.W., Brown. A.S. (2014). Elevated Maternal C-Reactive Protein and Increased Risk of Schizophrenia in a National Birth Cohort. *American Journal of Psychiatry*, early publication.

Cannon, T.D., Mednick, S.A. & Parnas, J. (1990). Antecedents of predominantly negative- and predominantly positive-symptom schizophrenia in a high-risk population. *Archives of General Psychiatry*, 47(7) 622-632.

Coffey, V.P. & Jessop, W.J.E. (1959). Maternal influences and congenital deformities: A prospective study. *Lancet*, 11, 935-938.

Cook, E.H. & Scherer (S.W. (2008). Copy-number variations associated with neuropsychiatric conditions. *Nature*, 455, 919-923.

Coger, R.W., Dymond, A.M. & Serafetinides, E.A. (1979). Electroencephalographic similarities between chronic alcoholics and chronic, non-paranoid schizophrenics. *Archives of General Psychiatry*, 36, 91-94.

Crow, T.J., Cross, A.J., Johnstone, E.C. & Owne, T. (1982). Two syndromes in schizophrenia and their pathogenesis. In F.A. Henn & H.A. Nasrallah (Eds.) *Schizophrenia as a Brain Disease*. New York: Oxford Univ. Press.

Crow, T.J. (1980). Molecular pathology of schizophrenia: More than one disease process? *British Medical Journal*, 280, 66-68.

Eagles, J.M. (1992). Are polioviruses a cause of schizophrenia? *British Journal of Psychiatry*, 160, 598-600.

Farde, L., Wiesel, F-A., Hall, H., Halldin, C., Stone-Elander, S. & Sedvall, G. (1987a). D2-receptor increase in PET-study of schizophrenia. *Archives of General Psychiatry*, 41:671-672.

Farde, L., Halldin, C., Stone-Elander, S. & Sedvall, G. (1987b). PET-analysis of human dopamine receptor subtypes using 11C-SCH23390 and 11C-raclopride. *Psychopharmacology*, 92, 278-284.

Faris, R.E.L. & Dunham, H.N. (1939). *Mental Disorders in Urban Areas*. Chicago: University of Chicago Press.

Fischer, M. (1973). Genetic and environmental factors in schizophrenia. ***Acta Psychiatrica Scandinavica (Supplement)***, 238.

Fuster, J.M. (1980). *The Prefrontal Cortex*, Raven Press, New York.

Girard, S.L. et al (2011). Increased exonic *de novo* mutation rate in individuals with schizophrenia. *Nature Genetics* (letters, published online 10 July 2011).

Golden, C.J., Moses, J.A., Zelazowski, M.A., Graber, B., Zataz, L.M., Horvath, T.B. & Berger, P.A. (1980). Cerebral ventricle size and neuropsychological impairment in young chronic schizophrenics. *Archives of General Psychiatry*, 37, 619-623.

Gottesman, I.I. & Shields, J. (1972). *Schizophrenia and Genetics: A Twin Study Vantage Point*. New York: Academic Press.

Gottesman, I.I. & Shields, J. (1982). *Schizophrenia: The Epigenetic Puzzle*. Cambridge: Cambridge University Press.

Gross, G., Huber, G. & Schuttler, R. (1982). Computerised tomography studies on schizophrenic diseases. *Arch. Psychiatr. Nervenkr.*, 231, 519-526.

Haracz, J.L. (1982). The Dopamine Hypothesis: An Overview of Studies With Schizophrenic Patients. *Schizophrenia Bulletin*, 8(3), 438-469.

Hart, A.B., Amazon, E.R., Engelhardt, B.E. Sklar, P., Kohler, A.K., Hultman, C.M., Sullivan, P.F., Neale, B.M., Faraone, S.V., Psychiatric Genomics Consortium: ADHD Subgroup; de Wit, H., Cox, N. J. & Palme, A.A. (2014), Genetic variation associated with euphorigenic effects of d-amphetamine is associated with diminished risk for schizophrenia and attention deficit hyperactivity disorder. PNAS, early edition.

Heston, L.L. (1966). Psychiatric disorders in foster home reared children of schizophrenic mothers. *British Journal of Psychiatry*, 112, 819-825.

International Schizophrenia Consortium (2008) Rare chromosomal deletions and duplications increase risk of schizophrenia. *Nature*, 455:237–241.

International Schizophrenia Consortium (2009). Common variants conferring risk of schizophrenia.. *Nature*, online July 1, 2009.

Jernigan, T.L., Zatz, L.M., Moses Jr., J.A. & Berger, P.A. (1982). Computed tomography in schizophrenics and normal volunteers. 1: Fluid volume. *Archives of General Psychiatry*, 39, 765-770.

Jones, I.H. & Frei, D. (1979). Seasonal births in schizophrenia: A southern hemisphere study using matched pairs. *Acta Psychological Scandinavica*, 59, 164-172

Kety, S.S., Rosenthal, D., Wender, P.H., Schulsinger, F. & Jacobsen, B. (1975). Mental illness in the biological and adoptive families of adopted individuals who have become schizophrenic: A preliminary report based on psychiatric interviews. In R.R. Fieve, D. Rosenthal & H. Brill (Eds.), *Genetic Research in Psychiatry*. Baltimore: Johns Hopkins University Press. Pp. 147-165.

Kringlen, E. (1967). *Heredity and Environment in the Functional Psychoses*. London: Heinemann.

Kyriakopoulos, M., et al (2009). Effect of age at onset of schizophrenia on white matter abnormalities. *The British Journal of Psychiatry*, 2009; 195 (4).

Lett, T.A., Chakavarty, M.M., Felsky, D., Brandl, E.J., Tiwari, A.K. et al (2013). The genome-wide supported microRNA-137 variant predicts phenotypic heterogeneity within schizophrenia. *Molecular Psychiatry*, 2013; 18, 443-450.

Levit, R.A., Sutton, S. & Zubin, J. (1973). Evoked potential correlates of information processing in psychiatric patients. *Psychological Medicine*, 3, 487-494

Lewis, M.S. (1990). Res Ipsa Loquitor: The author replies. *Schizophrenia Bulletin*, 16(1) 17-28.

Lidz, T., Hotchkiss, G. & Greenblatt, M. (1957). Patient-family hospital inter-relationships: Some general considerations. In M. Greenblatt, D. Levinson & R. Williams (eds). *The Patient and the Mental Hospital*. Glencoe, Ill: The Free Press.

Machon, R.A., Medmick, S.A. & Schulsinger, F. (1983) The interaction of seasonality, place of birth, genetic risk and subsequent schizophrenia in a high risk sample. *British Journal of Psychiatry*, 143, 383-388.

May, P.R.A., Tuma, A.H., Yale, C, Potepan, P. & Dixon, W.J. (1976). Schizophrenia: A follow-up study of results of treatment: II Hospital stay over two to five years. *Archives of General Psychiatry*, 33, 481-486.

McGue, M. (1992). When assessing twin concordance, use the probandwise not the pairwise rate. *Schizophrenia Bulletin*, 18(2) 171-176.

McNeil, T.F. & Kaij, L. (1978). Obstetric factors in the development of schizophrenia: Complications in the births of preschizophrenics and in reproduction by schizophrenic parents. In L.C. Wynne, R.L. Cromwell & S. Mathysse (Eds.). *The Nature of Schizophrenia: New Approaches in Research and Treatment*. New York: Wiley.

Mednick, B.R. (1973). Breakdown in high-risk subjects: Familial and environmental factors. *Journal of Abnormal Psychology*, April 22, 2009, 82, 469-475.

Mednick, S.A. (1970). Breakdown in individuals at high risk for schizophrenia: Possible predisposisional perinatal factors. *Mental Hygiene*, 54, 50-63.

Mednick, S.A. & Schulsinger, F. (1965). A longitudinal study of children with a high risk for schizophrenia: A preliminary report. In S. Vandenberg (ed), *Methods and Goals in Human Behaviour Genetics*. New York: Academic Press.

Morihisa, J. M.. Duffy, F. H.. & Wyatt. R. J. (1983). Brain electrical activity mapping (BEAM) in schizophrenic patients. *Archives of General Psychiatry*, 40, 719-728.

Mullen, M.J. & Murray, R.M. (1989). The impact of molecular genetics on our understanding of the psychoses. *British Journal of Psychiatry*, 154, 591-595.

Owen, F., Cross, A.J., Crow, T.J., Longden, A., Poulter, M. & Riley, G.J. (1978). Increased dopamine receptor sensitivity in schizophrenia. *Lancet*, 11, 223-226.

Pardes, H., Kaufman, C.A., Pincus, H.A. et al. (1989). Genetics and psychiatry: Past discoveries, current dilemmas, and future directions. *American Journal of Psychiatry*, 146, 435-443.

Pollack, M., Levenstein, S. & Klein, D.F. (1968). A three-year post-hospital follow-up of adolescent and adult schizophrenics. *American Journal of Orthopsychiatry*, 38, 94-109.

Pollin, W., Allen, M.G., Hoffer, A., Stabenau, J.R. & Hrubec, Z. (1969). Psychopathology in 15,909 pairs of veteran twins. *American Journal of Psychiatry*, 7, 597-609.

Pollin, N. & Stabenau, J.R. Biological psychological and historical differences in a series of monozygotic twins discordant for schizophrenia. In D. Rosenthal & S.S. Kety (Eds). (1968). *The Transmission of Schizophrenia*. Oxford: Pergamon Press.

Pulver, A.E., Moorman, C.C., Brown, C.H. McGrath, J.A. et al. (1990). Age-incidence artifacts do not account for the season-of-birth effect in schizophrenia. *Schizophrenia Bulletin*, 16(1) 13-15.

Regier, D.A., Myers, J.K., Kramer, M, Robins, L.N., Blazer, D.G., et al (1984). The NIMH Epidemiologic Catchment Area Program: Historical context, major objectives and study population characteristics. *Archives of General Psychiatry*, 41, 934-941.

Reiss, D., Plomin, R. & Heatherington, E.M. (1991). Genetics and psychiatry: An unheralded window on the environment. *Americal Journal of Psychiatry*, 148, 283-291.

Reveley, A.M., Reveley, M.A., Clifford, C.A. & Murray, R.M. (1982). Cerebral ventricular size in twins discordant for schizophrenia. *Lancet*, i, 540-541.

Reveley, A.M., Reveley, M.A. & Murray, R.M. (1984). Cerebral ventricular enlargement in non-genetic schizophrenia: A controlled fourth study. *British Journal of Psychiatry*, 144, 89-93.

Risch, N. (1990). Genetic linkage and complex diseases with special reference to psychiatric disorders. *Genetic Epistemology*, 7, 3-16.

Robins, L.N., Helzer, J.E., Weissman, M.M., Orvaschel, H., et al. (1984). Lifetime prevalence of specific psychiatric disorders in three sites. *Archives of General Psychiatry*, 41, (1984), pp. 949-958.

Rosenthal, D., Wender, P.H., Kety, S.S., Schulsinger, F., Welner, J. & Reider, R. (1975). Parent-child relationships and psychopathological disorder in the child. *Archives of General Psychiatry*, 32, 466-476.

Ross, C.A., Margolis, R.L., Reading, S.A., Pletnikov, M., and Coyle, J.T. (2006). Neurobiology of schizophrenia. *Neuron*, 52, 139–153.

Roth, W.T., and Cannon, E.H. (1972). Some features of the auditory evoked response in schizophrenics. *Archives of General Psychiatry*, 27:466-471.

Schobel, S.A., Chaudhury, N.H., Khan, O.A., Paniagua, B., Styner, M.A., Asllani, I. Et al (2013). Imaging Patients with Psychosis and a Mouse Model Establishes a Spreading Pattern of Hippocampal Dysfunction and Implicates Glutamate as a Driver. *Neuron*, 2013; 78 (1): 81.

Shi et al (ISC) (2009). Common variants on chromosome 6p22.1 are associated with schizophrenia. *Nature*, online July 1, 2009.

Singer, M.T. & Wynne, L.C. (1963). Differentiating characteristics of parents of childhood schizophrenics, childhood neurotics and young adult schizophrenics. *American Journal of Psychiatry*, 120, 234-243.

Slater, E. & Cowie, V. (1971). *The Genetics of Mental Disorder*. London: Oxford University Press.

Söderlund et al. Activation of brain interleukin-1ß in schizophrenia. *Molecular Psychiatry*, 2009; 14 (12).

St. Clair, David (2008). Copy number variation and schizophrenia. *Schizophrenia Bulletin*, (advanced access, Nov. 5, 2008).

Stefansson et al (2008). Large recurrent micro deletions associated with schizophrenia. *Nature*, 455, 232-237.

Stefansson et al (International Schizophrenia Consortium) (2009) Common polygenic variation contributes to risk of schizophrenia and bipolar disorder. *Nature*, letter online July 1, 2009.

Tandon, R., Keshavan, M.S. & Nasrallah, H.A. (2008). Schizophrenia, "Just the Facts" What we know in 2008. 2. Epidemiology and etiology. *Schizophrenia Research*, 102, 1-18.

Torrey, E.F. (1992). Are we overestimating the genetic contribution to schizophrenia? *Schizophrenia Bulletin*, 18(2) 159-170.

Torrey, E.F. & Bowler, A.E. (1990). The seasonality of schizophrenic births: A reply to Marc S. Lewis. *Schizophrenia Bulletin*, 16(1) 1-3.

Tyrell, D.A., Crow, T.J., Parry, R.P., Johnstone, E. & Ferrier, I.N. (1979). Possible virus in schizophrenia and some neurological disorders. *Lancet*, 1, 839-841.

van Kammen, D.P., Docherty, J.P., Marder, S.R. & Bunney, W.E. Jr. (1981). Acute amphetamine response predicts antidepressant and antipsychotic responses to lithium carbonate in schizophrenic patients. Psychiatry Research, 4 (3), 313-325.

Walker & McGuire (1982). Intra- and interhemispheric information processing in schizophrenia. *Psychological Bulletin*, 92(3), 701-725.

Walsh, T., McClellan, J.M., McCarthy, S.E., Addington, A.M. et al (2008). Rare Structural Variants Disrupt Multiple Genes in Neurodevelopmental Pathways in Schizophrenia. *Science*, 320: 539-543.

Watson, C.G. (1990). Schizophrenic birth seasonality and the age-incidence artifact. *Schizophrenia Bulletin*, 16(1) 5-10.

Watt, D.C., Katz, K. & Shepherd, M. (1983). The natural history of schizophenia: A 5-year prospective follow-up of a representative sample of schizophrenics by means of a standardised clinical and social assessment. *Psychological Medicine*, 13, 603-670.

Weinberger, D.R., DeLisi, L.E., Penman, G.P., Torgum, S. & Wyatt, R.J. (1982). Computed tomography in schizophreniform disorder and other acute psychiatric disorders. *Archives of General Psychiatry*, 39, 778-783.

Wender, P.H., Rosenthal, D., Kety, S.S., Schulsinger, F., & Welner, J. (1973). Social Class and Psychopathology in Adoptees. A Natural Experimental Method for Separating the Roles of Genetic and Experiential Factors. *Archives of General Psychiatry*, 28(3), 318-325.

Wong, D.F., Wagner, H.N. Jr, Tune, L.E., Dannals, R.F., Pearlson, G.D., Links, J.M. et al. (1986). Positron emission tomography reveals elevated D2 dopamine receptors in drug-naive schizophrenics. *Science*, 234 (4783), 1558 - 1563.

Other References

Arnold, S.E., Talbot, K., and Hahn, C.G. (2005). Neurodevelopment, neuroplasticity, and new genes for schizophrenia. *Progress in Brain Research*. 147, 319–345.

Bramon, E., Dempster, E., Frangou, S., McDonald, C., Schoenberg, P., MacCabe, J.H., Walshe, M., Sham, P., Collier, D., and Murray, R.M. (2006). Is there an association between the COMT gene and P300 endophenotypes? *European Psychiatry* 21, 70–73.

Brown, A.S. & Derkits, E.J. (2010). Prenatal infection and schizophrenia: a review of epidemiologic and translational studies. *American Journal of Psychiatry*, 167:261–280

Cannon, T.D. (2005). The inheritance of intermediate phenotypes for schizophrenia. *Current Opinions in Psychiatry*, 18, 135–140.

CATIE (Clinical Antipsychotic Trials of Intervention Effectiveness) (2005). Effectiveness of antipsychotic drugs in patients with chronic schizophrenia. *New England Journal of Medicine*. 353, 1209–1223.

Chen, J., Lipska, B.K., and Weinberger, D.R. (2006). Genetic mouse models of schizophrenia: from hypothesis-based to susceptibility gene-based models. *Biological Psychiatry*, 59, 1180–1188.

Coyle, J.T. (2006). Glutamate and schizophrenia: Beyond the dopamine hypothesis. *Cellular and Molecular Neurobiology*. 26(4-6), 363-382.

Craddock, N., O'Donovan, M.C., and Owen, M.J. (2005). The genetics of schizophrenia and bipolar disorder: dissecting psychosis. *Journal of Medical Genetics*, 42, 193–204.

Chen, J., Lipska, B.K., and Weinberger, D.R. (2006). Genetic mouse models of schizophrenia: from hypothesis-based to susceptibility gene-based models. *Biological Psychiatry*, 59, 1180–1188.

Craddock, N., Owen, M.J., and O'Donovan, M.C. (2006). The catechol-O-methyl transferase (COMT) gene as a candidate for psychiatric phenotypes: evidence and lessons. *Molecular Psychiatry*, 11, 446–458.

Freedman, R. (2003). Schizophrenia. *New England Journal of Medicine*. 349, 1738-1749.

Harrison, P.J., and Weinberger, D.R. (2005). Schizophrenia genes, gene expression, and neuropathology: on the matter of their convergence. *Molecular Psychiatry*, 10, 40–68.

Honea, R., Crow, T.J., Passingham, D., and Mackay, C.E. (2005). Regional deficits in brain volume in schizophrenia: a meta-analysis of voxel-based morphometry studies. *American Journal of Psychiatry*, 162, 2233-2245.

Katsel, P.L., Davis, K.L., and Haroutunian, V. (2005). Large-scale micro array studies of gene expression in multiple regions of the brain in schizophrenia and Alzheimer's disease. Int. Rev. *Neurobiology*, 63, 41–82.

Lymer, G.K., Job, D.E., William, T., Moorhead, J., McIntosh, A.M., Owens, D.G., Johnstone, E.C., and Lawrie, S.M. (2006). Brain-behavior relationships in people at high genetic risk of schizophrenia. *NeuroImage*, 33(1), 275-285.

McEvoy, J.P., Lieberman, J.A., Stroup, T.S., Davis, S.M., Meltzer, H.Y., Rosenheck, R.A., Swartz, M.S., Perkins, D.O., Keefe, R.S., Davis, C.E., et al. (2006). Effectiveness of clozapine versus olanzapine, quetiapine, and risperidone in patients with chronic schizophrenia who did not respond to prior atypical antipsychotic treatment. *American Journal of Psychiatry*, 163, 600–610.

Owen, M.J., Craddock, N., and O'Donovan, M.C. (2005). Schizophrenia: genes at last? *Trends in Genetics*, 21, 518–525.

Rapoport, J.L., Addington, A.M., Frangou, S., and Psych, M.R. (2005). The neurodevelopmental model of schizophrenia: update 2005. *Molecular Psychiatry*, 10, 434–449.

Riley, B., and Kendler, K.S. (2006). Molecular genetic studies of schizophrenia. *European Journal of Human Genetics*, 14, 669–680.

Straub, R.E., and Weinberger, D.R. (2006). Schizophrenia genes - famine to feast. *Biological Psychiatry*, 60, 81–83.

Timms, A.E., Dorschner, M.O., Wechsler, J, et al. (2013). Support for the N-Methyl-D-Aspartate Receptor Hypofunction Hypothesis of Schizophrenia From Exome Sequencing in Multiplex Families. *JAMA Psychiatry*, 70(6):582-590.

Turner, J.A., Smyth, P., Macciardi, F., Fallon, J.H., Kennedy, J.L., and Potkin, S.G. (2006). Imaging phenotypes and genotypes in schizophrenia. *Neuroinformatics* 4, 21–49.